Praise for Toxic Childhood

'Excellent book . . . practical, sensible and eminently attainable advice on how to detoxify childhood' Deborah Orr, *Independent*

'A fascinating account of the problems facing kids today . . . contains solid parenting advice on subjects ranging from diet to childcare' *Sainsbury's Magazine*

'A splendid book that draws together a vast swathe of the most authoritative research from a whole range of fields and disciplines . . . that together explain "the worsening behaviour of children and the explosion in numbers of special needs pupils"' *The Mother*

'A brilliant book, Toxic Childhood, demonstrating how deprived children bear the brunt of rapid social change, and the knock-on effect this has on Britain's streets, schools and crime rate'
The Week

'All too often we are told what is wrong with society/parenting/environment and more, but seldom told how we can do something to redress the balance . . . This is what the author set out to do, and she has succeeded. Read Toxic Childhood'
www.familyonwards.com

'Almost every page in this book raises something compelling about the way we are treating children. It is a worrying book, but not unhopeful or unhelpful, and everyone concerned with children can rest assured that Sue Palmer is on their side' *Carousel*

'A great book' *My Child*

'Every parent should read this book, as it does contain a wealth of information you should know' *Evening Herald*

'Absolutely essential reading for anyone who has, or who works with, children. It's like Eric Schlosser (author of the exposé *Fast Food Nation*) for parenting' Lovereading.co.uk

'One of the most talked about books on the market . . . teems with perceptive observations and sound advice' *Family Bulletin*

'One of the most inspirational books I have ever read . . . a must-read for all parents' The Coffee House, mumsnet.com

'More and more of us have begun to wonder, with real anxiety, just what it is that has gone so horribly wrong with childhood. How can we face the future with confidence if we lose faith in the way most of the children around us are raised? In this book, Sue Palmer tackles a range of areas and issues that affect growing bodies and minds. Bravely, she gives us the unvarnished, and often startling, facts. More cheeringly, she then offers us ways to think afresh about a host of matters to do with young people, their health, their upbringing and their education, which we would – both as individuals and as a community – be very foolish indeed to either ignore or dismiss . . .' Anne Fine, author and former Children's Laureate

'Just what we all need to be reading. The levels of anxiety about our children are reaching new highs and we desperately need this kind of careful analysis' Dr Rowan Williams, Archbishop of Canterbury

'One of the most powerful books of the year'
David Willetts, Shadow Secretary of State for Education

'This is a compelling book, well-researched and authoritative, with powerful messages in each of the chapters, and practical suggestions that are both helpful and realistic'

Marion Dowling, President of the
British Association of Early Childhood Education

'Essential reading for all those who work with children. It has fascinating and sometimes startling revelations about the damaging influences on the young within our society and offers some practical and very readable ideas and recommendations for all those who endeavour to give children the very best we can'

Gervase Phinn, author

'Sue Palmer brings together the information parents need all in one place – research that reinforces what most parents really believe. We're under so much pressure to sign up to a status quo that so often feels wrong; this gives us the courage to seek the best for our children' Wendy Thomas, mother, Southampton

'As a teacher with 15 years experience I can only agree about the devastating effect our lifestyles are having on children today. Many of the chapters had me in tears! The book should be made compulsory reading for all politicians, health visitors, social workers, teachers and parents!' Julia Colley, teacher, Essex

'Very well written and well researched'
Mick Brookes, President, National Association of Headteachers

About the author

Sue Palmer, MEd FRSA FEA, is well known to British teachers as a writer, broadcaster and consultant on the education of young children. She is a regular contributor to *The Times Educational Supplement* and other journals, and the author of more than two hundred books, TV programmes and software for three- to twelve-year-olds. She is also a popular speaker, addressing thousands of teachers each year across the UK and around the world, and acts as an independent adviser to many organisations, including the Department for Education and Skills and the BBC.

TOXIC
CHILDHOOD

How the Modern World is
Damaging Our Children and
What We Can Do About it

Sue Palmer

An Orion paperback

First published in Great Britain in 2006
by Orion
This paperback edition published in 2007
by Orion Books Ltd,
Orion House, 5 Upper St Martin's Lane,
London WC2H 9EA

1 3 5 7 9 10 8 6 4 2

A CIP catalogue record for this book is available
from the British Library.

ISBN-13 978-0-7528-8091-4

Printed in Great Britain by Clays Ltd, St Ives plc

The Orion Publishing Group's policy is to use papers that
are natural, renewable and recyclable products and made from
wood grown in sustainable forests. The logging and manufacturing
processes are expected to conform to the environmental
regulations of the country of origin.

www.orionbooks.co.uk

CONTENTS

ACKNOWLEDGEMENTS

There's no way of naming everyone who's helped with *Toxic Childhood* – but I owe particular thanks to the following: Tracey Abbott, Professor Jean Aitchison, Liz Attenborough, John Baker, Ros Bayley, Dr Jan Born, Dr Ann Buchanan, Mark Childress, Pie Corbett, Beth Crocker, Jill Curtis, Galina Dolya, Professor Margaret Donaldson, Marion Dowling, Peter Ellse, Clare Elstow, Suzanne Eva, Anne Fine, Helen Freeman, Tim Gill, Alice Gordeneker, Ann Gray, Ben Hamilton-Baillie, Dr Norbert Herschkowitz and Elinore Herschowitz, Professor Peter Hobson, Diane Hofkins, Warren S Jaferian, Dr Susan Jebb, Carole Kimberley, Dr Amanda Kirby, Jasper and Rita Kirkby, Cornelia Kurz, Professor Richard Layard, Tessa Livingstone, Ian Mallinson, Dr Jackie Marsh, Dr Christine Mcintyre, Paul Mikculcik, Clare Mills, the late Dr Sue Opie, Sue Palmer, Georgina Pensri, Diane Rich, Dr Alex Richardson, Anne St Aubin Roberts, Dr Juliet Schor, Professor Iram Siraj-Blatchford, Dr Pat Spungin, Professor Colwyn Trevarthen, Wendy Thomas, Amanda Torr, Jason and Natalie Walker, the late Dr Sally Ward, Cecilia Weiler, the late Dr Randolph White, Maureen Woodhouse, Sarah Woodhouse and Melanie Young. Thanks also to my agent Luigi Bonomi for his help and inspiration, my two painstaking researchers, John Lambert and James Baker, my assistant Ulrike Vaughan, and finally Peter and Beth for their patience and love during the three years that *Toxic Childhood* took over our home.

AUTHOR'S NOTE

This book, like most non-fiction, contains both fact and opinion. Establishing the facts involved many interviews with experts from fields as diverse as child development, physiology, economics and marketing, as well as conversations with parents, children and teachers from around the UK and mainland Europe. My two research assistants and I also waded through thousands of research papers, articles and press reports (only a tiny fraction of which are explicitly cited in the references), and what felt like half a library of books. This research also informed the opinions in *Toxic Childhood* which, along with any mistakes, are all my own. Most of the people I consulted agreed with me, some didn't – but they all helped enormously in assembling the evidence and creating the book.

PREFACE TO THE PAPERBACK EDITION

Since first publication of Toxic Childhood nearly a year ago, evidence of the damage that can be inflicted on children by a competitive, consumer-driven, screen-based lifestyle has continued to emerge. Indeed, just as the book went to press, research from Kings College, London, showed that children's conceptual understanding – that is, their common-sense appreciation of the world and how it works – has declined significantly.[1] In a battery of tests, eleven-year-olds in 2004 scored two to three years behind their counterparts in 1990 – a staggering deterioration in the space of fifteen years.

When I asked Michael Shayer, one of the researchers concerned, what he believed lay behind this alarming trend, he specifically cited changes in play and education. In the last ten to fifteen years, children's outdoor play – making mud pies, climbing trees, damming streams and so on – has markedly declined (see Chapter 2); what is more, as Dr Shayer pointed out, '1990 was the year that sand and water began to move out of infant classrooms' (see Chapter 7). The combination of sedentary screen-based entertainment at home and an over-emphasis on pencil-and-paper work at school means children are seriously deprived of the first-hand experience necessary for real understanding.

There has also been further evidence from the British Medical

Association of a gradual decline in children's mental health.[2] Their statistic published in summer 2006 that 20% of children and adolescents could expect to suffer from mental health problems is – in a prosperous, peaceful country – a shameful one. Even more shameful was the finding several weeks later that out of 25 countries in the European Community the UK had scored 21st in a survey of children's well-being.[3] The four countries scoring lower – Estonia, Latvia, Lithuania and Slovakia – were ex-Soviet states where problems for children could be explained in terms of ingrained poverty and deprivation. As the world's fourth richest country, the UK has no such excuse for its children's unhappiness.

And, of course, unhappy children tend to turn into unhappy, often antisocial teenagers. A report in autumn 2006 from the Institute of Public Policy Research labelled British teenagers the most antisocial in Europe, at or near the top of the charts on every measure of bad behaviour – drugs, drink, violence, promiscuity – and far more susceptible to the excesses of consumerism than youngsters elsewhere.[4]

However, alongside all these gloomy research findings, there are also many rays of hope. Shortly after publication of *Toxic Childhood*, I was contacted – on the same day – by two leading opinion-formers, one representing the world of science, one religion. The scientist was Baroness Susan Greenfield, Director of the Royal Institution, who has long been concerned about the effects of contemporary culture on the development of the brain. She was in the process of setting up an all-party committee in the House of Lords to draw attention to the neuroscientific implications of changes in childhood and education. The religious leader was the Archbishop of Canterbury, who has also now set up a working group – the Good Childhood Inquiry – to 'renew society's understanding of childhood for the 21st century'. This group is led by the economist

Professor Richard Layard, whose work on happiness and social capital underpins much of Chapter 10 of *Toxic Childhood*.

The interest and involvement of influential figures from such varied backgrounds suggests that the social and cultural 'drift' in which toxic childhood syndrome has flourished may be coming to an end. Further evidence of this change came in autumn 2006, when psychotherapist Dr Richard House and I collected signatures to a letter to the *Daily Telegraph* calling for public debate on child-rearing in the 21st century. One hundred and ten high-profile professionals, academics and writers put their name to the letter, which was widely reported in the media, attracting public support not just in the UK, but around the world. The issue of 'toxic childhood syndrome' was also picked up during the political party conference season, and it seems that the debate called for in our letter is now under way. All this is good news, as public awareness of the problems facing parents and children is the first step towards significant cultural change.

For me, however, the greatest hope has come from the individual parents and teachers I have met as a result of this book. When invited to speak about *Toxic Childhood* around the UK (and also in mainland Europe, the USA and South East Asia), I have encountered many people already determined to detoxify childhood in their own families and communities. Researching, writing and meeting audiences for *Toxic Childhood* has convinced me that it is through grass-roots action of this kind that real change will come about.

With very few exceptions, parents love their children and want the best for them – including a happy childhood and the chance to grow up bright, balanced and able to make their own particular contribution to society. Since parental love is one of the strongest forces on the planet, it shouldn't be too difficult for an advanced, technological culture to harness this love and produce bright, balanced, happy children.

And given sufficient information about child development, the freedom to act in their children's best interests, and the support of their local communities, I am sure that most parents can detoxify their children's lives. What is more, if that community support is effective, it can also detoxify the lives of all children – near and far – who will be friends and neighbours in the next generation's global village.

1   Philip Adey and Michael Shayer, report to the ESRC, 'Have the Norms for Volume and Heaviness for Year 7 Changed Since the Mid-70s?' January, 2006.

2   British Medical Association, *Child and Adolescent Mental Health – a Guide for Healthcare Professionals*, June 2006.

3   Professor Jonathan Bradshaw and members of the Department of Social Policy and Social Work, University of York, research report, 'The Well-Being of Children in the UK', 2006.

4   Institute of Public Policy Research, *Freedom's Orphans: Raising Youth in a Changing World*, November 2006.

TOXIC CHILDHOOD SYNDROME

She was standing on the steps of the Uffizi Gallery in Florence – a short, dark-haired girl, slightly overweight, sulkily licking an ice cream. I guessed from her face that she was no more than ten years old, but the angry scowl and scrunched self-consciousness looked more like a teenager, wracked with adolescent angst. Her clothes were too old for her too – a low-slung miniskirt and high-cut top, exposing a plump little midriff. And across her little girl's chest was printed a message to the world: 'I ♥ *my attitude problem*'.

In the building behind her were some of Western civilisation's greatest treasures – paintings by Botticelli, Leonardo, Michelangelo – which presumably her parents had dragged her across Europe (maybe across the world) to see. She clearly wasn't remotely interested. I suspect the only thing that small lost soul wanted to do was curl up in front of a widescreen TV and lose herself in something mindless – a cartoon, maybe, or one of the endless American sitcoms on the Disney Channel. Her feelings about life were written all over her: anger, self-obsession, boredom, lack of engagement – the multiple trademarks of the brat.

Poor child. Poor parents. Poor Western civilisation – indeed the whole of the developed world – which now teems with miserable little creatures, male and female, toddlers to pre-teens. In a global culture whose citizens are wealthier, healthier and more privileged than ever before, children grow unhappier every year. From the disgruntled and discontented to the depressed and dysfunctional, we seem to be raising a generation with nothing to love but its attitude problem.

What's happening to children?

The developed world, especially the most economically successful countries – USA, Japan, Germany and the UK – is suffering an epidemic of misery among its young. In 2004, an English research foundation recorded that behavioural problems in young people have doubled over the last thirty years and emotional problems have increased by 70 per cent. The American Psychological Association now estimates that one in five children and teens suffer from mental health problems, and the World Health Organisation expects that by 2020, neuropsychiatric disorders in children will swell by 50 per cent compared with other health issues, making them one of the five main causes of disability and death.

The knock-on effects of this epidemic are already obvious in statistics on drug and substance abuse among teenagers, along with binge drinking, eating disorders, self-harm and suicide (attempted and successful). Add these to the figures for teenage crime and anti-social behaviour, and there is an awful lot for the parents of a ten-year-old with an attitude problem to worry about. Occasional terrifying incidents – such as the Columbine High School massacre or the eleven-year-old in Japan who murdered her classmate because she didn't like her postings on the Internet – ratchet up the concern.

So what's going wrong? As one who's worked with children for thirty years – the last three of which have been spent researching this issue, and talking to experts on aspects of child-rearing around the world – I've come to the conclusion that there isn't one simple answer. We can't blame the parents, or the teachers, or the junk food manufacturers, or anyone else. This is a complex cultural problem, linked to the incredible speed of human progress. We've created an amazingly exciting global culture but over the last quarter of a century progress has accelerated so much that our species simply can't keep up. In a nutshell, our culture has evolved faster than our biology.

This clash between our technology-driven culture and our biological heritage is now damaging children's ability to think, learn and behave. And unless we do something about it, the twenty-first-century global village is going to be in trouble. To put it bluntly, the next generation may not be bright or balanced enough to keep the show on the road.

The 'special needs' explosion

What first started me fretting over this issue was the alarming escalation, over my time in education, of what are known as 'developmental disorders'. A number of learning difficulties, which didn't even enter the public consciousness until the late twentieth century, began to affect an alarming number of children.

First and foremost among these syndromes is ADHD ('attention deficit and hyperactivity disorder'), now the most common psychiatric condition affecting children in the USA. Up to 12 per cent of American children suffer from ADHD, which affects their ability to concentrate and control behaviour, and rates are soaring across the developed world.

Another group of learning difficulties rapidly reaching epidemic proportions is the 'dyslexia cluster'. Statistics suggest that around 10 per cent of children in the USA and the UK suffer from dyslexia (difficulty in reading), and other countries, including Japan, are reporting increasing numbers of cases. Dyslexia's close cousins – dysgraphia, dyscalculia and dyspraxia (difficulties respectively in writing, maths and physical coordination) – are also significantly on the rise.

However, the most recent – and extremely worrying – increase has been in autistic spectrum disorders (ASD), involving children's ability to relate to the world and communicate with others. Autism affects children in many different ways – hence the term 'spectrum'. At one end are 'high functioning' Asperger's Syndrome children – often academic high achievers but socially inept – and at the other are very severely autistic children, completely cut off by their disability and unable to communicate with the rest of the world. The unifying features of autistic spectrum disorders are difficulties in social functioning and communication, and unusual (often repetitive) behaviours. Dustin Hoffman in *Rain Man* illustrated them admirably.

In the early 1980s, the incidence of autism in the USA was about 1 in 50,000. By 2004 it had grown to 1 in 166, and the American Academy of Pediatrics reports that diagnoses are increasing by roughly 25 per cent every year. Estimates elsewhere vary from 1 in 100 children in the UK to about 1 in 600 in Japan, but they appear to be on the increase in all countries in the developed world.

It's possible that the huge increase in these 'special educational needs' is the result of increasing knowledge and understanding among doctors and teachers, meaning conditions that went undiagnosed in the past are now routinely recognised. Another possibility is that parents these days prefer to medicalise problems once simply labelled under-achievement. This argument is often put forward by critics of the growth in drug treatment for ADHD – mind-altering drugs such as Ritalin or Dexedrine, prescribed to correct the chemical imbalance in the child's brain.

Both suggestions probably have some truth. But even then the increases are phenomenal. In 2004 the American Academy of Pediatrics recorded on their website that '1 in 6 children are diagnosed with a developmental disorder and/or behavioural problem'. The thought that one in every half-dozen children in the most developed nation on earth is considered educationally and/or socially dysfunctional is extremely alarming. What happens in the USA today has a habit of happening in the rest of the developed world tomorrow. And today's special educational needs turn all too often into tomorrow's mental health problems, antisocial behaviour and crime.

Nature, nurture and behaviour

It's now widely accepted that developmental disorders have a genetic – or, at least, neurological – component. 'Nature' plays a major part, but it's also widely agreed that the way children are brought up inevitably influences their development. The nature-nurture debate about how much an individual's personality is due to one or the other is tediously familiar – indeed it's assumed a similar status during the twentieth century to the medieval debate about how many angels can balance on the head of a pin. But most scientists now take the view that, while genes are indeed significant, upbringing and outside influences make a great deal of difference. Nature and nurture are vibrantly interactive.

When a predisposition is strong – as in the case of those unfortunate infants locked into profound autism – nurture may have little effect. But in most cases the environment in which a child grows up will significantly affect the way any traits – good or bad – develop. In one particularly memorable American research project, two groups of identical genetically vulnerable monkeys were brought up in different circumstances and then given access to alcohol. The monkeys who'd had a tough childhood consoled themselves with drink, while those who'd been carefully cared for and mothered drank less than the average monkey.

So could there be something going on in the successful nations of the world that's making it more likely that genetically vulnerable children develop special educational needs? Might it be that – despite our economic success – childhood today is tougher than it was a few decades ago?

The reason psychologists call ADHD, the dyslexia group and ASD 'developmental disorders' is that, in terms of social behaviour and/or achievement at school, the children concerned don't develop at the 'normal' rate – something holds them back. There's a sort of developmental continuum we expect children to move along during the first ten or so years of life. At birth, they're all helpless little bundles of egocentricity, but as time goes on we assume they'll move slowly (with occasional understandable regressions) towards more 'grown-up' civilised behaviour. We don't consciously teach this civilised behaviour, except hopefully by example – we just expect it to emerge (or develop) as children mature, in the same way we expect them to walk and talk. Along the way, we also expect them to learn the basic skills covered in primary school – the Three Rs of reading, writing and reckoning.

If something is happening to interfere with the normal course of children's development – and thus contributing to the huge increase in developmental and behavioural disorders – you'd expect to see it affecting children in general, not just genetically vulnerable ones. And that's exactly what people have been seeing. Over the last couple of decades, I've heard reports from many thousands of teachers around the UK of a steady deterioration in the behaviour and learning potential of children in their classes, not just those diagnosed with a special educational need. Reports from educators in the USA, Japan and other developed countries bear it out. In *general*, children in the world's most successful nations are not as well behaved or as well equipped to learn as they were in the past.

Learning to behave

Of course, all children sometimes act up. When over-tired, over-excited or feverish, any child can regress to the level of a two-year-old on a bad day. But in a civilised society we expect a decline in self-obsession and an increase in grown-up behaviour as the years go by – the proportion of good days to bad gradually increasing, until by the time a child's age is in double figures, his or her behaviour is relatively stable. The fact that children then enter that long dark tunnel known as adolescence is, of course, something of a backward step, but if all's gone well in the preceding years, there's hope they'll come out of the tunnel unscathed. As St Ignatius Loyola, Miss Jean Brodie and Hillary Clinton have all pointed out, the most important learning happens well before the teenage years. This change from a tantrum-throwing two-year-old to a relatively civilised pre-teen depends on many things, but there are three key principles children must grasp on their journey, principles which have been at the heart of civilisation throughout human history.

The first is the ability to maintain attention even when something doesn't particularly interest them. All children – even very young ones – can focus for long periods on chosen activities (as parents forced to play endless games of peek-a-boo or 'pick up the rattle' know only too well). However, once children begin to socialise with others, they must learn sometimes to focus on other people's choices; and by six or seven, they're expected to focus on what the teacher is teaching them. If you can't attend – or if you're only prepared to attend to the things that interest you – you're going to have trouble at school.

The second is the concept of 'deferred gratification'. Children must grasp that the rewards for actions are not always immediate, and that sometimes people have to knuckle down to dreary, boring, repetitive tasks because they'll pay off later – perhaps in the fairly remote future. An experiment from the 1960s illustrates how important the appreciation and acceptance of deferred gratification can be. Researchers left four-year-old children, one by one, alone in a room with a plate containing a single marshmallow. The children were told that, if they wished, they could eat the marshmallow; but if they waited till the researcher's return, they'd be given a whole plateful of marshmallows. Some children cracked and wolfed down the single treat; others managed to resist temptation and held out for a plateful. Twenty years later researchers hunted down the subjects of this experiment, and discovered that those whose self-restraint had earned them multiple marshmallows had led more successful and happy lives than those who'd been impulsive.

The third principle is that living happily in a group of any size involves balancing your own needs against the needs of everyone else. This is summed up very succinctly in Mrs Doasyouwouldbedoneby, the name of a character in Charles Kingsley's *The Water Babies*. Doing as you would be done by, and thus making the wheels of domestic, institutional and social life turn smoothly, requires an awareness of others (the ability to empathise with their point of view) allied with the sort of self-control I've described above. Human beings who do not have these qualities are likely to have a very hard ride through life – and so are the people around them.

Children with profound developmental disorders – conditions that completely impair their quality of life (and, indeed, that of their parents) – don't grasp these principles and their behaviour remains sadly primitive. But 'normal' children progress steadily towards civilised self-control. Then there are the ones in the middle – those who make some progress but not enough, whose education begins to suffer, and who may have real problems 'fitting in'.

The point at which psychologists diagnose a developmental disorder is, of course, moot – indeed, everyone in education knows diagnosis is partially dependent upon a child's background (the apparent incidence of dyslexia, for instance, is much greater in affluent areas than in disadvantaged ones). But the point is that, year on year, fewer children make what used to be called 'normal' progress. Increasingly, children in general have problems focusing their concentration, exercising self-restraint and taking account of other people's needs and interests.

A twenty-first-century report card

Primary teachers are well qualified to assess the behaviour of pre-teen children, since they spend most of the day in their company, and can compare the way classes behave over time. Over the last couple of decades, UK primary teachers' concern about children's deteriorating behaviour – especially in schools in disadvantaged areas – has mushroomed. We have heard similar reports coming out of America for years, and I now hear them increasingly from teachers on mainland Europe. The general opinion is that, as the proportion of children with diagnosed special needs has increased, so has the proportion that doesn't have a specific diagnosable disorder but are just distractible, impulsive or badly behaved.

This shift has caused many problems for schools because distractible, impulsive children are difficult to teach. It's particularly difficult teaching them to read and write, since the various sub skills of literacy take a long time to acquire and – no matter how hard teachers try to jazz it up – involve plenty of dull, repetitive effort. The eventual rewards, however, are well worth having: beside the obvious advantages of being literate in a literate world, psychologists believe the very process of learning to read develops children's powers of thought and understanding. It's a classic example of the importance of deferred gratification.

Another major problem is that, as children's behaviour gets worse, teachers must spend more time and energy on crowd control. At the lowest level, they've noticed a decline in manners and respect for adults, with general 'cheekiness' and backchat making day-to-day classroom management more demanding. More significantly, there are many more incidences of rule breaking, violence and bullying, and all these discipline problems take up teaching time and distract from the business of learning.

Readers blessed with well-behaved offspring, or those who do not mix much with children at all, may think teachers are overstating the case. Janet Street-Porter, a British writer and broadcaster, used to feel that way – until she agreed to spend two weeks teaching eight-year-olds in a primary school. Ms Street-Porter is renowned as a forceful woman, capable of withering hardened BBC executives with a glance. In her new role, however – despite an armoury of guidelines for dealing with problem children – she found herself leaving school at the end of each day 'weeping with frustration that several of the worst offenders would simply run rings round me. Quite simply, they had no idea of discipline whatsoever'.

These opinions are reflected in teachers' comments across the developed world. Even in Japan, where a formal education system has meant that discipline was not a problem in the past, primary teachers now speak of widespread impulsive behaviour, including bullying (the Japanese word for this, *ijime*, didn't enter the public consciousness till the early eighties, but is now a household word). They also report an apparent lack of guilt among the children concerned – deeply worrying in a society where respect and honour is of supreme importance. What's more, over the last few years, literacy levels – always a source of pride in Japan, where dyslexia was once unknown – have begun to plummet. Why then, in all the most advanced and advantaged countries of the world, should children be growing less able to exercise self-control and more difficult to teach?

The blind men and the elephant

Like most teachers I meet, my first instinct was to lay the blame for deteriorating behaviour on television. To a literacy specialist it seems obvious that children who spend their days slumped in front of TV miss out on other important activities, such as conversation and reading for pleasure. Commentators have been complaining about reduced attention span ever since television became widespread in the 1950s, and over the last twenty years children's viewing has escalated wildly as TV became a round-the-clock global presence, with endless channels aimed specifically at them: Nickelodeon, Disney, Fox Kids, CBBC, Toonami and so on. I began to take a keen interest in the issue and often wrote about it for the educational press.

Then one day, while looking into reports that Ritalin prescriptions in the UK had increased ten-fold in a single decade, I bumped into another researcher, an expert on children's play. She put the apparent increase in attention deficit down to something quite different: the fact that many parents were too frightened to let their children go outside and run off excess energy. In conversation we discovered that, while her argument and mine were clearly linked – in both cases, TV was implicated – neither of us had hitherto given much consideration to the other's point of view.

Suddenly I noticed how many other experts seemed to be digging away at this issue. They began to turn up everywhere –newspapers, bookshops, the Internet – and each had his or her own speciality. They seemed to be all over the world – from the USA in the west to Japan in the east – worrying away at the same problem, despite differences in cultural traditions. Some put the change in children's behaviour down to diet or lack of exercise; others chose working mothers, marriage breakdown, defects in the education system, excessive consumerism or other effects of technological or social change. The world is full of experts on children's behaviour, and most of them seem completely oblivious of all the others.

The trouble is, expertise nowadays is increasingly specialised: researchers are trapped in their own disciplines, knowing more and more about less and less; social commentators are trapped in their own countries, addressing the minutiae of national concerns. So although there's worldwide concern about changes in children's behaviour patterns, investigation into the issue is proceeding like that of 'The Blind Men and the Elephant'. In the poem, each blind man caught hold of one bit of the animal – the trunk or the leg or the tail – and on the basis of this worked out his theory of what an elephant looked like. At present, each expert latches on to one element of the decline in children's behaviour and ability to learn, and in so doing we fail to grasp it in its entirety. We haven't observed the whole elephant.

The more I read, the more I became convinced that there was not just one cause behind the changes in children's behaviour, but a vast array of causes, all interrelated and deeply ingrained in contemporary culture – a complex and alarming mix. And it was affecting children across the developed world. This is why, three years ago, I stepped off my personal professional tramlines and began research into childhood in general.

The past is another planet

My first reaction was deep sympathy for contemporary parents. How in the world could they be expected to cope with the astonishing amount of information generated by these legions of experts? And if those same experts haven't worked out what 'the elephant' in the middle of all their research looks like, how are parents supposed to guess what's significant in their findings?

Bringing up children has never been easy, but nowadays it's a minefield. Twenty-first-century parents pick their way gingerly through the sound bites – junk food, sugar highs, couch-potato kids, pester power, battery children, electronic babysitters, technobrats, and so on – but with a distinct shortage of reference points. When my husband and I were bringing up our daughter twenty years ago, the world we lived in was not vastly different from the one in which we'd grown up ourselves. But since then, the pace of change has been phenomenal. In less than two decades, technology has transformed our homes: PCs, laptops, email, the worldwide web; cable, satellite and digital TV, camcorders, DVD; computer games, PlayStations, iPods; mobile phones, text messaging, camphones ... And everything happens much, much faster than it did in the past.

Social changes have been no less startling. Across the developed world, there are now far fewer extended family groups than there were, and more parents bringing up children alone; mothers are much more likely to work and, in a fast-moving, fast-changing workplace, the pressures of work for all parents have increased enormously; marriages are less stable and cohabitation and divorce widespread – even in countries, such as Japan and Spain, where such behaviour was unthinkable twenty years ago. The old certainties have gone, and 'moral relativism' doesn't make for easy parenting.

Technology has meant families across the developed world have more and more in common – an exciting development – but it also means that they have less and less contact with their own cultural past. Back in 1950, L. P. Hartley began his novel *The Go-Between* with the famous words: 'The past is a foreign country. They do things differently there.' These days the past isn't just a foreign country, it's another planet.

The Canadian media visionary Marshall McLuhan called this phenomenon 'electric speed'. It began with the growth of global mass media in the middle of the twentieth century, but has accelerated wildly – as evidenced above – since the 1980s. McLuhan predicted that the contraction of time and space within the global village would be a great leap forward for mankind, and in many ways he was right: for adults, it's an amazing period to be alive, and most of the time we manage to keep up with the electric speed of modern life.

But children are not fully developed adults – they still have to move along that developmental continuum, acquiring the habits of civilised behaviour. Focused attention, deferred gratification, self-control, empathy and other important lessons can't be learned at electric speed. Human development happens in 'slow time', and contemporary children need the same time-consuming, old-fashioned nurturing that small, highly intelligent primates have needed through the ages.

The elephant in the house

In the tumult of change, it's not surprising if some parents have lost sight of age-old truths about child-rearing, especially as many of the old reference points – lore from the extended family, cultural and religious traditions – have been swept away. But the problem is compounded because the cultural changes of the last quarter of a century have brought with them a toxic mix of side effects that have made the task of rearing children more difficult than ever before. Parents haven't had the time (or the clarity of information) to make adjustments for these side effects. As a result, every year children become more distractible, impulsive and self-obsessed – less able to learn, to enjoy life, to thrive socially. So even though it's more difficult than in any previous generation, good parenting is essential. In a complex contemporary culture, children are in greater need of parental wisdom, guidance and support than ever before.

The needs of a small human being are much the same as they ever were. They need physical nurturing (a healthy mind in a healthy body): nourishing food; plenty of exercise and play; adequate sleep. They need emotional and social support, which means time, attention, communication and love from the people closest to them. As they grow older, they must widen their social circle and learn cognitive skills, including the Three Rs. And throughout childhood they need moral guidance, to help them navigate the increasingly complex web of contemporary ethics.

My research suggests that children's development in every one of these areas is threatened by the side effects of technological and cultural changes. A great many – probably a majority – of our children have developed a taste for unhealthy food and a couch-potato lifestyle, and have related problems with sleeping. An unacceptable number also suffer from inadequate early emotional bonding, lack of interaction with their parents and a high level of emotional instability. Instead of stimulating, real-life experiences, contemporary children have TV and computer games at home, and – all too often – a narrow test-and-target-driven curriculum at school. Moral guidance has suffered as societies become increasingly confused, while children are constantly exposed to manipulative advertising and the excesses of celebrity culture.

Any one of the vast array of cultural side effects I discovered would be enough to trigger developmental delay in a genetically vulnerable child; the whole toxic brew could trigger it even in the most genetically robust of individuals. This is the 'elephant' standing full square in the living room of every family home in the developed world.

Toxic childhood syndrome

There's no point in standing around wringing our hands about this problem, or indeed in looking for someone to blame. No one intended it – the culture changed so rapidly that we're only just beginning to notice the extent of the collateral damage. Hand wringing and blaming are just a waste of precious time.

So I'm not suggesting we turn the clock back on our cultural revolution – and most of us wouldn't want to. Personally I *love* new technology and would hate to go back to an earlier age. Indeed, without email and the worldwide web, this book couldn't have been written. I love the buzz of twenty-four-hour living, the improvements in women's status, the comfort and convenience of our contemporary lifestyle, the excitement of change. But, in order to maintain the new global culture, we must acknowledge what it's doing to our children and work out how to detoxify their lives.

Toxic Childhood assembles evidence from a wide range of disciplines – from psychology and neuroscience to economics and marketing. The research involved took several years' work (by myself and two hard-working research assistants), hundreds of discussions with children, parents and teachers around the world, and – most importantly – interviews with scores of scientists and other experts, who gave generously of their time and expertise to explain the effects of 'toxic childhood syndrome' in their particular disciplines.

The more I found out, the clearer it became that trying to tackle any one of these elements independently of the others was a waste of time – they all swirl together in a toxic mix. So just improving a child's diet, for instance, isn't enough – all sorts of other things impinge on it: TV and marketing messages, exercise and sleeping habits, childcare arrangements, parenting style. Anyway, just as we can't know a child's genetic blueprint, so we can't guess which elements of contemporary culture might be particularly poisonous for each individual. Toxic childhood is a syndrome, and we have to tackle the *whole* thing, not just odd symptoms. The good news is that doing so isn't particularly difficult, shouldn't cost much (except in time and attention) and parents who are already detoxing their children's lives find it extremely rewarding and enjoyable.

Detoxing childhood

After each chapter, there are a few guidelines for 'detoxing childhood', taking age-old wisdom and adapting it to fit contemporary culture. However, I'm not a parenting expert and *Toxic Childhood* is not a child-rearing manual – one of the problems I recognised in my research was that the growth in 'parenting experts' has contributed to the syndrome – parents feel de-skilled and unable to trust to their instincts. Besides, in some countries, cultural traditions or enlightened social provision already point the way towards aspects of detoxification. Some of these are included as recommendations in the book. I hope parents will assess the evidence offered and interpret all the suggestions as seems most appropriate to their own children's needs, within their own culture and circumstances. I also point to other sources of information, books and websites that I've found particularly helpful in understanding the issues confronting twenty-first-century parents. The strength of the global village means that, as further recommendations arise, they too can be disseminated at electric speed.

But tackling toxic childhood syndrome is not simply about what individual parents can do – it's also an important social project, one that affects everyone in the developed world. Children are our most significant investment for the future, and the toxic cocktail described here is already undermining the social, emotional and intellectual development of an unacceptable number. Even if your own offspring have escaped unscathed, the world they're growing up in is full of others who've been less fortunate. As more children become distractible, impulsive and lacking in empathy, antisocial behaviour and violent crime will increase. If toxic childhood syndrome is not stemmed, it will pose an increasing threat to social cohesion.

We could, of course, try to solve the problem by doling out drugs, as already happens in the case of the growing number of children diagnosed with ADHD. I would be the last to deny that some families desperately need the relief that comes from a timely dose of Ritalin – living with a severely ADHD child can be utter hell. But as prescriptions soar (between 2000 and 2002, 68 per cent more mind-altering drugs were prescribed to children in the UK alone), we must ask ourselves whether pathologising childhood in this way is an acceptable option.

Apart from anything else, drugging a growing proportion of the nation's youth is an expensive option, and we don't know where it might lead. The rock stars Kurt Cobain and Courtney Love, both on Ritalin as children, became confirmed drug addicts. After Cobain's suicide, Love ruminated, 'When you're a kid and you get this drug that makes you feel that feeling, where else are you going to turn when you're an adult? It was euphoric when you were a child – isn't that memory going to stick with you?'

A much more sensible solution would be for medical, educational and political establishments to address the underlying causes of these changes in children's behaviour, and support parents in doing the best for their children. Governments across the world already recognise that investment in the next generation's physical, mental and emotional health is a worthwhile cause, but they often base their responses on research that doesn't take into account all the effects of cultural change – research from that other planet known as the past. Awareness of, and attention to, toxic childhood syndrome is essential if their investment is to succeed.

Big business needs to listen too. Large corporations have been slow to recognise that, when short-term profit undermines society's long-term prospects, it's not just the punters they're screwing, it's themselves. However, there are hopeful signs that, with sufficient public outrage and threats of litigation, they can be persuaded to change direction. It's even possible they'll recognise that there's money to be made in creating and marketing products that develop a healthy rather than unhealthy lifestyle for children. In helping big business along this road, parental pressure is an extremely powerful force.

*

In the end, though, the main responsibility for rearing children lies, as it always has, with parents. They have to wise up, stop being paralysed by a combination of rapid change, uncertainty and guilt, and concentrate on providing a secure, healthy environment in which their children can grow. The suggestions in this book are not rocket science, but if we care about the future of our global village, they're more important than rocket science. In defending the culture we've created, we have to recognise that the barbarians are not only at the gate, they're in the womb.

Mind the gap

'Something really awful will happen soon.'

I was eating lunch with a group of primary head teachers in a deprived area of the UK, listening to their chat about the children in their schools. They all nodded gloomily at their colleague's prophecy.

'It's inevitable,' someone answered. 'Things are getting so bad. What's tragic is that we have to wait for a terrible disaster before the rest of the country notices.'

I realised, as I pushed my salad around the plate, that they were predicting some shocking, headline-grabbing act of violence from the infants in their care. Murder, mayhem or destruction. By children under ten.

Young children in many rundown, inner-city areas of the UK are becoming increasingly feral. Visiting such places, I find them more terrifying every year. Many of the children don't have children's faces – they're pinched and angry, with dead eyes. For them, violence is a fact of daily life. Their parents – deprived, uneducated, often scarcely more than children themselves – are often junkies, alcoholics, involved in crime. Toxic childhood syndrome flourishes in such circumstances, and it's feeding this feral generation.

Any parents who've gone to the trouble of picking up this book are probably already taking steps to detoxify their children. In the last few years, as concern about children's health and behaviour has grown, there's been plenty of media coverage and advice. The problem exists across all social groups, but educated families are already getting to grips with it. Even the parents of children with genetic developmental conditions are sometimes able to discover and make specific lifestyle adjustments that help to normalise their child's behaviour, often at considerable cost to themselves in terms of time and effort. But uneducated parents – especially those in areas of great deprivation – are either too ill-informed or lack the personal competence to make any adjustments, despite the fact that the toxic effects on their children are greater than anywhere else. That's why, at the end of each chapter, I've added a PS entitled 'Mind the gap'.

This topic could, of course, be a book in its own right. For brevity's sake therefore, the postscripts are often personal, anecdotal and impressionistic. If you want to know more, you can either Google or go and see for yourself. But it's a subject we should all engage with. In the world's most successful countries the gap between the haves and have-nots widens every year. Politicians call it 'social mobility' – the extent to which a nation's citizens are able to move up and out of an impoverished childhood. While some countries, such as Sweden and the Netherlands, have slightly increased social mobility in recent years, in others – notably the USA and UK – the gap grows ever wider.

What's more, in most economically successful countries the birth rate among have-nots is soaring, while among educated classes it's falling. Demographic experts in developed nations are concerned about this widening gap, for two main reasons. First, it diminishes the home-grown educated workforce; second, if a growing section of the population has no stake in society (especially if the younger generation sees no way out of poverty) their disaffection could eventually threaten social stability.

There are moral and philosophical problems in considering how to detoxify other people's children, which is why those head teachers have to wait for 'something awful' to happen before action is taken. Liberal thinkers consider it politically incorrect to interfere in the lives of the poor; laissez-faire libertarians prefer to wait until deprived children are adults, then lock up the troublemakers, even though overcrowding in the prisons of developed nations is reaching crisis point. But there's a limit to how long we can ignore it. As the world continues to move at electric speed and the toxic influences on the children of the poor increase, there's every chance of serious civil unrest within a generation. If for no other reason than enlightened self-interest, it seems to me we have to notice this widening gap and take measures to close it. Just detoxing our own children's lives isn't enough.

CHAPTER ONE

FOOD FOR THOUGHT

In the early years of the twenty-first century, the people of the developed world have suddenly noticed we've been poisoning our children. The food we've let them eat over the last decade or so – ever richer in sugar, salt, additives and the wrong sort of fat – now contains very little actual nourishment. Instead of building healthy bodies, it's simply making children fatter and unhealthier by the year.

There's been less fuss about the fact that this food has also been damaging children's brains. In an international symposium on brain research and learning in Germany in 2003, delegates were told: 'If we do not pay attention to the diets of our children, we may be faced with a future of brain degenerating problems which are closely linked to learning problems.'

How could parents in the world's most highly developed, highly educated nations have allowed this to happen? It isn't as if we don't know what a balanced diet looks like – governments around the world produce guidelines like our food pyramid, often with flashy illustrations. Canada has its food rainbow; Germany its dietary circle (with a healthy glass of water in the middle) and China a food pagoda. In 2005, the US Department of Agriculture upgraded its food pyramid into a multicoloured, individualised animation – MyPyramid. This revamp was hailed by nutritionist Michael Jacobson as 'the strongest dietary guidelines yet produced'. So it's clear what children *ought* to be eating, but sadly that's not what they've been programmed to want.

In a multi-media world running at electric speed, it's not just parents who feed children – it's the whole culture. And even though most parents are now well aware of the dangers, it's going to be very difficult to turn the effects of that culture around.

Junk-food junkies

Despite all we know about it, highly processed junk food is still extremely popular throughout Westernised society, and among children in particular. In a quick-fix world, it's the fastest, easiest way to satisfy hunger – pre-prepared, readily accessible and requiring no effort. It doesn't even need eating implements: burgers, hotdogs, pizzas, pies and pastries are all finger-foods, and fizzy drinks can be consumed straight from the can. What's more, these finger-foods are 'tasty', because the high quantities of fat, salt and food additives disguise poor-quality ingredients. Fizzy drinks satisfy our human craving for sweetness (there's the equivalent of three tablespoons of sugar in each can), as do sugary snacks like biscuits and chocolate bars.

The addiction has been building up for some time, since fast-food outlets proliferated in the second half of the twentieth century and restaurants like McDonald's became associated with days out, treats and parties. As children grew increasingly keen on the taste of quick-fix meals, manufacturers responded by creating more products for the home: foods that are quick and easy to prepare in the microwave; ever-sweeter cereals; salty snacks to be popped into school lunch boxes or scoffed while watching TV; fatty foods suitable for 'grazing' throughout the day. The more of this stuff children eat, the more they want.

It's not an exaggeration to talk about contemporary children being addicted to junk. Psychologist Deanne Jade, founder of the National Centre for Eating Disorders, explains that highly flavoured food works in the same way as drugs. 'It changes our mood and it impacts on the chemicals and neurotransmitters in the brain in a similar way to alcohol, nicotine and cocaine.' The extent of physical addiction is considerably less, of course, but as the British nutritionist Dr Susan Jebb puts it, 'Children develop very strong learned preferences – junk food can become a psychological addiction.'

Sadly, it's usually parents who initiate children into the junk-food habit. Most adults have been conditioned by their own upbringing to see certain products as 'treats', which we enjoy and use to increase our feelings of well-being and self-esteem. Since we love our children, we want to give them treats too, and certain foods swiftly become associated with love, comfort and reward. This can start very early in life, when parents add sugary flavourings to children's drinks or provide fruit juice instead of water. As Susan Jebb points out, this is quite unnecessary – children are perfectly happy with milk or water if we don't give them anything else, just as they are happy with fresh, wholesome food if no one introduces them to the unhealthy stuff.

But it's not that easy. Even if mum and dad try to keep sugar, salt and fat intake down, other adults (grandparents, neighbours, playmates' parents) like to indulge children with 'treats', and the thrill of forbidden food makes it taste all the sweeter. As they grow older, children compare notes with friends at school, so they're soon aware of the range of goodies on offer. Add to this the impact of marketing – not just the obvious TV ads, posters and packaging, but the subliminal marketing wherever we go, such as vending-machine displays and product placement in films – and it seems practically impossible to keep children away from unhealthy food for long.

Marketing messages

In the last few decades, the marketing industry has made increasingly insidious inroads into consumers' minds, affecting the way we think and act. Most people in the developed world now believe that choice – in food as in all other consumer products – is a fundamental right. (In fact, for most of human history, choice hardly existed – most people ate, drank and wore what they could get, if they were lucky enough to get it.) As a result, many parents feel guilty when they deny their children the choice of their favourite junk meal. But, as celebrity chef Jamie Oliver put it when asked why he thought children shouldn't have any choice over their school meal, 'You wouldn't ask them what they wanted to read in an English class. If they'd asked me, I'd have chosen ... comics or porn.' Children do need the opportunity to learn to make choices, but it's up to parents to decide which choices to offer.

Marketing has also conditioned us to care about brands. Neuro-imaging technology has shown that for many Americans the mere sight of a can of Coca-Cola excites activity in sections of the brain associated with feelings of self-image, memory and cultural identity. Since the early 1990s, when it became clear that even two-year-olds recognise and ask for specific branded products, there has been a concerted effort to win the hearts and minds of juvenile consumers. A UK government report on children's food and advertising in 2004 found that children associate highly advertised, branded food with 'fun', influenced not just by the taste but by the colourful packaging and use of pictures, cartoons and characters from TV or films. It added that 'effectively marketed brands generate recognition, familiarity and even affection amongst children. Well-known brands can impart status/"cool" to the user.'

Marketing aimed at children – such as links to popular films and TV programmes, toys in cereal packets and 'Happy Meals', etc. – creates a very powerful form of 'pester power'. So when parents are conditioned by marketeers to feel that allowing choice shows love for their children, and children are persuaded by those same marketeers to choose certain products, it can be extraordinarily difficult to resist the pressure. And that pressure now is immense: marketing techniques have become enormously sophisticated in recent years, and parents are often unaware of the ways their children are being targeted.

A confidential report about one advertising agency's successful child-focused promotion – for a fruit-based sugary snack – recently caused a furore when it fell into the hands of a British journalist. The report described how the agency had used a 'viral' approach – designed to create interest in the brand by word of mouth before the launch. Their task was to ensure children recognised images associated with the snack ('mutant fruit characters'), and saw them as 'cool'. The first target, therefore, was not the children themselves, but older youngsters whose tastes would influence children. So they 'seeded' the characters, along with a secret language, at concerts, in magazines and in cinemas, to put the word on the street. Using gifts of clothing, they also adorned children's celebrities with pictures of the characters, thus gaining exposure on television shows and music channels that children watch. They featured their characters on Internet pop-ups and created micro-sites on popular children's websites. Only when demand had been created among the infant audience was the product also marketed to their parents, this time as a 'healthy snack'.

Trapped in the junk-food jungle

Wise parents keep ahead of advertising tricks and educate their children to do so too (see Chapter 8). But even where parents are able to withstand the marketing assault and convince their offspring that love is not the same thing as indulgence ('We **love** you; the marketing men just want your money!'), children also have to live in a world beyond the family. Peer pressure exerts a strong influence – children don't want to seem 'different' – and the wrong sort of packaging in your lunch box can be social suicide. Even schools have been drawn into promoting unhealthy food, through schemes where they received cash or equipment for collecting snack-food wrappers. Indeed, for years many schools throughout the developed world have relied on revenue from snack vending machines to pay their staff salary bills. The obesity issue has forced schools to review what these machines provide, and many now include bottled water and healthy snacks. But if they still offer the choice of fatty snacks, biscuits and fizzy drinks, children are more than likely to choose the junk.

In some countries, school lunches have actually fed the junk-food habit. In 2005, Jamie Oliver caused a national outcry in Britain with a TV series drawing attention to the type of food being fed to large numbers of the nation's children. The nutritional content of this food was summed up by the notorious 'turkey twizzler', a popular item on many school menus, consisting of reconstituted bits of poultry (probably the bits you'd rather not think about) mixed with fats and additives. Oliver's valiant efforts to change the eating habits of primary-school children made fascinating viewing, and caused the British government to establish much stricter controls on school food standards. But he also showed how difficult it can be to wean children off junk food. As his dinner ladies pointed out, the reason they served up turkey twizzlers and other nutritionally hopeless dishes wasn't just a question of cost and convenience; it was because the children refused to eat anything else.

The problem is that once children are hooked on unhealthy food, their sense of taste is suppressed by excessive amounts of salt, sugar and additives, making other foods taste bland and unappetising in comparison. This is when they turn into 'fussy eaters', holding adults to ransom to provide the type of highly flavoured food they crave. So even though most parents are now aware of the dangers of a poor diet, many – like the dinner ladies – still allow their offspring to exist on junk, simply because it's the only food they'll eat. The UK government's 2004 report into children's food and advertising notes that, despite all the publicity about obesity, the majority of parents defer to their children's food preferences: 'Only a minority of parents in our research seemed to exercise effective control over their children's food choices'.

Parents often find themselves loving their offspring 'not wisely, but too well'. When a child refuses to eat, panic can set in. To the heady mix of pester power, 'the right to choose', peer pressure and a quick-fix culture, is added parental panic that their children might waste away (or acquire one of those much-hyped eating disorders). So children across the world continue to be hooked on a diet that threatens the healthy development of both body and brain.

Sugar rush

The brain is a greedy organ, needing almost one-third of the blood pumped from the heart to supply it with the oxygen and nutrients it needs to work efficiently. Deprived of these nutrients, it won't work as well as it should, so a balanced diet is essential for growing, learning children. Filling up on the wrong foods doesn't just threaten their physical health, it threatens their brain chemistry and thus their capacity to learn.

One of the main dietary culprits is sugar, which children – left to their own devices – often use as a major source of dietary fuel. They start the day with a sugary cereal, and continue at regular intervals with cans of fizzy drinks, cakes and biscuits, chocolate bars and sweets. As a body fuel, sugar is worse than useless. It provides an immediate 'sugar high', which in many children can lead to hyperactivity and impulsiveness, so they're unable to settle down and learn in school. But this high soon wears off, leaving the body craving more sugar. The child then has the option of feeling cranky and miserable or refuelling with sugar for another high. Hence the regular sugary snacks.

There's no doubt that excessive sugar consumption has contributed to the obesity explosion. But even more significantly, the calories in refined sugar are 'empty calories'. Sugary drinks and snacks don't provide any of the nutrients and dietary fibre children gain from eating healthy snacks like fruit, vegetables, nuts, dairy produce and grain. This means children with a sugar habit are likely to end up deficient in the minerals and vitamins found in a balanced diet. For instance, in a review of studies in 2005 the British Nutrition

Foundation found that 50 per cent of children had a marginal intake of vitamin A and 75 per cent had a marginal intake of zinc, both essential nutrients.

A long-term study at the University of Southern California claimed that if children's diets lacked a variety of minerals in the first three years, the children were more likely to be irritable and aggressive at eight years old, more likely to swear and cheat at eleven, and more likely to steal and bully at seventeen. Over the years, studies of children with ADHD and dyslexia have frequently pointed towards various mineral and vitamin deficiencies, usually resulting in a surge in the sales of food supplements. But when human beings eat a balanced diet, supplements aren't generally necessary. Too much sugar is a sure way of putting the diet out of balance. In the words of Oxford scientist Bernard Gesch, 'There is evidence that nutrition can improve [developmental conditions].More importantly, if careful diet can be used to treat these, it's possible we can also prevent them in the first place.'

The additive cocktail

While children may be missing out on essential nutrients, they are usually getting high doses of inessential additives. Controversy has raged for years about the safety of additives, such as tartrazine, caffeine and monosodium glutamate, which are used to colour, flavour or preserve food, and certain additives are banned in some countries but not others. Since additives often have long, complex chemical names (not made any easier in the European Union by the convention of also giving them E-numbers), the whole subject can be bewildering to consumers, adding to parental confusion and concern about diet. A 2004 review of 283 snack foods popular with children in the UK found that the average snack contains more than five additives, 70 per cent contain flavourings or flavour enhancers, and one-third contain food colourings.

Recent studies suggest that the 'cocktail' of additives consumed in a diet of processed food and soft drinks could be a contributory factor in behavioural problems. British toxicologist Vyvyan Howard points out that additives are tested by food companies one at a time, and little is known about how they react in combination: 'A number of these substances are related very closely to transmitter substances in the brain, which is the way nerve cells talk to each other. If you interfere with that, you interfere with brain function.' But establishing whether this is the case, and then the exact nature of each additive's contribution, will be difficult and could take decades.

Research studies into the effects of dietary factors on brain function are few and far between (in a world financed mainly by commerce, it can be difficult for scientists to access funding), and the food industry is quick to find fault with them. There's also the problem of identifying which ingredients specifically affect particular children – indeed, it seems possible that different cocktails of sugar, additives and other ingredients have adverse effects on different children, and maybe even the same children at different times.

But we do know what the usual suspects are, and now that the obesity explosion has proved conclusively that an impoverished diet damages the human body, we must also take seriously its potential effects on the brain. On a UK news programme in 2005 about children with behaviour problems, the nutritionist Patrick Holford said, 'We're seeing outrageous imbalances in brain chemistry simply caused by eating the kinds of food that, sadly, millions of kids are eating – and nobody's doing anything about it.'

Fats and fish oil

An important ingredient in any balanced diet is fat – or at least the right sort of fat. As well as being greedy, the brain is a fatty organ – in fact, it's almost two-thirds fat. Some of the key nutrients it requires to keep it going are essential fatty acids, which the human body cannot make, and which we therefore have to ingest in the form of food. The demonisation of fats in general – due to the twin terrors of heart disease and obesity – have blinded many people to the fact that some fats are essential to health, especially for children, whose brains are still developing. Breast milk is 50 per cent fat, and paediatricians advise parents not to restrict fat intake in children under two, when brain development is at its most rapid.

As children grow older, the advice is that – like adults – they should avoid saturated fats (solid, hard animal fats like butter and lard) in favour of healthier vegetable oils, keeping fried food to a minimum. However, in the 1990s Japanese researchers discovered another important element in the relationship between children and fat. A research team headed by Dr H. Okuyama suggested that a deficiency in omega 3 fatty acids 'might be affecting the behavioural patterns of a significant part of the younger generation in industrialised societies'.

In the past, a typical human diet included two essential fatty acids: omega 3 (found mostly in oily fish), and omega 6 (found in vegetable oils, meat and dairy products). Our hunter-gatherer ancestors consumed these in about equal measures. Over time, as people ate less fish, the ratio has changed – nowadays, we consume up to twenty times more omega 6. Indeed, omega 3 has virtually disappeared from the diets of many people in the developed world – including many vegetarians.

There's mounting evidence that (among other contemporary ills) omega 3 deficiency is related to distractibility and learning difficulties. In a 2005 UK study, fish oil supplements made a noticeable difference to the concentration and academic achievement of ADHD and dyslexic children. Professor Tom Sanders, professor of nutrition at London University, has compared omega 3-rich brains to Pentium 3 microprocessors, while people whose brains have too much omega 6 are 'slow and sluggish, like a 20-year-old silicon chip'.

The wrong sort of fat

But there's a further worrying factor in the fat story. Many foods these days contain manufactured 'trans-fats' (often listed on the label as 'hydrogenated vegetable oils'). These are processed fats, which are popular with the food industry because they're cheap to produce and prolong shelf life. However, trans-fats pose the same health threats as saturated fats such as butter and lard. They now turn up in many foods, including factory-produced bread and microwaveable 'ready meals', and particularly in snack foods such as potato crisps, cakes and biscuits. Felicity Lawrence, author of *Not on the Label*, points out that consumers are often misled by the 'vegetable oil' tag on food labelling: 'They know they have to cut down on saturated fat, so they see chicken nuggets as healthier than beefburgers. But they are just as bad.'

In terms of children's health, trans-fats may be even worse than saturated fats. The fatty acids in trans-fats don't lubricate the brain in the way natural fatty acids do – in fact, they may actually inhibit brain function. Animal studies have shown trans-fatty acids alter the efficiency with which brain cells communicate with each other. In the words of Dr Alex Richardson, a physiology researcher at Oxford University, 'Every time children eat crisps, biscuits or cakes, they are filling themselves with what are, essentially, toxic fats ... They are replacing the essential fats that would make their brains and bodies work properly with ones that are clogging up the machinery.' She points out that this has been admitted by government food agencies around the world, but 'they are not shouting loudly'.

Perhaps the reason governments don't shout loudly is that so much of the food we eat today is laced with processed trans-fats – to remove it all from our shelves would leave the supermarkets half empty. It's therefore up to parents to listen to the scientists and vote with their feet on their children's behalf in terms of harmful junk food. According to Dr Ann Kelley, professor of neuroscience at Wisconsin University, 'Those particular types of food – the fat and the sugar – are really the culprits. They're responsible for the behavioural changes that occur, the obesity and also the brain changes that look like addiction.'

The decline of the family meal

There's another huge influence on contemporary children's eating habits that I've so far failed to mention: the changes over recent decades in family structures and working habits. This subject is covered in Chapters 5 and 6, but its effects are felt in every single chapter in the book. In terms of diet, the greatest impact has been the decline of the family meal.

Throughout human history, eating has been an important social event, and in countries where food traditions are still highly valued, enjoyment of food is closely related to the circumstances of eating: preparation and presentation, family gatherings and mealtime conversation. But in developed nations, meals have become increasingly solitary experiences, with preparation often involving little more than piercing a film lid and switching on the microwave. The habit of 'grazing' on snacks throughout the day means that in many homes set mealtimes have all but disappeared; in others, there is not even a dining table.

A 2005 UK survey of 2000 families showed that 20 per cent never sat down to a meal together, and three-quarters of the rest ate while watching TV. And usually they aren't even watching the same TV. Many families around the world would identify with American journalist Sheila Pell's description of a typical mealtime – husband and children eating in different rooms in front of different televisions, while she perches alone in the middle, tucking into a microwaveable snack meal: 'Like much of the nation, everyone in the family is so busy that we long ago became used to eating in shifts. Dining has become dinner, interrupted. It is often a staggered affair, where people wander in on their own schedules, gaze into the refrigerator as if it were a 1950s automat, and make a selection. Our seating arrangements evolved out of this moveable feast.'

The highly significant social shift from communal to solitary eating has happened almost without comment, a knock-on effect of many other cultural changes happening at electric speed. These include the rise of dual-income households; the availability of pre-prepared meals; the increase in television channels so that each family member wants to eat in his or her own personal space, and, of course, children's addiction to junk food, which means they're not really interested in sharing something 'gross' with the rest of the family – they'd rather 'grab a burger and chill out' on their own.

No one realised, as the cult of the individual TV dinner grew, the extent to which children's solitary eating habits would begin to affect their overall development. When one day we woke up to find ourselves eating like Sheila Pell's family, people began to worry, and to look for the reasons behind the change. It's easy to blame parents, or the food industry, or marketeers or television (although, to be fair, most people blame parents). But, in fact, no one meant this to happen – it just did. In the words used by an Internet wag to sum up the Buddhist attitude to evil: shit happens. The decline of the family meal is a serious part of twenty-first-century shit.

Meals, manners and marijuana

The loss of shared mealtimes raises a host of issues. For a start the family meal was an opportunity for parents to model desirable behaviour: table manners, consideration for others and sensible eating habits. Teachers in Western countries frequently complain nowadays that children can no longer handle a knife and fork. A 2005 survey of a thousand pre-teens eating in a restaurant chain in the UK found that 20 per cent eat with fingers more than cutlery, 49 per cent use only a fork and three-quarters don't put their knife and fork together at the end of a meal. It doesn't seem to be much better in

Japan – a country famed for its addiction to manners – where nutritionist Dr Yukio Hattori complains that nearly 40 per cent of children can't use chopsticks properly. As social psychologist Pat Spungin puts it, table manners have an important social function: 'It's an important social skill to be able to sit at a table and not embarrass yourself and other people with your manners – to not lean over people and grab things, not take the last potato and to recognise that other people are with you.'

Family meals also affect social development: in a world where opportunities for adults and children to talk together grow fewer and fewer (see Chapter 4), a regular shared meal is the ideal opportunity for chatting over the events of the day, swapping gossip and planning future activities. This type of social interaction cannot start too early, but as Karen Pasquali-Jones, editor of *Mother & Baby* magazine, has pointed out, as parents increasingly use television as an electronic babysitter, even toddlers are beginning to eat alone. As she says, 'Toddlers need the experience of sitting up at a table. It not only encourages them to eat properly; it improves their speech and social skills and encourages them to try new foods.'

At the other end of the age range, researchers at the University of Minnesota found that the more frequently teenagers ate with their parents, the less likely they were to smoke, drink, use marijuana, or show signs of depression. There's even a research study showing that the only common denominator among National Merit Scholars of all races and social classes is that they eat dinner with their families. It doesn't take a rocket scientist to recognise that regular family get-togethers have a socialising and civilising effect on children of all ages.

Feeding a family

Family meals also tend to be healthier. Japanese nutritionist Asako Aramaki points out that people who eat with chopsticks tend to eat a more balanced diet than members of the 'hashi-nashi zoku' (chopstickless tribe), who are 'particularly careless about eating a good breakfast ... take dinner at irregular hours and nibble constantly at snacks during the day.' Shared mealtimes, of course, allow parents greater supervision of the food children eat (and when they eat it) and opportunities to counter the fussy-eater syndrome, thus weaning them off junk food.

If possible, the best way to avoid fussy eating habits is to stop them before they begin, by ensuring children eat a wide variety of food from the earliest age. In Italy, there's a long-established detailed feeding routine for babies, weaning them off milk and on to a range of tastes. This seems eminently sensible. As pointed out earlier, parents have control over children's diet in the first few years and it's not till the age of two that children really begin to be fussy about food. Evolutionary biologists explain that this is when they become aware that unfamiliar foods might be poisonous – and marketeers tell us it's the age at which they become aware of brands. The collision of old and new 'instincts' is a powerful one.

Once children have become addicted (or even quite partial) to junk foods, changing their eating habits is much more difficult, and without careful forethought parents' efforts could be counter-productive. The combination of work-frazzled adults and junk-demanding children could easily mean that mealtimes turn into a battleground – and unless family meals are a pleasant social occasion, no one's going to benefit. Indeed, it's possible that struggles with parents over food can, in the long term, drive children into eating disorders (although other elements are undoubtedly involved – see Chapter 8).

A brief battle-plan for detoxing junk-food addicts, culled from discussion with a range of experts, is provided on page 42, but its success depends on parents sticking to three key principles:

- Mealtimes should be enjoyable.
- Everyone eats the same meal – no special dishes.
- Parents decide which choices to offer to children.

To convince children to be more experimental, experts suggest the repeated offering of 'a little taste' during the family meal. If the child enjoys it, you offer more. If not, the key is not to push it – but *not* to offer an alternative dish. If you provide plenty of bread, rice, vegetables or other staples to choose from the child won't go hungry. The next time you eat that dish, offer 'a little taste' again, and so on. The American nutritionist Ellyn Satter has a useful rule of thumb for establishing mealtime harmony: adults decide *what*, *when* and *where* children eat; children decide *how much*, and even *whether*.

For working parents, preparing and sharing a pleasant meal each evening is clearly not easy to arrange – but it's worth putting in some thought on the subject. The ideal would be to arrive home at a regular time themselves, and build up a repertoire of simple meals using fresh ingredients that can be prepared relatively quickly. There are plenty of recipe books with suggestions for quick, healthy suppers. But if they can't always be there themselves, parents could at least ensure that whoever minds the children in their absence – hopefully other committed adults – reads clearly from the same nutritional and behavioural hymn sheet (see Chapter 6).

The key elements are consistency and regularity – agreed attitudes to food and behaviour at table, and an agreed regular mealtime – so children know what to expect and when and where to expect it. This might seem an effort to organise, but it's a question of priorities. When their children are ill, working parents move heaven and earth to ensure correct medication is administered at the right time. Regular healthy meals on a daily basis are as significant for children's long-term health as medication is for acute conditions – and in this respect, as in every area of child-rearing, consistency is essential. The nutritionist Susan Jebb believes that establishing eating habits to keep children in good shape for the rest of their lives is 'a key way to invest in their futures'. As she explains, 'They are not called "eating habits" for nothing – habits are ways of behaving which have become very deep-seated and are therefore difficult to change. Habits acquired in childhood tend to stay with you life-long.'

Cutting back on snack attack

Regular family meals are the best way to provide children with a balanced diet – and with ring-fenced 'family time' in which to consume it – while also making them less likely to gorge on unhealthy snack foods. Indeed, if you're going to the trouble of cooking, it's essential they don't eat snacks in the couple of hours leading up to the main meal. If children come to the table full, they'll have a far higher fussiness quotient. This is another reason for insisting on a regular mealtime: so that everyone knows when food is going to arrive on the table and, out of courtesy to the cook, snacks within an hour or so of that time are banned.

Children do, however, sometimes need snacks to stave off hunger – for instance on arrival home from school. Susan Jebb recommends the best way to ensure these are healthy snacks is to make your home a junk-free zone. This removes the temptation for anyone – including adult role models – to snack on unhealthy food. I found the following list of suggestions on an Australian government website, and have stuck it inside a kitchen cupboard door: fresh and dried fruit; crackers with cheese or peanut butter; yogurt; raisin bread, fruit loaf, toasted muffins; dips and biscuits or vegetable sticks; plain biscuits, scones or buns. I intend to add to it as I think of others – popcorn, sardines on toast and boiled egg have already been tagged on the end. Similarly, to save children from the soft-drinks trap, have only water, milk, diluted fruit juice or hot chocolate available.

If food at home is kept relatively junk free, parents can afford to be more relaxed outside the home. A total ban on junk food isn't a good idea, as it leads to interest in the forbidden foods. Allowing the over-fives occasional burgers and snacks when out shopping or eating out as a family is unlikely to do much harm, and ensures they're worldly-wise about such things among their peers.

*

The essence of this chapter is that adults have to take back responsibility for what children eat. We have to reassert the grown-ups' right to decide what, in terms of nutrition, is good for growing bodies and brains. 'Choice', the siren call of the marketing men, depends upon informed decision-making, and children don't know enough about nutrition to make informed decisions. Adults must therefore make choices on their behalf, to counteract damaging marketing messages.

This doesn't mean coercing children to eat particular foods, which could be just as damaging in other ways. It means ensuring attractive healthy options, associating these with pleasant family rituals, and thus gradually weaning children away from an unhealthy diet. If the significant adults in every child's life genuinely believe healthy food is better than junk, then we'll make the effort to provide food that nourishes our children rather than poisoning them.

DETOXING MEALTIMES

- Serve the main meal of the day at a regular time, and eat together as a family as often as possible, even if only one parent (or even a parent substitute) can be there.

- Make a list of healthy meals your family enjoys, and add to it as you find new ones. Then you won't have to think so hard when deciding what to cook.

- Don't make different dishes for different members of the family – all eat the same food.

- You decide what, when and where your child eats; let the child decide how much, or even whether.

- Teach table manners by:

  – deciding with other adults and older children what to emphasise and why
  – modelling good manners yourself
  – building up younger children's eating skills and manners gradually – focus on one aspect at a time and give plenty of praise when they get it right.

- Eat in a TV-free zone. Concentrate on the food and the chance to chat (see Chapter 4 for ideas on what to chat about).

- Don't allow any snacking for an agreed period, say 90 minutes, before a meal.

- Don't let mealtimes turn into battlegrounds: aim for enjoyable social occasions.

- Try not to panic if your child goes through a 'fussy' stage. Not eating a balanced diet for a while is unlikely to be too harmful (see the doctor and look into food supplements if you're really worried). Getting into battles over food is more likely to do long-term harm.

- As often as possible, let your child help with planning (e.g. choosing new dishes from recipe books), shopping and preparing meals.

- Be laid back. Meals are a time for enjoying your family's company, so try to make them pleasurable occasions.

- If you're not going to be at home, make sure everyone responsible for your child's meals knows and keeps to your ground rules.

TURNING CHILDREN INTO HEALTHY EATERS

- Start as you mean to go on – for instance, from the beginning provide water or milk rather than sugary drinks. If you later include fruit juice, dilute it.

- Keep an eye on your children's behaviour in relation to food, and try cutting out any foodstuffs that seem to create a bad reaction – check the labels to work out what ingredient (especially additives) might be the cause.

- Follow healthy eating guidelines, such as the Food Pyramid, but remember that low-fat products are inappropriate for young children.

- Ensure children have both omega 3 (e.g. oily fish, flax oil/linseed oil) and omega 6 (animal fats, nuts, vegetable oils) – if necessary, look into fish oil supplements.

- Avoid trans-fats (e.g. hydrogenated vegetable oil).

- Help children recognise the difference between *your* interest in their health and fitness, and the marketeers' interest in your money.

- Don't use food – especially unhealthy snack foods – as a reward or treat. Try to persuade grandparents and others to follow this rule too.

- Parental example is very important. If you have a sensible, balanced attitude to food and eating, your child will pick up on it – but if you gorge on unhealthy snacks, they'll want to as well. Raising a healthy child is great motivation to sort out your own eating habits.

- Don't keep any junk food or unhealthy snacks in the house. Have a selection of healthy snacks available (but no snacking before meals).

- When shopping or watching ads, alert your children to unhealthy food. For instance:

  – the more 'pre-prepared' the product, the more likely it is to contain damaging ingredients (e.g. frozen peas are probably OK; frozen pizza probably isn't)
  – the longer the list of ingredients, the more suspicious you should be
  – be wary about long shelf life, very unnatural colours, 'cool' packaging

– just because something claims it's good for you doesn't necessarily mean it is: vague claims like 'full of goodness', 'wholesome' and 'nutritious' are probably disguising something (for instance, for 'energy' or 'glucose', read 'sugar').

- Don't ban junk food altogether – allow occasional snacks, drinks and fast food (for instance, when away from home) – but don't view them as 'treats'.

HOW TO DETOX A JUNK-FOOD ADDICT

This takes time, so don't expect too much too soon. Use the techniques listed above, and at mealtimes try the following:

- Offer a mixture of new foods and the healthiest of children's old favourites (gradually transferring to home-made burgers, fish cakes, pasta sauces, etc).
- Offer 'tastes' of new foods to start with, not whole portions. If the child doesn't like it, don't insist. Wait a month or so and offer the same dish another time ... and again, and again.
- Present food as attractively as possible. Borrow the marketeers' ideas, e.g.

  - cut food into interesting shapes, make 'faces' or other pictures on the plate
  - invent names to make dishes sound special ('Cheesy Delight', 'Sardine Special').

- So your child doesn't go hungry, make sure there are plenty of 'staples' on the table, e.g. rice, pasta, bread or potatoes and vegetables or salad.
- Soups, stews, casseroles and smoothies are great for disguising unfavourite vegetables (switch to mince or grate on the food processor). This can help familiarise a fussy eater with a new taste.
- Some children prefer vegetables raw (for instance, with a dip).
- Always have water at the table for drinking (this is good for adults too – if you're drinking wine, intersperse with glasses of water). Make it more enticing by adding ice or serving in fancy glasses or with a special straw.
- Don't force or bribe your child to eat – for instance, don't offer dessert as a reward for finishing a main course. Ellyn Satter recommends that if you're having dessert you put out a single portion for each person *before* the meal, and children can eat their dessert first if they prefer. But only a single portion – no seconds.
- Fresh fruit is a healthy dessert. You can make it special by peeling, cutting into shapes, cooking (baked or stewed fruit) or creating a fruit salad.
- *See* Satter's book (see page 44) for many more ideas.

PARENT POWER: CHANGING THE WAY WE EAT

Public opinion is a potent force. International reaction to the film *Super Size Me* stung McDonald's into changing its menus; support for celebrity chef Jamie Oliver's campaign forced the UK government to improve school meal provision. When people get together they can change the world.

Parents may come in all shapes, sizes, colours and creeds, but they're united by one overriding ideal: they want their children to grow up happy and healthy. Working together, parents could become the world's most powerful and positive pressure group. So as well as detoxing your own child's diet, look for ways of helping detox the culture they live in:

- Talk to other parents about children and food. Tell them what you know; find out more. Support local, national and international campaigns to improve food quality.
- What is your child's school doing to promote healthy eating? If they haven't already done so, suggest they:

  – provide water coolers and/or milk to drink and discourage (or preferably ban) the consumption of sugary drinks on school premises

  – provide healthy snacks (e.g. toast, fruit, homemade scones and biscuits) at break times and stop children from bringing unhealthy snacks as tuck or packed lunches

  – provide appetising, healthy school lunches and encourage all children to eat school lunch (one of the best ways to do this is to make the bringing of packed lunches an unattractive option, e.g. by providing less pleasant facilities for eating them)

  – provide a pleasant, calm environment for school lunches, and use them as an opportunity to develop good manners and civilised behaviour

  – interest children in food production and preparation by growing food in school gardens, keeping hens, etc., with clubs to involve the children in gardening, caring for livestock

– involve children in devising menus, preparing food, simple cookery lessons and cookery clubs.

- If you have particular expertise in any of these areas and time to spare, offer help with school and child-care activities (see Chapter 7).
- Support campaigns to tackle the effects of marketing – for instance, the banning of all advertising to children under twelve (as has already happened in Sweden) – see Chapter 8.

Further reading

Dr Alex Richardson, *They Are What You Feed Them* (Harper Thorsons, 2005)

Ellyn Satter, *Child of Mine: Feeding With Love and Good Sense* (Bull Publishing, 2000)

Jeannette Orrey, *The Dinner Lady: Change the Way Your Children Eat, for Life* (Bantam Press, 2005)

Useful websites

Latest US food guidelines: **www.mypyramid.gov**

Independent research findings on food and behaviour:
www.FABresearch.org

The Center for Science in Public Interest: **www.cspinet.org**

Sustain (the alliance for better food and farming) is running a Children's Food Bill campaign: **www.childrensfoodcampaign.co.uk**

Mind the gap

Ten years ago, when I first began visiting schools around the UK, I was struck by the size of children in poorer areas of the country. I'd expected them to be small and undernourished, but many were huge, heavily built and lumbering. They were indeed malnourished, the products of a high-fat junk-food diet.

There are many reasons why poorer families feed their children less well than others: transport problems that prevent them shopping around or buying in bulk for economies of scale; the cost of buying fresh and organic products; a lack of knowledge about healthy eating and more susceptibility to marketing messages. So while recent health campaigns, films and television programmes have made an impact on diet in wealthier homes, many children in poor homes remain trapped in poor eating habits.

A nursery nurse working in a school in a deprived area of the country sent me this note:

'As I live near the school where I work, I shop at the same store as most of the parents. I've noticed that many buy poor-quality or cheap basics such as white bread and a small and limited variety of fruit and vegetables, but seem quite happy to spend more money on branded expensive cakes, chocolates, snacks, etc ... In school we give free fruit and milk at break time. Some parents insist their children will not eat fruit and send them with a chocolate biscuit or crisps every day. An even larger number of children don't have the free milk provided and bring high-sugar, coloured drinks.'

In a recent international comparison of social mobility (the extent to which children from poor homes are able to overcome the circumstances of their birth and prosper in the educational system) two of the most successful countries were Spain and Finland. I've recently visited both these countries and eaten school meals in each. The food was fresh, locally sourced, highly nutritious and appetising; all the children ate it (no packed lunches); and teachers sat down to eat with them, insisting on the sort of civilised behaviour you'd expect at a pleasant family dinner. The contrast between this and the noisy eating areas, highly variable school food and junk-filled packed lunch boxes in the UK and USA (two countries with very poor social mobility) was stark.

Schools in the UK try valiantly to pass on the message about healthy diets, but in deprived areas it's an uphill battle. A headteacher told me recently that, as part of a healthy food campaign, his school began to provide milk, fruit and toast for the children at break time, but the campaign was undermined because some children continued to bring in crisps, chocolate bars and sugary drinks. After much debate, it was agreed the only way to stop the drift back to unhealthy food was to ban it. Within hours, one father was in school threatening the headteacher with (a) violence and (b) a trip to the European Court of Human Rights if he didn't reinstate his daughter's right to eat junk.

But schools in poorer areas of the USA and UK, where healthy eating campaigns *have* been successful, report considerable improvements in children's behaviour. It seems the best way to make a real change in the eating habits of under-privileged children would be for the government or individual schools to be heavy-handed about school meals. If there were a national policy of compulsory school lunches for all (as is often the case in private schools), campaigning middle-class parents would soon ensure high-quality appetising food, all children would have access to at least one healthy meal a day and parents would be let off making packed lunches. It sounds a good deal to me.

CHAPTER TWO

OUT TO PLAY

Centre-screen, a lion is basking in the sun. Three young cubs tumble, prowl and pounce around him – play-hunting, play-fighting and occasionally launching themselves at their father, until he loses patience and brushes them away with a mighty paw. Into this picture edges the natural historian David Attenborough, speaking softly into the mike so as not to disturb the family group. 'Play,' he breathes sonorously, 'is a *very serious* business.'

It certainly is. Those lion cubs are learning some of the most important lessons of their lives. They're developing the physical control and coordination they'll need for the hunt; they're establishing the social pecking order within their family pack; and they're discovering – in a safe, controlled environment – what it's like to take risks … and what happens when you step over the line. What's more, they're enjoying it. The glorious thing about play is that it's *fun*: the young of every species are designed by nature to learn fundamental physical, social and emotional lessons through sheer enjoyment. As the Scottish poet Robert Louis Stevenson put it over a century ago:

> *Happy hearts and happy faces*
> *Happy play in grassy places –*
> *That was how, in ancient ages,*
> *Children grew to kings and sages.*

Unless, of course, they are denied the opportunity to play outside, or lured away from Stevenson's 'grassy places' to some sort of virtual unreality.

One major side effect of the technological revolution has been, for many children, the replacement of age-old play activities (running, climbing, pretending, making, sharing) with a solitary, sedentary screen-based lifestyle. This is an alarming development. TV and computer games have many merits, and our lives would be much poorer without them, but they aren't a substitute for real life – and if children are to develop healthily in mind and body, neither are they a substitute for real play.

This change in children's play habits has happened over a single generation, and two side effects of contemporary culture have helped it along. First, the development of technological (and entirely indoor) options mentioned above, the pros and cons of which are discussed in Chapters 8 and 9, have provided a seductive alternative to outdoor play. Second, a huge increase in parental anxiety has led to restrictions on children's physical activity, their play and their freedom to roam beyond the confines of home, school and other supervised environments. Part of this anxiety is rational – for instance, a huge increase in traffic on the roads means the outdoor environment becomes less safe every year, and with more parents out at work there are fewer 'eyes on the street' to watch out for children's welfare – but part of it is highly *irrational* and is itself a consequence of our multimedia culture.

The fear of fear itself

One summer afternoon in 2002, two little girls went out for a walk in an English country village ... and disappeared. For weeks, the world's media camped out in Soham, Cambridgeshire, and the last photograph of ten-year-olds Holly and Jessica shone out from TV screens across the developed world – until the discovery of their bodies in a ditch wiped out all hope. A couple of months later, the TV cameras moved to Washington, USA, where deranged snipers were picking off adults and children from their car, leaving unnerving messages that no child was safe. The faces and voices of terrified parents spoke directly to mothers and fathers all over the world. Fast-forward two years to Boxing Day 2004 and the devastating tsunami in South East Asia that tore children from their parents' arms, whirling them to their deaths. The horror of those hundreds of thousands of deaths and the agony of the bereaved fathers, mothers and children left behind shocked the whole world. But it didn't just shock us; it affected the way our brains work.

We can now view (and repeatedly re-view) distressing images of terrible events as if they are actually happening in front of us. This has a much greater effect on our mental stability than hearing or reading about them. Neuroscientists have found that horrific pictures affect the emotional centres in the brain, and the more frequently they're viewed, the more they induce feelings of anxiety. When you read news, or listen to the measured tones of a newsreader, your responses are less immediate, more open to reason. What's more, in reading a newspaper, you can choose which stories to look at, while television news involves sitting through the whole thing – and studies show that the majority of television news stories are negative, depicting issues such as conflict and abuse.

Psychologists researching the World Trade Center attack on the people of America found that the more TV people watched, the more likely they were to suffer psychological effects, even though they had no personal connection with the atrocity. Terrorists have been swift to capitalise on this finding, and to use TV as a primary instrument of terror. Indeed, the vile acts of destruction and suicide bombings that increasingly dominate our screens are designed not so much to draw attention to a grievance, but to crank up international anxiety and destabilise Western societies.

Television coverage of horrific news about children and families forces parents to confront their worst fears over and over again. The fact that this coverage continues remorselessly, night and day, in the corner of one's own living room – or in the bedroom just before sleep – makes it even more powerful. So, even though we know the chances of our children being murdered by a maniac, hit by a sniper's bullet or taken from us by some terrible natural disaster are infinitesimally small, we are still afraid. We have fallen victim to the worst fear of all: fear of fear itself.

When a National Lottery was introduced in Britain in the 1990s, its TV slogan, accompanied by a pointing cosmic finger was, 'It could be you!' Whenever any terrible event happens to children – however far away – we now know about it immediately, share vicariously in the parents' anguish, and think: It could be my children. As one newspaper columnist put it in the week of the Beslan school siege in Bellorussia, 'That was the overpowering feeling as we watched the images of women, their faces contracted with stress and grief ... the men outside the siege school swearing at their impotence. It could have been us.'

Children too are becoming more fearful. Despite restrictions on other types of television programming during the daytime and early evening, there's no restriction on the content of the news. Young children cannot distinguish between real events in real time and drama or video footage: to them, what's happening on TV is happening now. Neither do they understand geographical distance: as far as they're concerned, these scary events could be going on just down the road. As TV coverage of catastrophic events grows ever more graphic and all-pervasive, psychiatrists have become concerned about the levels of stress and anxiety it can raise in children. In the words of Eric Vernberg, Professor of Clinical Child Psychology at the University of Kansas, 'The news media may inadvertently amplify and increase traumatic exposure ... by showing graphic and emotionally laden images of terrorist acts and the aftermath; in previous eras, the public could only imagine such a scene of violence, whereas today we can experience it over and over again in Technicolor.'

So parental anxiety and children's fears go hand in hand, and the outside world begins to seem an infinitely frightening place. This is in spite of the fact that, for most of us in the developed world, life is generally safer than it's ever been.

Putting fear in its place

Anxiety is insidious. It amplifies rational fears and stimulates irrational ones. There seem so many things to worry about now – health issues, all sorts of possible accidents, crime and violence, paedophiles and other people with evil intent, natural disasters – and all of these receive copious coverage in the media. But when the gathering paranoia begins to threaten children's emotional, social and intellectual development, we have to confront the problem.

One obvious way to avoid unnecessary anxiety is to limit exposure to distressing news. I'm not advocating ostrich-like head-in-the-sand behaviour – everyone needs to know what's going on in the world, and to wise up to real risks – but we don't need to invite constant messages of doom and destruction into our living rooms, and we certainly don't need to wallow in the misery of other people. The best advice seems to be to read the news rather than watch it, keep an eye on the content of TV news when children are up and about, and definitely don't keep tuning in to distressing reruns.

We also have to be aware that there's a huge market in safety, so it's in the interests of the marketing men to keep anxiety on the boil. All parents need to take sensible precautions, of course, but there's a limit. *Washington Post* journalist Laura Stepp concluded it was breached by an advertisement for a 71-piece child-safety kit (including sponge tape to lash over the sharp edges of furniture) featuring the reminder that 'accidents are the No. 1 killer of children today'.

Indeed, attempts to make life super-safe frequently backfire. It's recently become clear that the asthma boom of the last two decades (and perhaps increases in allergies and other diseases of the auto-immune system) is related to excessive levels of cleanliness in contemporary homes. When all the everyday bacteria are wiped out, children's bodies don't get the chance to build up resistance. Too great a preoccupation with safety can be as harmful as too little, and wrapping children in cotton wool carries a very strong risk of suffocation.

How fear turns children into couch potatoes

Healthy development of both body and mind depends on activity and experience. From the very beginning, babies learn about the world around them through touch and movement. To refine their physical control and coordination, they need plenty of opportunity to flex developing muscles. If parental anxiety gets in the way, development is inhibited.

For instance, the 'Back to Sleep' campaign (aimed at preventing Sudden Infant Death Syndrome or 'cot death') advised that babies should be put to sleep on their backs, but parents who overreact to the advice become frightened of placing their children on their stomachs. Dr Amanda Kirby, director of the Dyscovery Centre for Specific Learning Difficulties, believes this may help account for recent increases in dyspraxia, since babies won't get adequate exercise unless they also spend time lying on their fronts and sitting up in baby seats. 'Children need to exercise all their bodies,' she says. 'If an adult did exercises just for the biceps, and none for the triceps, he'd have flabby triceps.'

If babies are never put down on their fronts they'll be slow to lift themselves on their arms, and then to crawl, and some will never crawl at all. The act of crawling – alternately leading with opposite arms and legs – helps to open up connections between the two sides of the brain, vital for later learning. Opportunities to move about – touching, grasping and exploring objects in a carefully monitored environment – are also essential for babies' developing brains. Dr

Christine Macintyre, an expert in children's physical development at the University of Edinburgh, points out that 'poor movement is part of all the specific learning difficulties and syndromes such as Asperger's'. Yet in many contemporary homes, parents obsessed with cleanliness or accident prevention often decide it's safer to stop them. Children now spend much more time strapped 'safely' into baby seats, high chairs, car seats and strollers than ever before.

Once old enough to be up and moving, small children by nature want to walk, run and climb – and some are genetically programmed to need more of this type of physical activity than others. Without sufficient opportunities to work off excess energy, any child (genetically vulnerable or not) will be frustrated and fractious. But in a home full of electronic equipment – TVs, DVDs, computers, music centres, phones – lively physical play can prove both dangerous and expensive. And with the amount of traffic zooming around nowadays, even in rural areas, play outside in the street or lane is definitely off limits for toddlers.

This sort of activity is therefore increasingly confined to 'specialist environments' – playgrounds, activity clubs or, if you're lucky, the family garden – where toddlers require supervision. As parental time is nowadays at a premium (quite apart from work demands, all that electronic equipment around the house keeps adults pretty busy), many young children spend precious little time in the sort of places where they can indulge their need for active play. It's much easier to let them watch other people moving about on TV. Even getting back and forth from play places seldom involves much physical activity. Time pressures and fears of traffic mean small children are usually transported by car, or strapped, for safety reasons, into a stroller, even when they are perfectly capable of walking.

If the weather's good, some parents have another reason for keeping children indoors: fear of the sun. A decade's worth of warnings about ultraviolet rays mean they've become paranoid about skin cancer. But like the Back to Sleep campaign and sensible hygiene rules, this issue calls for a bit of common sense. Apart from the importance of outdoor exercise, children of all ages need exposure to sunlight to meet their body's requirement for vitamin D. Although in hot sunshine children should take precautions (the fair-skinned particularly need good dollops of suncream, broad-brimmed hats and advice to keep in the shade), there are too many benefits to outdoor play to let fear keep our children indoors.

Researchers in Scotland recently concluded that today's three-year-olds weigh more than their counterparts 25 years ago, not so much through over-eating (up to three, most parents are still in general control of their children's diets) but because physical activity levels have dropped dramatically. Their study showed that, despite a widespread perception among parents (and even health and education workers) that young children are spontaneously active, pre-schoolers are now as inactive as office workers. And these early bad habits clearly persist, because the couch-potato three-year-olds were just as inactive when the researchers checked up on them two years later.

It's around the age of three, when children enter pre-school, that interest in junk food usually begins in earnest. So this is the point – as lack of exercise and an increasingly unhealthy diet collide – when the fuse on many children's personal 'obesity time bombs' is ignited. From now on, the more sedentary they are, the more time is available for screen-based snacking and grazing. And the more overweight and sluggish they become, the less interested they are in taking exercise. These two side effects of our technological culture begin to swirl together in the toxic mix, and we can't tackle one without bearing in mind the effects of the other. What's more, as future chapters will show, the toxic brew is enriched by many other contributory factors.

Getting children off the couch

There's an easy way to get children off the couch (and out of the stroller and car seat) while simultaneously defusing parental anxiety. It is simply to spend more time in their company, introducing them to non-sedentary activities. This doesn't have to be taxing or tiring and it doesn't need any special equipment. For instance, walking with children through the streets rather than driving provides physical exercise, a chance to chat and an opportunity to develop awareness of road safety skills through example and experience. Indeed, children need many opportunities to watch adults model road safety procedures if they're eventually to cope for themselves on today's busy roads, and learning about road safety can't start too early. Safety campaigners point out that the highest number of deaths and injuries occur when children are in their early teens, because they begin travelling independently without having acquired deep-seated pedestrian road skills.

Sadly most of us are now so used to using the car for all journeys that the thought of walking is off-putting. It can, however, provide opportunities for interaction that simply aren't available when you're driving. When my daughter was at pre-school we didn't have a car, so we had to walk a mile or so there and back each day. I still remember impromptu games of hide-and-seek in the churchyard we used as a short cut; squirrel-spotting and hiding peanuts for them to find as we passed through the park; inventing stories about the people we saw regularly in the streets. All these and many other silly games arose naturally and delighted us both, although often we just ambled along in companionable silence. (Mind you, sometimes it wasn't very companionable – not every moment spent with one's child is one of unalloyed joy ... but the two generations also have to learn how to cope with not getting along with each other.) Anyway, after a couple of years we got a car, and I have no more memories of our trips to school – except, of course, the misery of the traffic.

Spending time with young children in safe outdoor environments gives them a chance to run about and let off steam – and it doesn't have to be a special outing. But activity doesn't necessarily mean outdoor exertion. As soon as children are old enough, letting them help with everyday chores – such as making beds, emptying rubbish and preparing food – provides shared time for chat and develops physical dexterity and competence. Parents often spend a fortune on expensive 'educational games', forgetting that there are many significant life skills to be learned using resources to hand in every home. One mother I met said her toddler's favourite occupation was helping fill the dishwasher; another remembered a happy day defrosting the fridge: 'We started off making snowballs, and ended up paddling.' The list of 'life skills for a ten-year-old' in Chapter 5 is a starting point for activities you can first model, then share, and finally hand over to your offspring.

The point is that spending time with children doesn't usually require parents to *do* anything special – just to be with them, getting on with whatever needs doing. What's more, shared time can reduce parental anxiety: it's reassuring to know you've repeatedly modelled safety procedures, and over time you can actually watch a child grow in confidence and ability. As for the children, they get to wallow in what they most crave – parental time and attention – while learning skills to carry into their own time and play. A woman told me recently how she drops her little girl off at tap-dancing class and her son at golf, then manages to snatch half an hour in the gym before picking them up again. I suspect the children would much prefer to spend time with their mother, rather than paid minders – and some sort of shared exercise would be healthier and more enjoyable for all of them than that weekly frantic round trip.

More focused family activities – such as swimming, ball games, cycling, riding, climbing or just walking the dog – also help keep everyone fit and healthy. In the Netherlands, where practically everyone cycles everywhere and you frequently see family groups speeding down the cycle lanes, there's one of the lowest levels of obesity in the developed world. And these active family pursuits don't need to be expensive – indeed, psychologists and paediatricians all agree that parents' major expenditure on their offspring should be in the form of time rather than money. Amanda Kirby finds it sad that people who visit her centre often feel they're not 'good parents' if they're not spending money: 'They've been made to believe by marketing that they have to pay for a package called "creativity" or some sort of programme to make their children healthy. I find they're often relieved to be given permission just to go swimming or throw a ball about. We seem to have forgotten the secret of just playing with children, just having fun ...'

PE, playtime and paranoia

There's now concern across the developed world about children's dwindling interest in physical exercise. This has been clearly recorded in Japan, where the Central Council for Education has monitored children's development annually since the 1960s and noted a steady deterioration in physical abilities, beginning in the mid-eighties. Children can no longer run as fast, jump as high or throw and catch a ball as well as they did in the past. The Central Council puts this decreasing physical strength down to changes in lifestyle, including more playing of video games, less space for physical activity and an inadequate diet, and concludes, 'We are now playing a high price for what we have unconsciously lost.' A survey of children's physical skills in Switzerland in 2004 recorded similar findings.

Internationally, the situation has also been fed by changes in attitudes to physical education (PE) in schools during the latter part of the twentieth century. Firstly, a generally liberal educational establishment, influenced by increasingly vocal and anxious parents, has become less keen to enforce participation in school sports and outdoor activities – even in Japan, where the tradition of *rajio taiso*, communal callisthenic exercises, which used to be compulsory each morning of the school vacations, is dying out in some areas.

Secondly, as school curricula throughout the developed world have become ever more exam-orientated (see Chapter 7), there have been changes in both the time available for PE and the way the subject is taught. With the emphasis on literacy, numeracy and other academic subjects required by law, there are now fewer opportunities for physical education in the school day than there were in the past. PE itself has often been 'academicised', even in the pre-teenage years, with teachers required to concentrate on the development of technique rather than general exercise and enjoyment. When lessons are about curricular targets, rather than opportunities for children to run, jump, be active and let off some steam, those who aren't keen on PE – including the overweight or out of condition – are difficult to motivate. 'Fear of injury' then provides a good excuse for reluctance to join in.

Thirdly, another source of fear – fear of litigation – is affecting PE in the same way it affects the rest of the curriculum. As well as influencing what happens on the sports fields, fear of injury also leads to constraints on what children can do at playtime and a reduction in outdoor excursions and challenges which could, if anything went amiss, lead to lawsuits. The health and safety brigade now stalks the corridor, playground and sports field, attempting to eliminate all risks from children's lives. All that happens, of course, is that schools become bland and unexciting places. When teachers have to fill in a dozen pages of risk assessment forms before taking their class out on so much as a nature walk, many just decide not to bother. In recent years, keeping gerbils, games of conkers, snowball fights, even using egg boxes for making craft models have all been banned in one British primary school or another on safety grounds.

The irony is that there's actually been very little litigation about this sort of thing. But some insurance companies have exploited the possibility that there *might*, so the health and safety lobby grows ever stronger ... and our children grow ever weaker.

And it's not just physical development that's threatened by the changes in society's attitude to PE. As well as promoting physical control and coordination, sporting activities – particularly team games – have always been valued for their contribution to children's social and emotional growth. For many children, especially boys, learning to work as a team on the playing field teaches important lessons about cooperation, rule-following and self-control. For some, success in competitive sport can offset the damage of failure in the classroom – indeed, the boost to self-esteem can sometimes help restore failing academic fortunes.

If schools' attitude to sport is ambivalent, PE lessons fail to motivate, and fear of injury interferes with playground games and after-school clubs, these benefits are lost for many children. Sadly, for those who do catch the sporting bug, an over-emphasis on competitiveness can be just as damaging – when children model their behaviour on that of many sports personalities seen on TV, the values of cooperation, rule-following and self-control are unlikely to figure highly.

This complex web of social conditions and conditioning will take some time to unravel, but parental awareness is a good start, and there are some suggestions for how schools and society might address the underlying issues in Chapter 10 and *Detoxing Childhood* (page 308). In the meantime, there's another pressing problem to consider that's much nearer to home.

The decline of the free-range child

Until recently, children did not have to rely on organised games and activities for their physical, emotional and social development. As they reached school age there was another way they grew in physical strength and learned about themselves and how to relate to others. It was called 'going out to play'.

Nowadays, our generalised adult anxiety has created a culture in which children's freedom to roam, whether to the park for an informal kick-about or just for a general mooch around with friends, has been greatly curtailed. Research at Lancaster University in 2004 found that compared even to the 1990s, today's ten- and eleven-year-olds are given a smaller and more clearly specified area in which they can play freely, are monitored much more closely by their parents, and have their play curtailed at the first hint of danger. The same growing restrictions are happening across the developed world.

This means children no longer experience what writer and play expert Tim Gill calls 'everyday adventures', those small but significant experiences through which they learn about the world, develop their physical coordination and control, and grow in independence. Everyday adventures are an unpredictable but essential part of growing up – they are opportunities to make judgements, take risks, learn how to make friends and elude enemies. But they depend upon the freedom to be out and about, not closeted at home.

In stark contrast to these everyday first-hand escapades, today's children have ersatz adventures courtesy of television or computer games. These adventures are not real – the children aren't moving in real space, interacting with real people, or taking real risks: if it all gets too dull or too scary, they can just switch off. Screen-based activities don't prepare children for the real-life risk assessments human beings must make on a day-to-day basis – judging speed and distance when crossing the road or driving a car, for instance, or assessing how far to trust other people with their own safety. Without the preparation of play and other independent activities involving rel-atively 'safe' risks, some children may eventually become excessively reckless and others excessively timid.

Places to play, people to play with

The loss of opportunities for outdoor, loosely supervised play is also likely to have long-term effects on children's social development.

Learning how to make friends, play as part of a group, and resolve minor conflicts used to take place out of adult view, meaning children could take responsibility – and make mistakes – without incurring immediate adult judgement. Many of children's playmates now are screen-based virtual friends, from whom they don't learn social skills. And practically all real juvenile socialising goes on under the eagle eye of adults, who are naturally swift to intervene if things look dicey. Some children are thus being labelled 'naughty' very early in their social careers (and then going on to fulfil the prophecy), while others are learning to call for help at the first sign of danger. The epidemic of bullying recorded in many countries over the last decade may be partly due to over-supervision, which helps to create both bullies and victims.

The loss of outdoor play and everyday adventures is particularly significant for children who have a tendency to be easily distracted or impulsive. They often need to run off excess energy and develop self-confidence through confronting physical challenges. In school, these children may be trapped in a vicious cycle of poor school per-formance, leading to poor self-image, leading to poor behaviour. They need access to other environments and experiences, away from constant adult censure. But all too often the few open spaces left – parks and playgrounds – suffer from the same health-and-safety paranoia that affects the rest of children's worlds. A report from the UK Child Accident Prevention Trust in 2005 pointed out that, 'the fear of being sued and insufficient understanding of risk assessment ... contribute to local authorities making playgrounds boring, or removing them altogether'.

There are still some communities in the developed world where children can play out in interesting, semi-supervised environments, without adults constantly on their backs, and we should be seeking to build on their success. A German father emailed me details of his neighbourhood, predominantly made up of young families. With all adults keeping an eye out for all children, houses in cul-de-sacs and the frontage street a go-slow zone for cars, it feels safe to let the children roam: 'It's not uncommon for me to be sitting on the patio reading on a spring or summer afternoon, only to have my kids invade with eight or ten other kids to play on the swing set in the backyard. Half an hour later they're all at the next-door neighbours' jumping through the sprinklers; perhaps later the boys split off to ride their bikes while the girls play with their Barbies on the lawn. The whole situation certainly gave me a new appreciation of urban and suburban design once it sank in.'

Sadly, however, in more and more suburbs and in cities everywhere, fears about safety have led to a growing perception that parents who let their children play in the street are uncaring and irresponsible, and that any youngster out unsupervised must be an ill-disciplined 'feral child', probably up to its neck in truancy, drug-running and crime. Our children are increasingly battery-raised – cooped up in their homes, living virtual lives, or in the car, being transported from club to class to club – rather than enjoying the free-range existence they could expect even twenty-five years ago.

Re-establishing children's right to roam

The first steps in tackling this damaging culture are the anti-anxiety measures described earlier. Parents must work on banishing their own irrational anxiety and, by spending time in their children's company, on providing them with the life skills necessary to assume greater independence, including a full training in road safety and how to avoid 'stranger danger'. The more time parents and children spend together, the more they'll both be able to trust children's judgement and their ability to cope alone. As children grow in self-control and self-confidence, it becomes easier to let them flex their wings in a relatively unsupervised environment.

Opportunities from an early age for loosely supervised play with friends will also develop self-confidence. Issy Coles-Hamilton of the UK Children's Play Council believes this sort of experience is essential if children are later to feel confident enough to make their own decisions, and not be forced by peers into doing something that doesn't feel comfortable. 'If you ban friends or keep your child in, they'll never learn to evaluate risk. And just telling them "Don't do this" isn't an answer. What you should be saying is, "This is what to expect if you do this".'

Once you feel it's time (and the time will vary depending on the individual), the first step to a free-range childhood is simply a question of letting your child out of your sight for a limited time – to go alone to the local shop, or to the park with a friend, or to walk with chums to school or after-school club. Some parents – and I have to admit, I'd probably be one – may feel better if their offspring carries a tracking device or mobile phone. After all, it seems only sensible to make use of technology to facilitate outdoor play (although, except in dire emergencies, phones should be used for texting only, as there's a possibility their use can damage the developing brain). Once you've done this a few times and your child has demonstrated confidence and competence in being away from you, you can gradually extend the level of freedom to roam.

Extending children's free-range existence can also involve parents in a little socialising themselves, because as play expert Tim Gill says, the best sort of security is getting to know your neighbours. We need to know there are people who will 'keep an eye out' for children, and to whom they can turn in emergencies. The most obvious starting point is other parents in the neighbourhood with whom you can share supervision and, as children begin to wander a little further afield, agree curfews and geographical boundaries. Informal contacts like this might widen to take in grandparents and any retired neighbours with the time to watch out for local children. Best of all would be if residents' associations could be drawn into the quest, so that 'keeping an eye out for the children' became a means of strengthening community relations.

In over-crowded, over-trafficked, post-industrial societies, however, parental and community efforts also need backing up with policy and action from the authorities, to ensure that the world out there is as safe as it possibly can be. We need to know that effective measures are in place to control the small number of people who wish to harm children, and we need many more attractive, safe open spaces where children can play.

Safer streets

Despite having lived with motorised traffic for over a century, we still haven't sorted out the vexed question of which should come first, pedestrians or cars. While it's fair to expect pedestrians to keep off major roads, it's also reasonable to expect cars to give way to people in built-up areas. Initiatives to keep heavy traffic out of residential areas, traffic calming measures and very low speed limits are a start, but traffic accident figures make it clear that much more could be done. Urban designer Ben Hamilton-Baillie points to evidence that where traffic speed is kept to around 20 mph (30 kph), pedestrian safety is vastly improved. For one thing, an impact at that speed is unlikely to be fatal; for another, drivers and pedestrians can still make eye contact at 20 mph, and that sort of human contact tends to make drivers more considerate.

Some European countries, notably Germany and the Netherlands, are exploring the concept of 'home zones' – residential areas where the needs of pedestrians are considered more important than those of motorists. Another successful innovation in Scandinavian and Dutch cities is 'shared space', where cars and pedestrians have equal rights to the road, traffic signs are removed, and the design of the street works alongside interaction with pedestrians to make drivers drive safely. These measures have achieved significant reductions in accident figures, while the UK, which is swamped by road signs and traffic furniture, has the second worst road casualty figures in Europe for child pedestrians.

Schools could also do their bit to help improve road safety by organising systems to replace 'the school run' that bedevils so many European cities. It's a foolish irony that, by driving their children to school 'for safety reasons', parents add massively to the traffic problem. The long-established yellow school bus system means this is far less of a problem in the USA, and similar systems have been trialled successfully in rural areas in the UK. In built-up areas, the system of 'walking buses' widely used in Japan is worth considering: parents drop their children off at a walking bus stop at an agreed time and older children supervise the walk to school.

However, revitalising city children's play involves much more than traffic calming. The seminal German study *The Child in the City* in the late 1990s pointed out many other disadvantages of growing up in built-up areas, above all the lack of opportunities to 'test and train motor and social abilities'. Provision of real, attractive open play spaces requires cooperation between children's services and planning departments, backed by financial commitment from governments.

Happy play in grassy places

Stevenson's poem stresses the importance of '*grassy* places' for play, and contact with nature is a critically important part of the equation. Even the most convinced city-dweller knows that greenery is important for lifting the human spirit, and it seems particularly important for children. Indeed, a research study at the University of Illinois has suggested that contact with nature can have a significant 'detoxing' effect on children with attention deficit disorders, and 'the greener the setting, the greater the relief'. In contrast, researchers found that indoor activities like watching television, or outdoor activity in paved or non-green areas increased attention deficit.

This is, of course, no real surprise. The benefits of a trip to the countryside for older children are well known. From American summer camps to British 'Outward Bound' courses to the Japanese *sanson ryugaku* (which sends teenagers from the big cities to rural schools for a taste of life in the countryside), such opportunities clearly contribute to physical fitness, self-confidence and problem-solving abilities – what the Japanese call 'power for living' (*ikiru chikara*). But going away from home for prolonged visits isn't an option for the under-tens, who need the security of family contact and familiar haunts – they need green and grassy places close to home.

As technology burgeons, however, many adults who enjoy a pleasant stroll in a carefully tended park find other aspects of nature rather untidy and unhygienic, and prefer to have them cleared away. According to author Alex Kerr, the Japanese lead the way in this respect, tarmacking over as much of their environment as possible. In some areas, trees are shorn of foliage before the end of summer because residents find fallen leaves dirty and messy. Not surprisingly, therefore, researchers recently found that many children in Tokyo and the surrounding area have little experience of nature. Not only had the majority never eaten a nut or berry pulled from a tree or drunk water from a natural stream, but more than half these children from the Land of the Rising Sun (52.6 per cent) had never seen a sunrise or sunset. Thirteen years ago the figure was 41 per cent. I suspect city-dwelling children across the developed world – and even some in rural areas – are just as ignorant about nuts, berries, fresh water and the sun's comings and goings. It would be interesting to know how many children in New York, Paris or London have had the chance to make mud pies or daisy chains, build a den or a bonfire, dig a hole, dam a stream or collect bugs, tiddlers or conkers.

Fortunately, there are counter-movements committed to greening urban and suburban areas. For instance, in Canada the Evergreen movement is a national charity working for community naturalisation – with government assistance – by transforming school grounds, publicly accessible land and home landscapes. Planners in Freiburg in Germany have stopped installing artificial play equipment and begun creating 'nature playgrounds', full of logs, mounds, ditches and other natural features. A playground recently developed in Scotland is made of a combination of natural and man-made features – fallen trees, boulders, sand, water and structures such as a willow maze and a dugout canoe. If parents are convinced of the importance of outdoor play, the pressure they could exert would be a powerful force in the greening of post-industrial landscapes across the developed world ... and a few more 'grassy places' would be a boon for everyone, children and adults alike.

All this also has implications for the provision of supervised play facilities in school buildings after school hours (see Chapter 6). National and local providers need to look hard at the environments provided for this extended care, and the quality of the staff they employ to supervise them. Corralling children in paved school yards surrounded by grey city streets is simply not good enough.

One possible way forward is to extend the influence of playworkers and play rangers – professionals devoted to encouraging and facil-itating children's independent play. The playwork movement is already widespread in Scandinavian countries such as Norway and Denmark, and is growing internationally. As well as working in day centres and after-school clubs, providing less intrusive supervision than that of teachers or untrained helpers, playworkers can also be assigned to particular open spaces for community use. Here then are the twenty-first-century professionals who could begin the re-establishment of eyes on the street. Not only could they keep a general eye on the children who play in their areas, they could also run activities, help make open spaces more inviting to everyone, and encourage people to take ownership of the area in which they live.

*

If the key message about food is that adults, especially parents, must reassert control over what children eat, the key message about play and exercise is that once children are of school age we must begin to relinquish excessive anxiety-driven control over this aspect of their development, so that by the end of the primary years they are fit, self-confident, socially competent and growing in independence. Improved attitudes to PE at school would help, but even more important are opportunities for youngsters to run, play, move and grow independently in their own space, learning to make their own choices with steadily diminishing adult attention. So, rather than keeping them safe from a supposedly threatening outdoors, the job is to make the outdoors safe – and exciting and inviting – so our children can once again go out to play.

DETOXING THE GREAT OUTDOORS

- Reduce anxiety by watching less TV news, and don't have the news on during the day when the children might watch it. *Read* the news rather than watching it.
- Resist irrational fears, and balance worries about letting your child play outside with the knowledge of how important outdoor play is.
- Help children become streetwise and safe by walking around your local community with them so you can demonstrate road safety. (By not taking the car you will also incidentally help cut traffic congestion.)
- Make sure you go out with your child in bad weather too, dressing appropriately. Children need to experience all kinds of weather, and if you model wimpishness they'll learn it.
- Explicitly teach about road safety rules and 'stranger danger'. Make sure your child knows what to do in emergencies, and remind them regularly.
- Look for safe places where your child and friends can play outside: in your or neighbours' gardens, in parks, recreation grounds, local 'wild places', even on the pavement outside home, if the street's generally free of traffic.
- Help children get to know your local environment by getting out and about in it with them, pointing out potential dangers and helping them choose safe routes.
- Make sure children know how to travel by bus, train or tram by doing it with them lots of times.
- When children start going out alone, ask them to let you know where they're off to and with whom. Ask them to check in regularly with you or other trusted adults, particularly if there are any changes of plan. Make this such a routine that they wouldn't dream of forgetting.
- Make contact with other local parents and arrange to 'keep an eye out' for all the children in your neighbourhood. If possible, try to involve more of the local community. Agree ground rules about play, curfews, out-of-bounds areas and so on.
- Accept that occasionally accidents happen – and keep your fingers crossed that the only accidents affecting your child will be minor ones, and useful learning experiences. (Actually, no matter how hard you try to remove risk, accidents *will* happen – so there's no point in losing sleep about them.)

HOW TO AVOID COUCH POTATO SYNDROME

- Ensure your child has plenty of opportunity for free movement and exercise at all stages in development.
- Babies and toddlers:

  - Give babies opportunities to lie on their tummies and backs (but put them to sleep on their backs).
  - Create safe spaces for toddlers to run, play and tumble – preferably both indoors and out.
  - Don't panic about the dangers of dirt and mud – remember that children reared in 'super-clean' environments may fail to develop resistance to everyday infections.
  - Don't always put your child in the buggy – let him or her walk.

- Spend time with children doing 'ordinary things' like household chores, shopping or cooking – don't try to fill every moment with 'quality time' (see list of life skills in Chapter 5).
- Establish clear rules and routines for safety in the home, garden, street and so on as early as possible (see Chapter 10) so your child knows and accepts the boundaries, and can move around freely within them.
- From as early as possible, share family activities such as walking, swimming, cycling, exercising a dog.
- Introduce your child to exercise by playing with them and demonstrating skills, e.g.

  - three- to six-year-olds: dancing, catching a ball, bat and ball, playground and party games
  - six upwards: skipping, hula hooping, team games, jogging, aerobics to music, etc.

- Provide opportunities children of all ages to play with peers – both indoors and out – in a loosely supervised environment (with adults on hand, but not monitoring every move). As children grow older, encourage them to go on 'everyday adventures' and take 'safe risks'.

- Encourage children to sort out problems during play for themselves – don't rush to intervene before they've had the chance. Teaching 'conflict resolution' helps (see Chapter 4).

- If at all possible, walk your child to school. If it's too far, drive part way and walk the rest. When your child is old enough to walk with friends (or in a 'walking bus'), encourage him or her to do so.

- Encourage children to take part in sports and join activity clubs, dance classes, etc. Always turn up to support them if they're in a match or display. Give plenty of praise not just for winning, but for joining in, trying and taking part.

THIRTY-THREE THINGS A CHILD SHOULD DO BY THE AGE OF TEN

In 2005, as part of their Dirt is Good washing powder promotion, the manufacturers of Persil washing powder surveyed 1,000 adults to compile this list. You can probably add several more of your own.

Roll down a grassy bank

Make a mud pie

Prepare a modelling dough mixture

Collect frogspawn

Make perfume from flower petals

Grow cress on a windowsill

Make a papier-mâché mask

Build a sand castle

Climb a tree

Make a den in the garden

Paint using hands and feet

Organise a teddy bears' picnic

Have a face-painting session

Bury a friend in the sand (but not completely!)

Bake some bread

Make snow angels

Create a clay sculpture

Take part in a scavenger hunt

Camp out in the garden

Bake a cake

Feed a farm animal

Pick some strawberries

Play Pooh sticks

Recognise five bird species

Find some worms

Cycle through a muddy puddle

Make and fly a kite

Plant a tree

Build a nest from grass and twigs

Find ten different leaves in the park

Grow vegetables

Make breakfast in bed for Mum and Dad

Create a mini-assault course in the garden

PARENT POWER: GREEN AND PLEASANT PLACES TO PLAY

For children to be able to play out safely in a post-industrial society, policy-makers must be alerted to their needs. At present, in many countries children's needs are very low on the political agenda. This could be changed very rapidly if parents decided to vote for people who promise – and deliver – the following:

- traffic calming measures/car-free streets/very low speed limits/'shared space' design in residential areas (especially in new housing) – children are more important than cars
- greening of the environment – planting trees, conserving any open spaces (derelict ground, made safe, is great for 'everyday adventures')
- better parks and parklands, and playworkers to supervise open spaces of all kinds and build a sense of community
- daycare and after-school care facilities, properly supervised, that involve outdoor activities in exciting environments
- schools that aren't frightened (or too burdened with red tape) to provide physical exercise and fun outdoor activities as part of children's education
- international laws and policing to ensure that those who threaten children's safety are apprehended and their activities stopped (see also Chapter 9).

If you have the time and energy, campaign for these improvements yourself. Consult the web and local information sources (library, school, advice bureau) to find local pressure groups or get together with other interested parents, grand-parents, etc, and start your own.

Further reading

Christine Macintyre and Kim McVitty, *Movement and Learning in the Early Years: Supporting Dyspraxia (DCD) and Other Difficulties* (Paul Chapman Publications, 2004)

Tim Gill, *No Fear: Growing Up in a Risk-Averse Society* (Calouste Gulbenkian Society, 2007)

Sally Goddard Blythe, *The Well-Balanced Child* (Hawthorn Press, 2004)

Mary Gavin, Steven Dowshen and Neil Izenberg, *Fit Kids* (Dorling Kindersley, 2004)

Richard Louv, *Last Child in the Woods: Saving Our Kids from Nature-Deficit Disorder* (Algonquin Books, 2005)

Useful websites

Learning Through Landscapes (LTL): **www.ltl.org.uk**
Children's Play Council: **www.ncb.org.uk/cpc/**
Canadian Evergreen Project: **www.evergreen.ca**
Home Zones: **www.homezonenews.co.uk**

Mind the gap

One of my earliest memories is playing in the street outside my grandmother's
back-to-back cottage in Salford, one of the poorest areas of Manchester. I can't
have been above four, and some big girls (maybe six- or eight-year-olds) were
teaching me hopscotch. In those far-off days there was little danger from traffic
and older children were often left to look after the little ones.

A few years ago I revisited the same street, to run a training course for
teachers at the school where my gran was once the cleaner. It's still a very poor
area, but you don't see small children playing out any more. Their parents are
too worried by the high levels of drug-related violence and antisocial behaviour
by young teenage and pre-teenage gangs. And in places like this, such fears are
perfectly reasonable.

The area where my gran used to live looks like a war zone. Amid the litter in
the alleyways behind the houses are broken bottles and discarded hypodermics,
and on the day I visited there was a burned-out car a couple of streets away, the
remnant of nocturnal joy-riding by a gang of lads. The teachers at the school
warned me to empty my own car completely while I was away from it, so I
wouldn't get the windows broken. When I protested that no one would want to
steal a load of grammar books and other teaching stuff they shook their heads.
'You'd be surprised,' they said. 'Anything they might be able to flog for drug
money.'

I've visited similar areas in many parts of Britain, communities in which
civilised behaviour has broken down to the extent that young children can't
possibly venture out of doors unaccompanied, while older children (from about
the age of eight) wander in gangs, creating mayhem for local residents. You
don't leave big girls looking after the little ones any more – you really don't
know what they might do to them. Small children here are usually kept safe
indoors at all times – tragically, health problems as a result of excessive hygiene
are more common in these poorer homes than wealthy ones. But presumably, by
the time most children are eight or so, many parents have given up or lost

interest in trying to protect them – or the children have become so ungovernable that they break out of captivity and begin to run wild.

Sadly the parents seldom do much to widen their young children's horizons. Many make little effort to escape from the area even for a day: in rundown estates only a few miles from the seaside you often find large numbers of children have never been to the beach; in the inner cities, many children never visit the great city parks a bus ride away from home. Uneducated parents often don't see the point of family outings – they're too trapped in the misery of the here and now.

As usual, schools do their best to compensate, organising trips to the countryside, weeks at camp schools and so on. Recently, though, I've heard tales of parents refusing to let their children go on such excursions – not because of costs (schools will quietly waive fees in the case of real need) but because of safety fears. To their rational fear of the great outdoors near home, add irrational fear generated by media coverage.

Schools and other agencies also try to provide opportunities for children to play out and experience nature nearer home, by building adventure playgrounds, creating school gardens, vegetable patches or wild areas. All too often, their efforts are destroyed by vandals – those roaming gangs of disaffected teens and pre-teens. Sometimes children help their teachers build gardens or play areas during the day, then go to great lengths overcoming security measures to help their older mates wreck them at night. I once stood in the shell of a school burned down by its own needy pupils, and listened to the headteacher (a nun) explain gently, 'It's not personal. They just have this deep need to destroy.'

So where does it spring from, this cycle of ignorance, poverty and violent destruction, which transform an environment into somewhere no child can go out to play? In my experience, it takes about ten years to turn human children into impulsive, unempathetic animals, so desperately antisocial that they destroy their own habitat. And the best way to do it is rear them in captivity, malnourish them on junk and expose them to all the other aspects of toxic childhood outlined in this book.

So the best way to break the cycle is to detox childhood. Read on.

CHAPTER THREE

TIME FOR BED

> Sleep ...
> Sleep that knits up the ravelled sleeve of care;
> The death of each day's life; sore labour's bath;
> Balm of hurt minds; great nature's second course;
> Chief nourisher in life's feast ...

Do you get the impression that Shakespeare enjoyed a bit of shut-eye? If current research is on the right track, it's not surprising. Sleep, practically ignored by scientists for centuries, has recently started hitting the headlines in neuroscience – and since it appears to be the key to both memory and creativity, it's of great significance for children's thinking and learning.

Yet sleep is not high on the twenty-first-century agenda. When I asked teachers around the UK which aspects of contemporary childhood they think damage children's progress at school, 'lack of sleep' was very near the top of their list. Personally, I think it's not just children's lack of sleep that causes the problems. It's lack of sleep – or, at least, lack of good-quality rest – for adults too (and that includes teachers). In a 24/7 world where sleep has been sidelined, tiredness is heavily implicated in the toxic mix affecting contemporary children.

Sleeping problems have been on the rise ever since electric light became widespread and darkness was banished from our lives. Human beings had already learned to extend their waking hours by the regular absorption of caffeine (in coffee, tea and, most recently, fizzy drinks), to which most of the developed world is now addicted. Gradually, through the twentieth century, people have slept less and less, and rushed about more and more. Indeed, we now seem positively to resent time spent sleeping, or even resting. As science writer Paul Martin points out in his book *Counting Sheep*, 'Having nothing to do is seen as a sign of worthlessness, while ceaseless activity signifies status and success. Supposedly unproductive activities are deprioritised or delegated. And according to prevailing cultural attitudes, sleeping is one of the least productive of all human activities.' It seems that when electric speed was added to electric light, the developed world moved from mere sleep avoidance to chronic sleep deprivation.

Ten years ago the US National Commission on Sleep Disorders Research found 'a convincing body of scientific evidence and witness testimony indicates that many Americans are severely sleep-deprived'. They estimated that about a quarter of the nation (70 million people) was affected at that time, with damaging consequences for their mental and physical health, performance at work, quality of life and personal relationships. By now the numbers must be astronomical, and duplicated across the developed world.

Tired families

Consider how tiredness impacts on the average family. Tired parents, home late from work, don't have the energy to cook a meal and entice a recalcitrant child into eating something nourishing. Tired children are cranky and unpleasant, and more likely to kick up a fuss if they don't get their own way. In these circumstances, only the saintliest of parents sticks to the dietary advice in Chapter 1: most will soon be back to throwing a ready meal into the microwave for the adults, heating up nuggets and chips for the children, then slumping exhausted in front of the TV – or preferably a couple of TVs, so the kids don't moan and grizzle about what the grown-ups want to watch.

Tiredness thus draws whole families into the vicious circle of poor nutrition and lack of exercise. The sluggishness that comes from poor diet feeds further exhaustion, which leads to more quick-fix junk food and telly-slumping ... and so on, ad infinitum. And all this overlaps with another vicious circle. This is the one where exhausted parents attempt wanly to convince their children it's bedtime. And the children – over-tired and brattish – play up more and more, until their parents give up the unequal struggle and let them watch 'one more programme' or play 'one more computer game'. The next morning everyone wakes up tired again ... and on it goes, the two vicious circles overlapping into a vicious Venn diagram, with a worn-out family trapped in the middle.

Age group	Recommended hours of sleep	Average hours of sleep recorded in NSF poll
Infants (3–11 months)	14–15 (over 24 hours)	12.7
Toddlers (12–35 months)	12–14	11.7
Pre-schoolers (3–6 years)	11–13	10.4
Elementary school age (7–11 years)	10–11	9.5

A 2004 poll by the US National Sleep Foundation (see above) found that children of all ages seem to be sleeping far fewer than the lower level of recommended hours per night; at weekends, children apparently sleep even less than in the week. And since the poll was 'self-reported' (that is, children and parents volunteered information on sleeping hours), I suspect the true figures may be even lower. The researchers also pointed out that many parents seem to be unaware that their children are missing out on sleep. In a sleep-deprived society, we simply don't value it enough to notice.

A good night's sleep

Scientific interest in sleep was reawakened a decade or so ago by the development of magnetic resonance imaging (MRI) techniques, which allow researchers to watch what is actually happening in the brain. Now that neuroscientists are discovering more about the significance of sleep with every passing day (and night), maybe the rest of us will start taking it more seriously.

It's long been known that there are several distinct kinds of sleep, happening in cycles throughout the night, but it's now becoming clearer what the brain is doing in each of these stages. When we first fall asleep, our brain wave patterns slow down and we drop into something called Stage 1 and 2 sleep. This is quite shallow, so sleepers are easily awakened by activity around them. These stages tend to last longer in adults than children, who only take about five minutes to move into the next stage – slow-wave sleep (Stages 3 and 4 sleep).

Once someone is in Stage 3 or 4 sleep, they're very deeply asleep and difficult to rouse. (This is when you can carry children out of the car and put them to bed without waking them.) Although much of the brain seems to close down during slow-wave sleep, parts are still active, processing new information. In children, slow-wave sleep is also important for physical development, being the time when growth hormone secretion reaches its peak.

A phase of slow-wave sleep lasts around 80 minutes; after that, sleepers rise back up through the four levels to a state much closer to consciousness. This is called REM sleep (Rapid Eye Movement – because the eyes dart about beneath the eyelids), and it's here that most dreams seem to occur. Brain activity is much higher in REM sleep than slow-wave sleep, especially the areas of the brain associated with emotion.

During the course of the night, sleepers move through four or five sleep cycles – dropping down into deep slow-wave sleep and drifting up into REM sleep. They spend longer in slow-wave sleep during the first half of the night, but in the second half of the night they get more REM sleep. Not unnaturally, people are much more likely to wake during a period of shallower REM sleep, and, if so, they may well remember fragments of their dreams.

Learn while you sleep?

So why is sleep so important in terms of children's learning? The most obvious reason is its effects on mood and behaviour. Every parent knows from bitter experience that over-tired children are cranky and unpleasant. Unlike adults, who grow drowsier when they're tired, sleepy children often get more 'wired' and uncontrollable. This, of course, means that sleep-deprived children at school tend to be badly behaved and difficult to teach, while children who've had enough sleep are more likely to be pleasant and alert, finding it easier to concentrate and thus to learn. Sleep specialist Dr Gillian Nixon of the Australasian Sleep Association directly ascribes many of school children's difficulties in concentrating and problems with behaviour to lack of sleep: 'We're definitely undersleeping as a world population. All of our lives are getting busier, and children aren't sleeping as well as they should.'

But as well as putting children into the right frame of mind to learn in the first place, recent research shows that sleep is also essential *after* the event. It's now clear that skills, facts and ideas acquired during the day are transferred into long-term memory by the brain during sleep. Scientists can see this on their MRI pictures. When someone returns to a new skill or learning task after a night's sleep, different places light up in the brain from the ones that lit up when the learning first took place, proving that the memory of what they've learned has been transferred to another part of the brain.

It turns out that sleeping time, when everything's relatively quiet because no new input is being received, is when the brain reorganises and tidies information – transferring new stuff into long-term memory and pruning out what's no longer required. US neuro-scientist Terry Sejnowski compares falling asleep to leaving your house when workmen come in to renovate it: 'You don't want to live in the house while the construction's going on because it's a mess.' Every night, when children go to sleep, the workmen come in and sort out all the stuff that's been dumped in their brains during the day.

If you think about it, this is a great deal of stuff. Children have to learn a vast array of practical skills – from walking and talking to riding a bike. This sort of practical learning ('learning by doing' without much conscious awareness of what's being learned) is known by scientists as 'procedural' learning. They also have to learn facts and information, which involves concentration and intellectual self-awareness. And if they're lucky, they'll also learn how to make connections between the ideas they absorb, developing the skills of imaginative, creative thinking.

Why it's important to 'sleep on it'

Researchers have found that REM sleep is involved in procedural learning of practical tasks. It seems that during REM sleep the brain reruns experiences from earlier in the day – experiments have shown that patterns of activity in the brain during REM sleep precisely match those shown when people were actually practising the task. Procedural learning happens in chunks, and REM sleep appears to strengthen the processes, leading to better chunking. After REM sleep, when you practise again, the chunks can get bigger, so the more REM sleep the better.

To be effective, the REM sleep must occur within at least 24 hours of the learning – otherwise it doesn't improve performance at all. Young children do a great deal of this sort of practical learning, so it's not surprising that the younger the child the longer it spends in REM sleep, and likewise, the older we grow, the more our REM sleeping time reduces. Not surprisingly, babies and toddlers need lots of little naps to consolidate all their learning.

Slow-wave sleep, on the other hand, seems to be important for academic tasks involving concentration and conscious awareness of what's being learned – the sort of factual learning older children do at school. Again, the brain appears to replay the information they've studied, this time during slow-wave sleep, and in the process transfers it to long-term memory. It's therefore very important to 'sleep on it' when you've studied something, as even small reductions in slow-wave sleep have been linked to a decrease in memory function.

It may also be that 'sleeping on it' is involved in creative thinking and problem-solving. The German sleep researcher Jan Born recently gave some of his students a repetitive number task containing a hidden short cut. None of the students noticed this short cut while first practising the task, nor on returning to it after eight hours awake, but those who repeated the task after eight hours' sleep often spotted the short cut very quickly. Born suspects that, when we return to a problem after sleeping on it, the fact that information has started transferring from one part of the brain to another renders us more able to have a creative 'insight': 'What may be happening is that, due to this reorganisation, after sleep you get a slightly different perspective. So you can view the information from two perspectives, which means you could make a problem-solving leap.' Maybe some of Shakespeare's genius was simply that he knew when to take a nap.

Hush, little baby ... stopping sleep problems before they begin

Given sleep's significance in relation to learning, we should all be taking much more interest in seeing that children get plenty of it. Unfortunately, as the survey results outlined earlier in the chapter suggest, this isn't happening. Another US survey estimated that around half of pre-school-age children have sleeping problems of one sort or another. The advice of the experts is that the sooner children get into a good sleeping routine, the better for all concerned. But in the words of Tessa Livingstone, executive producer of the BBC's *Child of Our Time*, who watched many babies adjusting to life outside the womb, good sleep habits 'don't just happen. Parents have to show their children how to sleep.' She found that those who work at it 'double their chances of having a baby who sleeps through the night, every night'.

As most parents know to their cost, newborn babies' sleep habits are chaotic – they may sleep a lot, but hardly ever when you want them to. However, according to the National Sleep Foundation, by six to nine months the vast majority of babies should be sleeping through the night as well as having a number of short naps during the day. This transformation depends upon establishing good sleeping habits, and helping the child become a 'self-soother', able to fall asleep independently without needing a parent to be there.

Self-soothing is important because babies who can be persuaded to fall asleep without parental presence should be less perturbed when they wake in the night – with any luck they'll just blink a bit in the darkness and drop off again. So parents who hang around singing lullabies till they're sure their children have passed into the land of Nod may actually prevent them from becoming efficient self-soothers, because children who rely on adult assistance to fall asleep are more likely to cry for attention if they wake up later. Self-soothing is also a very important first step towards 'self-regulation', one of the keys to successful child-rearing (see Chapter 10).

The babies who haven't read the book

All this sounds fine in theory, but it's less convincing in the middle of the night when your baby is screaming uncontrollably and you can't remember the last time you slept for longer than an hour.

Neuroscience has confirmed that babies vary greatly in temperament, some being much more anxious and 'fussy' (especially low-birthweight babies or those born to mothers under stress in the later months of pregnancy) and therefore much harder to turn into self-soothers than others. This is why many parents find following the advice of parenting manuals – especially those with very hard and fast rules – makes them feel a dismal failure. And, almost inevitably, the more of a failure the parent feels, the more distressed the baby becomes.

Like every aspect of child-rearing, looking for a one-size-fits-all solution is a waste of time. All children are different, as are all parents. In the past, when people were reared in extended families within close communities, they witnessed the raising of many different children and had a reasonable idea of what could be expected at particular ages. This gave them the confidence to adjust and adapt child-rearing procedures to suit their own circumstances. Most contemporary parents, however, have little, if any, experience of children before bringing home their own from the hospital.

Working on the assumption that science is now the only available substitute for experience, it's useful to know that, according to psychologists, the best parenting style for our contemporary global culture is 'authoritative'. That's *authoritative* – not authoritarian – and it means being confident, consistent, caring and firm (see Chapter Ten). Research suggests that authoritative parenting works well for all children, but particularly for the anxious, fussy ones – probably because it means the parent takes control of the situation. Once parents are able to deal with their own anxiety, children can learn to deal with theirs and the chances of a good night's sleep for everyone are then considerably greater.

The trouble is, parents who are in thrall to a parenting manual are not in control – they've relinquished control to an author who knows neither them nor their baby. Confident parenting does not come from slavish adherence to someone else's rules but from being well informed about the way children develop, and about the techniques and resources available, then making your own judgements. When trawling through books on helping children to sleep, I preferred those that offered a range of suggestions, so that individual parents could choose the methods that suited their own and their babies' personalities. Educated parents would probably also find it useful to know something about the neuroscientific background of child development, so well-researched demystifying books on this subject are useful too (for example, the Herschkowitz book referenced on page 101).

Sadly, without sufficient information, the commonest way parents lose control is to hand it over to the baby. The more the baby cries, the more the parents panic and allow their offspring to set the agenda. The bottom line is that it's up to adults to train their baby (gently) into sleeping habits that will benefit the whole family, rather than letting the baby train parents into behaviour that leaves everyone exhausted and distressed.

Time for a nap

The importance of sleep schedules and self-soothing relates to daytime as well as night-time sleep. Babies and toddlers also need to take naps of thirty minutes to a couple of hours long, between one and four times a day. Again, babies vary, and parents have to be sensitive to their own children's needs, working out when and how long seems to be optimal. The number of daytime naps required changes over time, so this also involves awareness of changing needs – usually, by eighteen months, toddlers are down to one nap a day, lasting between one and three hours.

Naps are important. As paediatric sleep specialist Marc Weissbluth points out, 'when children do not nap well, they pay a price'. He cites research showing that four- to eight-month-old infants who don't nap well have shorter attention spans or appear less persistent when engaged in activities. As they grow older, these children are likely to be 'non-adaptable' or hyperactive. Napping also seems to consist mainly of REM sleep, which, as described above, is necessary to consolidate the hands-on physical learning of early infancy. So babies and toddlers need naps, both to restore energy and good temper and to consolidate the huge amount of learning they do every day.

However, our present-day resentment at wasting time asleep means that these days we don't attach much benefit to naps. All too often, children's napping habits conflict with childcare arrangements or other facets of modern life, and the naps have to be curtailed or abandoned altogether. Children themselves may become resistant to napping, perhaps because an increasingly sedentary lifestyle means they don't have sufficient exercise to make them physically tired, or enough real-life stimulation to tire them mentally. And if they spend too much time in front of the TV, the artificial stimulation of constantly changing images may make it more difficult for them to switch off.

The psychologist Marie Winn suggests that TV may affect children's napping habits in another way. She reckons that before the advent of the electronic babysitter, parents had a powerful motivation to encourage their offspring's napping habits – to provide a little uninterrupted time to complete other chores, or to have half an hour to themselves. If the baby can be kept busy staring at the TV, there's less incentive to insist on naps.

One way and another, establishing good sleeping habits from the start is probably harder today than it's ever been – but in a high-octane, super-stimulating world it's also probably more important than ever before.

Sleepy schoolchildren

As children grow older, they naturally become more interested in staying up late to find out what's going on in the infinitely interesting adult world. If they aren't good sleepers, this is when 'bedtime resistance' – difficulty falling asleep or night-time awakening – can get out of hand.

In a 2002 US study up to 40 per cent of the parents of school-age children reported behavioural sleep problems such as 'bedtime struggles' and 'prolonged and/or frequent night awakenings'. A year later a UK survey estimated that as many as two-thirds of children weren't getting enough sleep, including one in eight who were sleeping less than the eight hours recommended for adults (this figure rose to one in four when both parents were out at work). There are similar findings across the developed world, including a 2004 Japanese survey which recorded a third of under-tens staying up until after 10 p.m. and 17 per cent of the same age group until after 11 p.m., suffering accordingly the following day.

Many factors contribute to the problem. Diet may play a part – for instance, children who are sensitive to certain additives may find settling to sleep more difficult. One particular additive, found in most fizzy drinks, is proven to keep people awake: caffeine. Indeed, three cans of Diet Coke deliver as big a caffeine hit as a regular espresso. As the French essayist Jean-Anthelme Brillat-Savarin said in 1825, 'It is the duty of all mamas and papas to forbid their children to drink coffee, unless they wish to have little dried-up machines, stunted and old, at the age of twenty', but many parents, diligent about banning coffee, are unaware of the caffeine cocktail available in fast food and soft drinks. The Sleep Foundation website has a Caffeine Calculator, for checking out the caffeine content of many types of drinks and food.

A number of studies have recently connected lack of sleep with obesity, possibly because poor sleepers secrete less leptin, an appetite-reducing hormone released during sleep, or because they have more time awake during which to consume unnecessary calories. Common sense also suggests that lack of outdoor play and exercise may contribute to sleeping problems, since the muscular fatigue induced by exercise should lead to better quality sleep.

Snoring and other worries

Another common condition associated with disturbed sleep is snoring, and research has found that children who snore are more likely to have learning problems at school. Constant loud snoring may be a symptom of sleep apnoea, a condition in which sleep is disturbed because the sleeper actually stops breathing periodically throughout the night. But it may also be the result of enlarged tonsils or adenoids – leading to frequent infections and bunged-up noses – or to an allergy, perhaps relating to processed foods or environmental pollution (and possibly enhanced by our over-clean homes – see page 52). When I worked with special needs children, I noticed that many (especially dyslexics and ADHD-sufferers) suffered from snuffles and runny noses – but I'd always assumed these were connected with hearing problems rather than disturbed sleep. Perhaps it's a mixture of both.

As sleep specialist Marc Weissbluth points out, in the past snoring was often 'cured' by an operation – doctors tended to recommend the removal of tonsils and adenoids for recurrent throat infections. These days the medical profession is less enthusiastic about invasive surgical procedure. However, Professor Jim Horne of the Loughborough Sleep Research Centre cites research findings that 20 per cent of children with mild to moderate ADHD appear to have sleep disturbances due to chronic colds, enlarged tonsils or breathing problems, and in his opinion the removal of tonsils or adenoids may often solve the behavioural problem. This is an area where medical and educational professionals could usefully work together.

Other reasons for sleep disturbance include emotional difficulties and anxiety, which can cause nightmares, insomnia or bedwetting. As we'll see in succeeding chapters, many contemporary children have powerful reasons to be emotionally disturbed, and emotional problems are among the most difficult to solve. But one of the main ways parents can develop emotional resilience in their children is to provide stability and security. And one of the best ways of doing that is to buttress family life with calm regularity and reliable routine.

A regular bedtime

All child development experts point to the significance of regularity and routine in children's lives, and the more difficult the children, the more they need familiar, comfortable routines. I suspect many of the problems today's children have in going to sleep and staying asleep are simply the result of our contemporary lifestyle. Parents who frantically juggle work and domestic duties often lose sight of the importance of ensuring a regular sleep schedule and bedtime routine. Yet both they and their children would benefit from the predictability of established routines, not only at bedtime, but for mealtimes, weekday mornings and any other regular parts of family life. The more the mechanics of such occasions are carried along by habit, the more one's brain is free for conversation and enjoying family time. On the other hand, when life is chaotic and no one's sure what to expect, discord and disharmony ensue.

Sleep specialists specifically point to the significance of a routine for preparing for sleep. The connection between properly organised bedtimes and behaviour at school is clear, with researchers reporting 'spectacular improvements in manageability' of ADHD children when bedtime was improved, adding that, 'our clinical impression in these cases was that the changes were too rapid to be accounted for by other changes, such as parental discipline tactics'.

A good bedtime routine involves a comfortingly familiar winding down towards sleep, providing a sense of security while encouraging the child to relax (see page 98). Sadly this sort of restful ritual is a long way from the reality of many families' evenings, with children staying up waiting for parents to return from work, then becoming excited by their arrival and understandably reluctant to break up the reunion. So either parents vainly try to put them to bed, and bedtime becomes a battleground, or the children stay up far too late and eventually drop off out of exhaustion.

However, just as working parents have a responsibility to provide regular meals for children, they can't afford to ignore the importance of a regular bedtime. Parents who work late really have only two options: to adjust their working hours so that at least one parent is home in plenty of time to supervise bedtime routines; or to sacrifice seeing their children in the evening and ensure someone else settles them down to sleep. If supervision has to be spread among a number of adults over the course of the week (and, in the case of very young children, it should be as few as possible) everyone involved should share a behavioural hymn sheet – every child should be able to look forward to a familiar bedtime ritual each night.

The more 'difficult' and temperamental children are, the more they need the security that comes from regular routines – and the more disruptive any departure from that routine will be. This has implications for parents' social life. If children don't find bedtime and sleeping easy, the disruption caused by holidays or special late-night excursions can play havoc with carefully established procedures. Parents who've struggled to put a regular bedtime into place may find it pays not to disrupt the routine too often. Otherwise, they may have to retrain their child from scratch each time, which is wearing for everyone.

The monsters in the bedroom

Many children go through a phase of worrying that lions, dragons or other monsters are lurking under the bed. I love the idea suggested by a friend of using Monster Repellent Spray (see page 98) to see off these chimera every evening. Children's fears may seem silly to adults, but they're very real to them, and brushing them off as nonsense doesn't help. Parents are only too happy to indulge childish fantasies about the Tooth Fairy and Santa Claus, so there's no inconsistency in collaborating in the brisk disposal of monsters if it helps soothe a child for sleep.

There is, however, another sort of monster that's established itself in children's bedrooms around the developed world, which parents have unfortunately collaborated in putting there. Electronic equipment such as TVs, computers and so on can be wonderful additions to family entertainment, but they have no place in the 'restful darkened room' prescribed by the sleep specialists. Instead of a calm winding down to sleep, many children settle down in bed to the accompaniment of flashing bright lights and the unsoothing soundtrack of the television.

The ill-effects of bedroom TV have been catalogued since the end of the 1990s, when researchers found that sleeping problems in children aged between five and nine were more likely among those who watched a lot of television, especially just before sleep. They pointed out that having a television set in the bedroom 'may be an important contributor to sleep problems in school-age children'. Yet TVs have continued to find their way into children's bedrooms – survey results in the US and UK range from 30 per cent of four-year-olds and under up to 80 per cent of over-fives, and the figure appears to be going up year on year – with computers and other equipment not far behind.

Meanwhile alarming research findings have continued to mount up. American researchers suspect that bright lights on television sets and computers can reset the circadian clock, changing the sleep-wake cycle. A TV in the bedroom may not interfere with the sleep patterns of an adult, who's already learned – in an earlier, less frenetic age – how to drop off and, hopefully, stay asleep. But lights from TVs or computers can be a powerful force in preventing the development of good sleeping habits in children. Italian scientists have also found that these lights block the secretion of the sleep hormone, melatonin, which usually begins as it gets dark outside.

From the University of Columbia in the USA, there's evidence that too much television-watching has a knock-on effect on sleep problems later in life. They found that late-night TV leaves children in a state of 'heightened alertness' at a time when their minds should be winding down, preventing them from developing natural sleep patterns which would otherwise become ingrained, so they're more likely to have sleep problems throughout their lives.

Other technological gadgets can be just as harmful. A Belgian researcher found the sleep of young teenagers was disturbed by incoming text messages on their mobile phones, and also that they slept at a different level because they were constantly aware of the phone, waiting for communications. His conclusion that this leads to a different – presumably shallower – level of sleep is very worrying, as it's during deep slow-wave sleep that academic learning is transferred to long-term memory. Since a 2005 British survey showed that more than half of pre-teenaged children now have mobile phones (including a quarter of children under eight), it's fair to assume that it's not just adolescents who are having their sleeping patterns disturbed in this way.

There's also suspicion among researchers as far apart as Australia and Switzerland that mobile phone use may suppress the body's production of the sleep hormone melatonin, thus interfering with sleep in another way – a further reason to keep them out of children's bedrooms. Yet a mother working evening shifts recently told me that she and her eight-year-old daughter both have video-phones so mum can ring up at bedtime to say goodnight.

The message from all the research is clear: if children are to get a good night's sleep and develop healthy sleep habits, the electronic paraphernalia of modern life – television, computer games, telephones and the rest – must be removed from their bedrooms. The sleep experts are all in accord that children need a quiet, darkened, calm environment in which to become effective sleepers. What's more, there are many other pressing reasons why electronic gadgetry in the bedroom is not a good idea, which will all be explored in Chapters 4, 8 and 9.

*

Many aspects of contemporary culture seem to contribute to problems with sleep, and research shows clearly that these problems impact on children's learning and well-being. But this particular example of our cultural evolution outstripping our biological needs is not just affecting children. There's mounting evidence that post-industrial society in general has gone too far in the direction of enforced wakefulness – we could all benefit from calming down, dragging ourselves away from the flickering screens and getting an hour or so more shut-eye per night.

Benjamin Franklin's famous aphorism still makes sense: Early to bed and early to rise makes a man healthy, wealthy and wise. Maybe it would also make everyone – adults as well as children – more attentive, self-controlled and civilised.

DETOXING SLEEP HABITS

- If you're a new parent, start as you mean to go on, and establish good sleep habits early.

  − If your baby is particularly difficult to soothe, find out why (see *A Good Start in Life*, page 101) and investigate a range of ways of helping to calm him or her (see *Sound Sleep*, page 101).
  − Ensure a calm and quiet end to the day, preferably dimming the light, so your baby begins to associate this time with sleep.
  − Put babies down to sleep while they're drowsy and leave them to fall asleep by themselves. Don't feel you have to stay and sing lullabies, or even 'just be there', till they've dropped off − you want them to become 'self-soothers'. See bedtime routines on page 98.
  − Once babies can sleep through the night (i.e. for between 5 and 8 hours), if they wake and cry, don't pick them up immediately. Give them a chance to settle down without your intervention.
  − Create regular daytime and bedtime sleep schedules. The need for daytime naps changes over time, so be sensitive to your child's sleep patterns. By 18 months, most toddlers are down to one nap a day, lasting between one and three hours.
  − Remember that you are the one doing the training − don't let your baby train you into habits you'll one day regret.
  − If you've tried all the recommended techniques and your child still has problems, check with your doctor or paediatrician.

- Ensure your child is getting adequate sleep (see the chart on page 80).
- Don't let children have TVs, computers or electronic equipment in their bedrooms. Hold out over this until your child's age is *at least* in double figures. The one possible exception for older children is a tape recorder or CD player for talking books (see Chapter 4).

- If your child is a frequent snorer or has disrupted breathing patterns, consult your doctor (especially if there are problems at school).
- Don't let your child have caffeinated drinks after about 4 p.m. Keep an eye on other foods to see if any cause 'hyper' behaviour, and avoid these foods at all times, but especially in the evening.
- Be utterly consistent about the rules for bedtime. Occasionally you will have to adjust timings, routines, etc as your child grows older – do this in negotiation with your child, but ensure you make the final decision. This is an area, like diet, where adults have to take responsibility to act in the child's best interest – and the child often has other ideas.

HOW TO DETOX A PROBLEM SLEEPER

The key is to establish a bedtime routine that suits you and your child and stick to it as far as humanly possible.

- Begin the wind down to bedtime by removing your child from TV or other technological distractions.
- A bedtime routine should be gentle and calming and might involve:

  - a drink of warm milk
  - bathtime, teeth cleaning, etc
  - a bedtime story and/or songs (see also Chapter 4)
  - a security object, such as a blanket or soft toy
  - a darkened room, if necessary with a nightlight
  - soft music (the same gentle lullaby or soft music on CD every night can be a way of conditioning a child to feel sleepy)
  - a particular form of words for goodnight, with your goodnight kiss.

- If your child is fearful of 'monsters', let them watch you give the room a quick spray with 'Monster Repellent' – a water-filled plant spray bottle appropriately labelled.
- If your child's afraid of the dark, turn off the light while you're still in the room, and sing or tell them a story in the twilight.
- Don't wait for your child to go to sleep – and don't be cajoled into 'one more story'.
- Use a signal (such as a timer or your phone alarm) to limit time at the bedside to a previously agreed amount – that way there's no question about when to give the goodnight kiss and leave. You can just say 'Oh dear, time's up,' and it's the timer's fault you have to go, not yours.
- Try to ensure your child's bedroom is not only quiet and dark, but cool. A warm bed is more attractive and restful if it's much cooler outside it.
- When children refuse to settle, don't reward them with your attention. You have to find a system that keeps them in bed until they fall asleep with as

little attention as possible (see *Little Angels*, page 101, for a variety of approaches).

- Training children out of bad habits takes time and absolute consistency. Once you've chosen and started your routine, don't waver.
- If at all possible, make sure the bedtime routine is well established before interrupting it with holidays, trips or late-night excursions. If not, you might end up having to start the whole training programme from scratch.
- If you go away on holiday, try to keep to the routine as much as possible.
- Ensure everyone who puts your child to bed knows and sticks to your routine and schedule. Write it out and post it up where babysitters, etc, can easily refer to it.

PARENT POWER: SLEEP GUIDELINES

In a culture that has lost sight of the importance of sleep, it would help enormously if the government issued and publicised guidelines about children's needs. Many parents simply don't know how much sleep their children need and others would welcome support in creating and applying routines.

- If you're a new parent, ask your midwife or health visitors for guidelines on sleep requirements at various ages. If these aren't available in published form or on a website, ask why not.
- If your child is of school age, ask if the school prospectuses could include information on the sleep requirements of children at different ages, the significance of regular bedtimes and routines and the importance of keeping TVs and other electronic equipment out of children's bedrooms.
- If the school uses a 'home-school contract' setting out the rights and responsibilities of parents, children and school, suggest it includes a requirement to follow sleep guidelines, giving more power to parents' elbows about bedtime.

And remember that you, as a parent, need a good night's sleep almost as much as your child. If the conflicting demands of work and childcare are preventing this, perhaps you need to review your priorities (see pages 191–192).

Further reading

Sarah Woodhouse, *Sound Sleep: Calming and Helping Your Baby or Child to Sleep* (Hawthorn Press, 2003)

Norbert and Elinore Herschkowitz, *A Good Start in Life: Understanding Your Child's Brain and Behavior From Birth to Age Six* (University of Chicago Press, 2004)

Dr Tanya Byron and Sacha Baveystock, *Little Angels: The Essential Guide to Transforming Your Family Life and Having More Fun With Your Children* (BBC Books, 2005)

Useful websites

US National Sleep Foundation **www.sleepfoundation.org** and **www.sleep-forkids.org**

SleepNet (everything you ever wanted to know about sleep but were too tired to ask) **www.sleepnet.com/children2000.html**

Mind the gap

Attitudes to bedtime schedules and routines are a good measure of parents' general approach to child-rearing. On the whole, educated parents, although laxer about bedtime than science would suggest is sensible, nevertheless attempt to rule the roost in this respect. Judging by what they tell their teachers, the experience of children from poorer homes is much less organised.

A few years ago the Chief Inspector of Schools in England caused a furore by claiming that many young children led 'disrupted and dishevelled' lives. Asked for statistical evidence, he was unable to provide it – parents don't tend to invite researchers into their homes to record how they're neglecting their children or, alternatively, letting those children run rings round them. The Chief Inspector's anecdotal evidence came from the same place as mine – thousands upon thousands of teachers worried to death about the chaotic lives led by the children in their classes.

Whether statisticians have precise figures or not, the main reason for lack of regularity and system in the homes of disadvantaged families is not difficult to work out: parents whose own lives are chaotic and stressed are unlikely to be able to organise and apply schedules and routines for their children. I frequently hear stories of children from such homes falling asleep in class or arriving late for school (or not arriving at all) because they've overslept.

Anecdotal evidence also points strongly to the contribution of TV to these chaotic sleeping habits. In the poorest families, children almost inevitably sleep in rooms lit up by the TV, either because they share a room with their parents or – if they're lucky enough to have a room to themselves – one of the first items of furniture they're bought is a television to keep them out of their parents' hair (see Chapter 10). Even five-year-olds often report watching stunningly unsuitable late-night programmes.

The poorer the home, the greater their dependency on TV, it seems. The agony aunt for the *Sun* says her correspondents rely on the TV for company, information, relaxation – and respite from their children. In many such homes it's so important that it's never switched off. A correspondent in an industrial area of the north of England, whose job in the fire service takes him out in the depths of the night, records that the light of the TV flickers constantly in the windows of most homes, even when all else is darkness.

The children in such homes need the security and well-being that comes from a regular bedtime and a calm, restful night's sleep more than any others. Their parents also desperately need quiet time while their children are in bed to recoup from the day. Recommendations from government and schools on the importance of bedtimes, sleep schedules and naps for young infants could be really helpful to Mind the gap parents.

CHAPTER FOUR

IT'S GOOD TO TALK

It's never been easier to communicate. Technological advances over the last quarter-century mean we can now seek out like-minded people around the world through websites and blogs, register our opinions and order goods via interactive TV, commune across vast distances by email or video-conferencing, chat with family or friends wherever we happen to be by means of a mobile phone ... We have even discovered, in text messaging, a unique human ability to communicate by thumb.

Ironically, the more technology has allowed us to talk to each other, the less we seem to talk to our children. As well as worrying about children's lack of sleep, the teachers I meet are particularly concerned about two other factors: lack of conversation at home, and too much television. They see these two elements as highly correlated.

Language development is not an issue that generally worries parents – indeed, when I raise it with them, many wish their offspring would talk *less* rather than more. Young children go through a 'language explosion', which can be quite exhausting. But it's not childish prattle, endless toddlers' questions or pre-teen backchat that teachers are concerned about. It's children's ability to connect and communicate socially, to listen attentively and with comprehension, and to use language for learning – and according to teachers these skills appear to be declining across the social scale.

Language, literacy and learning

In fact, this is where I came in. My interest in toxic childhood syndrome developed from concern about children's language and literacy skills. At the end of the 1990s, I was an adviser to the British government's National Literacy Strategy, a nationwide drive to raise standards in reading and writing. Within a few years, we realised that the Strategy wasn't working – at least, not as well as it should have, considering the money and effort that were pumped into it.

As government ministers fretted, and literacy experts squabbled over the rival merits of different teaching methods, I became interested in what teachers were telling me on my lecture tours around the country. Everywhere I went it was the same story: four- and five-year-olds were coming to school with poorer language skills than ever before; they weren't arriving with the repertoire of nursery rhymes and songs little ones always used to know, and children of all ages found it increasingly difficult to sit down and listen to their teacher or to express complex ideas in speech or writing.

Almost unanimously, teachers put these developments down to the effects of all-day television, which arrived in the UK in the mid-1980s, and the proliferation of channels that come with cable and satellite TV. I started researching the subject and, as recounted earlier, realised there was a lot more to it than that.

I also discovered that this issue was bothering teachers across the developed world. As long ago as 1990, psychologist Jane Healey noted gathering complaints from American teachers about children's dete-riorating language ability. German researchers have recently found disturbing levels of language difficulty in primary-aged children and in a 2003 survey of teachers in Japan, well over half agreed with the statement: 'Academic Japanese-language capability of students is lower than it was in our school years.' One Japanese primary teacher commented, 'Even fifth- and sixth-grade students cannot speak in complete sentences,' and a middle school teacher said, 'I feel as if some students do not understand Japanese'.

That term 'academic language capability' is a useful one. It's not that children are unable to understand their mother tongue, or communicate their everyday needs – indeed, in terms of backchat and 'speaking up for their rights', contemporary children are way ahead of previous generations. But academic study requires more sophisticated language to express increasingly complex understanding and ideas.

Most children develop this sophisticated language through learning to read and write. Reading introduces them to a widening range of vocabulary and language use, while writing provides opportunities to use and master 'literate language' themselves. These skills are the bedrock of almost all academic learning, and the gradual process of learning to read and write – the 'getting of literacy' – is arguably the most critical stage in children's education (see Chapter 7).

There's a strong and growing body of evidence that the seeds of success in literacy are sown in the very first year of a baby's existence. Strange as it seems, positive interactions between parent and babes in arms can lay the foundations for future success at school. But they can lay many other foundations too. It's not just education that depends upon good communication skills – the development of language is bound up very closely with our sense of identity and self-esteem. Children who can communicate well tend to feel good about themselves, while those who are tongue-tied often feel embarrassed and inferior: the ability to connect with others is a hugely important social skill. Many psychologists believe that early parent-child communication is one of the most critical elements in nurturing a happy, healthy, resilient child.

Here's looking at you, kid

Communication begins when a newborn baby gazes at its mother's face while cradled in her arms. (Of course, it needn't be the mother – a father, grandparent, or any other 'primary care-giver' will do just as well, as long as they really love the child. But as it's usually mum who does the cradling, I'll stick to traditional terminology.) Babies are fascinated by faces, and their mother's face is particularly attractive, being associated with food, warmth and comfort. The mother's smiles, songs, crooning and 'baby talk' as she feeds, carries or comforts her baby are soon rewarded with an adoring gaze and reciprocal smiles, coos and babble from the baby itself.

Professor Colwyn Trevarthen, a child development specialist from New Zealand, calls this mother-baby interaction 'the dance of communication'. Initially based on physical closeness and eye contact it is critical to mother-baby bonding and the child's developing feelings of security and self-worth – what is known in psychological circles as 'attachment'. The more a child is attached to his early care-givers, the greater his chances of developing as a balanced, secure adult. As child psychiatrist Robert Shaw says, attachment is 'as central to the developing child as eating and breathing'.

To begin with, the dance of communication is mostly to do with body language – in social species like ours, non-verbal communication (including eye contact, smiles, other facial expressions, pointing and gestures) is as important as talk, and children learn from every interaction. Mothers naturally exaggerate their expressions and gestures – often using rhythmic movements and sounds as part of the communicatory dance – and infants respond by copying. Although children cannot speak themselves at this early stage, they become accustomed to the sounds of their mother's language, and are already tuning their ears and brains to their mother tongue.

The dance soon develops into 'conversations' about what mother and baby see around them. For instance, the mother says, 'Look at that doggy!' and her child looks in the direction she's looking and pointing. Mother says, 'He's a lovely doggy, isn't he?' and – over time, with enough repetition of this sort of scenario – the child connects the furry creature they're both seeing with the repeated word 'doggy'. One day, when he's developed sufficient control of lips, tongue and vocal cords (usually around about the first birthday), the child will have a go at saying 'doggy' himself, and mum's excitement and praise will encourage him to try more words. In the meantime, his contribution to the 'conversation' is attention and body language, perhaps along with some excited babble, which makes his appreciation clear.

All this may seem obvious, but in fact it's a uniquely human interaction, and one that probably underpins a great deal more than learning what a doggy is. By recognising his mother's intention when she gestures to the dog, the baby is in effect 'reading her mind', something non-human animals simply don't seem to do. The mind-reading potential of human beings is currently an extremely hot topic among neuroscientists, psychologists and philosophers – indeed, it may be that parent-child interactions of this kind are the key to understanding how human beings think.

The cradle of thought

In 2003, a professor of developmental psychopathology called Peter Hobson published a book about parent-child interaction which, if he's right, puts the dance of communication at the heart of child development. In *The Cradle of Thought* he argues that children's capacity to think, understand and reason arises out of the emotional attachment between parent and child, and their communicative dance.

For Hobson the dance is a triangular arrangement – the parent is at one corner of the triangle, the child at another and the outside world at the third. Secure in the parent's presence, the child looks out at the world, then back at the parent; the parent looks at the world, then back at the child; their mutual gaze acknowledges a mutual experience – they've both seen the same bit of world. Attachment, interaction and communication. Hobson argues that, through taking part in this emotionally embedded triangle of interrelatedness, children acquire three key insights.

First, there's the dawning realisation that child and parent are separate beings, looking at the same bit of world from different viewpoints – the child is simultaneously attached to and separate from the parent. This is a supremely important insight, because it's the beginning of empathy. If the mind-blowing discovery that other people have their own points of view is rooted in emotional security and pleasurable communication, the chances of the child later extending empathy to a widening range of people are much greater.

The next insight is the infant's recognition of his own personal perspective, different from the parent's ('She's looking at it from there, and I'm looking at it from here – this is *my* point of view'). The child thus becomes conscious of himself as a thinker, an intellectual self-awareness that underpins rational thought and behaviour. It's a charming thought: millions of infant minds throughout the millennia experiencing their own spontaneous recognition that 'I think, therefore I am'.

Finally, the realisation that it's possible to have more than one perspective points children towards symbolic play ('If I can look at this box in different ways, I can *pretend* it's a car ... brum, brum!'). Soon they'll delight in using dolls as symbols for babies, sticks for horses, and cardboard boxes for cars. Symbolic play lays the foundation for understanding the many systems of symbols used in our culture, including numbers and letters. Psychologists believe it's also critical for the development of imagination and creative problem-solving abilities.

So the shared gaze of parent and child, along with their shared pleasure of interaction, could be the answer to questions that have vexed philosophers since time immemorial: What does it mean to think? What is it to be human? What is the root of learning? But it also points to other questions: Why do some people think less effectively than others? Why do some seem to have less 'humanity'? Why do others have problems with learning?

Peter Hobson has some suggestions here too. His journey towards *The Cradle of Thought* was via long-term research into autism. He believes an autistic infant's genetic make-up prevents him from acquiring the three insights described above. The autistic child may be able to learn, but not to back up that learning with 'human' understanding. What's more, Hobson suggests that if opportunities to participate in emotionally satisfying interactions are missing in their first eighteen months, even children *without* such a genetic vulnerability may have difficulty in acquiring one or more of the insights. He cites the example of the unfortunate babies raised with little human contact in Rumanian orphanages under the Ceaucescu regime – many more than would be expected in a normal population developed autistic-like behaviour.

There's a growing body of neuroscientific research connecting successful early attachment with the development of neural networks in the prefrontal cortex of the brain – the area associated with rational thought, decision-making, social behaviour and self-control. If Hobson is right, the implications for early childcare are profound. What if a normal child isn't exactly neglected but opportunities for shared gazing and communication are limited? What if parents don't have time, or are too busy, or simply don't know how important it is to interact with their babies? The life we lead today doesn't exactly encourage parents to engage in the communicatory dance – in some ways, it positively discourages it.

How contemporary culture interrupts the dance

In an earlier, less frenetic age, most new mothers had time to devote to the dance of communication – or they delegated someone else to the job: the rich employed nannies; the poor enlisted the services of older siblings or other members of the extended family. Nowadays, it's not so easy. For the many mothers who feel obliged to return to work soon after their babies are born, time for cradling, crooning and pointing at doggies is limited, but – with fewer extended families around and a scarcity of daycare choices – it may be difficult to find someone to whom the child can attach emotionally in its mother's absence. Early communication, with all its attendant developmental implications, may be neglected from the very beginning.

The issue of daycare is discussed in Chapter 6, but even when a mother is at home, there are now many demands on her time which keep her from the 'dance'. Health workers on home visits frequently report seeing mothers with a baby in one hand and a mobile phone in the other, or failing to make eye contact with their suckling infant because they're simultaneously checking the email or watching *Oprah* on TV. These mothers are not uncaring or unfeeling – just products of our busy, multi-tasking contemporary culture and utterly unaware of the communicatory needs of their tiny children.

Organisations such as the UK's Talk to Your Baby, run by the National Literacy Trust, are now trying to raise awareness of the importance of switching off the TV, computer or mobile phone and concentrating – for at least some of the day – on looking at, talking to and singing to babies. Singing seems to be particularly important – the rhythmic movements associated with age-old songs – bouncing a baby on your knee while singing 'Bye, Baby Bunting', rocking a cradle to 'Rock-A-Bye Baby' – seems to affect the patterning of the brain and may have important implications for later social and cognitive development.

The lack of interaction between contemporary mothers and children often continues when they go outdoors. Perhaps because they think children are more stimulated by watching the world go by, many parents use baby-slings facing outwards, so eye contact is ruled out, and the triangle of relatedness is broken. Then when children graduate to pushchairs, these often face away from the pusher: lightweight, foldaway pushchairs generally face outwards, because the dynamics of the design require the baby's weight to be behind the front wheels.

It seems ridiculous that something as simple as pushchair design could affect children's development, but it's one more element in the toxic mix. Before foldaway pushchairs arrived on the scene about thirty years ago (in response to massively growing car ownership) parents ferried their offspring about in old-fashioned prams, which allowed them to look at and talk to the infant as they walked. From the point of view of a small infant, looking at and communicating with mum is much more productive and stimulating than silently watching the hotchpotch of movement in a busy street.

I watched a mother pushing her baby son through our local park the other day. She was being a 'good mum' and chatting away to him about their surroundings – the squirrels, the trees, my Bedlington terrier ('Look at that doggy!') – and he was totally unaware of her attempts at communication. Facing away from her, he couldn't see where she was looking, so the triangle was broken. Her attempts at communication were lost and her words were meaningless, just another noise among many that added nothing to his experience of the world.

Tuning in or turning off

Even when children and parents can see each other, there's another potential reason for communication failure: constant noise that interferes with children's ability to hear their parents' speech. Outdoors there is traffic noise, increasing every year; indoors, in many homes, there's the day-long noise of television. There is gathering evidence that noise impedes children's educational progress (for instance, schools on airport flight paths tend to have lower-than-average test scores) – this appears to apply in homes as well, as children from homes where the TV is on all day are less likely to read at age six.

For fifteen years at the end of the last century, child language expert Dr Sally Ward investigated babies' listening skills in Manchester, England. In 1984, 20 per cent of the nine-month-old infants she tested were unable to listen selectively; by 1999, the proportion had almost doubled. I met her in 1997, when she predicted that 'by the early years of the new millennium, around half the nation's one-year-olds will be unable to listen satisfactorily to the sound of their mothers' voices against the noise of the television'. Children who don't learn to listen – and thus pick up on where parents' attention is focused – are likely to have problems acquiring language and, if their awareness of speech sounds is affected, they'll probably also have difficulties with literacy skills.

Sure enough, in the early years of the new millennium, a survey of UK headteachers found that 74 per cent were concerned at deteriorations in children's speaking and listening skills; another found that 89 per cent of nursery workers were similarly alarmed; and my own survey (see Appendix) showed that more than 90 per cent of primary teachers were seriously worried about lack of talk at home and too much TV.

Sally Ward conducted an experiment with some parents from her study. She simply asked them to turn off the television for half an hour a day, and talk to their children. When they knew why it would be helpful, all the parents were keen to do this, but they had one panic-stricken question, 'What shall we talk about?'

Over the second half of the last century, as extended families died away, simple ancient wisdom that had passed through the generations since time immemorial died away with them. Many of today's parents – and even grandparents – have never witnessed the rearing of children, except perhaps the odd snippet on TV, and the details of their own childhood are now hazy, so how would they know what to talk about? They haven't watched an aunt, a sister, their own mother with a younger sibling, chanting as she dressed the baby ('That's one button, two buttons, three buttons ...') or rocking an infant to sleep with an ancient rhyme. Indeed, as the child of a nuclear family, the only reason I know such rhymes myself is that we tuned in to a radio programme called *Listen With Mother*, which broadcast rhymes and stories every afternoon (sadly, the BBC dropped this in the 1970s because it was 'old-fashioned'). Many of the generation of parents reared since TV became an all-day presence have lost track of this cultural treasure trove.

These old rhymes, songs and jingles may sound nonsensical to contemporary ears, but the reason they've been passed through the ages is that they're ideal for introducing children to the rhythms of language and tuning their ears to language sounds. The rhythmic patterns seem to be particularly important – American researchers have found that a young child's ability to keep a steady beat is one of the best predictors of future success at school. Many of the experts I spoke to, in both linguistics and developmental psychology, commented on the huge importance of music and song in developing children's social and communication skills.

If parents don't know the old nursery songs and rhymes, there are plenty of CDs and many collections on the web. However, in the first couple of years these should be for parental reference only – children need to listen to and learn from a fellow human being, not a machine. Our adult love affair with technology has led many people to believe it can act as a substitute for human interaction. It can't – at least, not with little children. A machine with lots of bells and whistles and buttons to press may easily engage a child's attention, but it isn't genuinely responsive. It has no human warmth, eye contact, facial expression or interest in the child's needs – there is no emotional connection.

The American Academy of Pediatrics (AAP) recommends that children under two should not watch television. As a seasoned BBC executive remarked to me, they are almost certainly 'on a hiding to nothing' on this one. TV is such a universal part of our culture that it would be impossible to stop babies and toddlers from seeing it. However, parents should try to limit exposure (see Chapter 9, 'The electronic babysitter'), and they should certainly make time for human entertainment in a quiet environment. The recent craze for baby signing is one way of promoting parent-child interaction and communication, especially for educated parents who find traditional childish pursuits tedious. But from the child's point of view, and in terms of developing language and listening skills, the tried and tested methods are best. Jigging on a parent's knee, chanting, singing – or collapsing into giggles as they play 'This little piggy went to market' over and over again – is intensely pleasurable for small children, while the constant rhythm, rhyme and repetition tunes their bodies to balance, their ears to sounds and their minds to pattern, opening up the neural networks that lead to fluent speech.

The language instinct

Human beings are the only animals on earth with the power of speech. It's over half a century since Noam Chomsky suggested we're genetically programmed to acquire language, just as songbirds are programmed to acquire songs. Neuroscience has since backed up his hypothesis. Unless children are physically or neurologically impaired, or reared in circumstances of extreme deprivation, every one of them learns to speak – usually uttering the first word around the age of one. Language comes as naturally to human beings as smiling, standing or walking.

However, despite being hardwired for language, human babies don't actually learn to speak a particular tongue unless they get plenty of experience of it. (In just the same way, songbirds need to listen to other songbirds in order to sing fluently and freely.)

The quality of the engagement and talk surrounding a growing child determines the levels of language, listening and – eventually – literacy that child is able to reach. If children are reared in a 'language-rich' environment, they will probably develop good language skills; if their background is 'language-poor', they probably won't.

A major component of a language-rich environment is at least one adult who spends time genuinely interacting with the child and focusing on the child's needs and interests, so that the language is meaningful to him, and using the exaggerated, simplified language that linguists call 'parentese'. This requires interest and commitment on the adult's part, and many contemporary adults find it difficult (or frankly boring) to 'come down to the child's level'. Perhaps they've been educated out of the ability to communicate naturally to tiny children, but for their children's sake they really need to educate themselves back into it – any of the books recommended at the end of this chapter would help.

When children begin to talk themselves, the best way to encourage more talk is to follow their lead, repeating a child's words, guessing at their meaning and extending the idea. For instance, 'Milk all gone.' 'Has the milk all gone? Oh yes, you've drunk it all up. Do you want some more?' There's no need to get hung up about correctness – children need to experiment with language, which means not worrying about making mistakes. Repetition of the child's words using the correct form shows the adult has understood, and provides a model the child can imitate. By repeating and expanding, parents encourage children to experiment more and more with language, and to grow in confidence in using it.

The power of words

Opportunities for interactive talk with children at all stages in their development abound in daily life. The suggestions in previous chapters – family meals; sharing everyday activities, outings and chores; bedtime routines and stories – are all natural opportunities for shared time and communication. They also provide subject matter for conversations – talking about what you're doing and why you're doing it, pointing out anything interesting, involving the child as much as possible.

Although the minutiae of domestic life may be commonplace for adults, it is still new and original for young children – and seeing it through a child's eyes allows adults to rediscover all the small wonders forgotten in our usual busyness: the sounds, textures, shapes and objects in our homes; how simple gadgets work; the exigencies and effects of the weather; the way a nearby tree changes through the seasons; the buildings, people, pets in the local neighbourhood. As children grow older, they also love talking about themselves and their family – chatting about shared memories, hearing stories about their parents' childhoods and learning snippets of family history. Dr Pat Spungin, social psychologist and founder of Raising Kids, believes this is an important element in developing a strong sense of identity.

When conversation flags, shared time provides an opportunity for singsongs, reciting rhymes together, number games (starting with counting stairs, cars, cans of beans and graduating to 'Think of a number, double it', etc, etc) or, whenever time permits, play. Any sort of play is an opportunity for parents to model behaviour and chat about and around the game: 'peek-a-boo' or 'show me the toy' with a baby; painting, playdough-modelling or bouncing a ball with a toddler; playing with soft toys, dressing up and role-play with pre-schoolers; card and board games with school-age children. To return to David Attenborough's quote: for young children, 'play is a very serious business' – symbolic and creative play not only develops physical competence, it underpins their later success at school.

None of the conversational opportunities suggested here are expensive – indeed, with young children, the more sophisticated the purchase, the less it usually engages them. Most parents have had the experience of watching an expensive present cast aside because the child was more interested in the wrapping paper or the box it came in. Our consumer society leads us to believe that the more costly and complex an item is, the more its value – this is not the case with children. Although in a way it is true: human beings are complex and these days their time is costly, and time with the human beings most special to them is what children most need and crave.

As the child grows older, the best sort of talk encourages creative thinking, and the use of language to communicate those thoughts. In 2004, a UK study described the most valuable educational experience for pre-schoolers (and I'm pretty sure it would apply to school-age children too) as 'sustained shared thinking' with an adult – this, of course, is mediated through sustained shared talk. One of the researchers, Iram Siraj-Blatchford, explained to me that the key is 'to open up language, rather than shutting it down'.

Adults so often ask closed questions, where there's only one right answer ('What colour is that?' 'What was the girl's name?' 'How many blocks do you have?'). Children either get such questions right, and that's that, end of exchange; or they get them wrong, and that's the end of the exchange too – though this time the child feels bad about it. Much more productive are speculative questions: 'I wonder what would happen if … ?' 'What do you think he might do?' 'Wouldn't it be interesting if … ?'

Parenting classes and books such as Adele Faber and Elaine Mazlish's *How to Talk So Kids Will Listen, and Listen So Kids Will Talk* recommend similar approaches to help children express their feelings. Instead of questioning a child, or providing instant solutions, they suggest acknowledging the way the child is feeling by giving the emotion a name ('Gosh, that must have been *disappointing*' or 'You sound really *frustrated /angry/irritated*!') and offering support with minimal but genuinely interested responses ('Mmmm?' … 'I see' … 'Yes') while the child talks through the issue, hopefully arriving at a personal solution. It is such open-ended approaches to talk – in which the adult respects and pays real attention to the child's contribution – that eventually lead to social awareness, self-esteem and independent thought.

I'm often asked by parents what they can do to help their children succeed at school. The simple answer, born out by research, is talk and listen. Or maybe that should be listen and talk.

How technology can dumb our children down

In all communication and language, the key is interactivity. From the very start, children learn language through human engagement, as illustrated by the story of a little American boy, Vincent, told to me by linguistics professor Jean Aitchison. Vincent's parents were both deaf and communicated in sign language. Their baby, however, was born with normal hearing ability, so from the very start his parents made sure he watched TV, expecting him to learn spoken language from the speakers on screen. Vincent didn't learn to speak a single word; but he did become fluent in American Sign Language, his real-life interactive 'mother tongue'. When he was eventually exposed to real-life spoken language at the age of three, his progress in learning to speak was painfully slow.

Language is only meaningful to a small infant if it is part of genuine experience. One of the more alarming developments of contemporary culture is the increasing use, across the developed world, of television as an electronic babysitter, with children watching alone while parents are engaged elsewhere. Vincent's experience shows that very young children *don't* learn language from TV – they learn it from people.

As they grow older, good quality television (see Chapter 9) will almost certainly expand their horizons and develop vocabulary – and researchers have found that repeated watching of a favourite video by pre-schoolers also means repeated hearing, which can be helpful to language development. But it should still be carefully monitored and limited, because 'receptive listening' is only one side of the language equation – real learning requires children to use the language themselves. Without opportunities to 'practise' any new vocabulary they acquire, children will rapidly lose it.

When first researching this issue, I thought the 'electronic babysitter' syndrome would be a problem mainly in socially disadvantaged households. A speaking engagement in a very expensive prep school put me right. The staff at this school – which sent many of its pupils on to Eton, where Princes William and Harry were educated – recognised the problem immediately. As one teacher put it, 'Here it's not mummy and daddy plonking the child in front of the television – they're both out earning shed-loads of money to pay the fees – it's the Lithuanian au pair!' Teachers in schools serving wealthy families around Europe have given similar reports: where childcare staff don't share a first language with the children, the electronic babysitter comes into its own.

And it's not just TV that takes parents away from their children – technology distracts us in many ways. One constant complaint from children I meet is the extent to which it now interrupts family time. Eight-year-old Lily expressed it very well: 'We'll just be settling down to something – a story or something – and her phone'll go. So then she goes off chatting, and I'm sitting getting jealous, so I just go and put the telly on.' Just as many nursing mothers don't realise that multimedia multi-tasking can deprive their children of essential early communication, parents of older children are often unaware of how much email, phones and their own favourite TV programmes come between them and their offspring. Since researching this chapter, I've made a conscious effort to treat my family with the same respect I would a business acquaintance – switching to answerphone during 'family time' and leaving the email to stew. It's scary how difficult this can be – we are now so much at the mercy of our machines. No wonder children often give up on us and disappear off to watch TV on their own.

If the television is in the child's bedroom, its ill effects are increased. A TV in the bedroom often leads to children watching alone, eating alone, preparing for bed alone ... practically all opportunities for family conversations are eroded. The knock-on effects on language development, alongside those on sleeping patterns described in the last chapter and problems with social isolation and emotional development to be covered in Chapters 8 and 9, make bedroom TV a key factor in toxic childhood syndrome. Now that televisions have apparently made their way into about three-quarters of pre-teenage children's rooms, it will not be easy to reverse the trend, but there are some suggestions for winkling them out on page 129.

Stories and screens

Bedroom TV has also hastened the decline of another cultural tradition: the bedtime story. There's a huge difference between listening to a story told or read by a loving adult and watching one on a screen, which is how a growing number of children now end their day. Not only is the screen-based version less emotionally satisfying, it's also less likely to develop children's linguistic and intellectual powers. Stories on screen are mostly visual – viewers *watch* the characters and the setting, following the plot with their eyes. For many contemporary children a story has no verbal narrative thread, just fragmented dialogue, sound effects and background music.

This can cause problems when they start learning to read. If the language of books is unfamiliar and their ears untrained to narrative, they may struggle to make sense of it – almost like learning another language. They may also lose out creatively, because if they only ever encounter stories on screen, where ready-made images are provided, children don't learn to 'make pictures' for themselves in their heads – in other words, to use their imagination. Neither do they learn the shape and feel of written sentences, the patterns of literate language that will allow them to express their own thoughts in writing.

Studies have repeatedly shown that children whose parents read to them tend to become good readers themselves, as well as gaining the many other advantages that literacy conveys. Cuddling up to share a picture book is a source of endless delight to toddlers – and even older children who can read for themselves benefit from hearing good books read aloud. The children's author Robert Louis Stevenson recommended that children of all ages need to *hear* stories, for how else will they learn 'the chime of fair words, and the march of the stately period'?

At this point, I must admit that I have not always practised what I preach. In my capacity as a literacy specialist, I was once on the radio rhapsodising about the importance of reading to children right up to their teens. My daughter, who was nine at the time and listening at home, turned to her childminder and said, 'Huh, she hasn't read to me for ages.' It was embarrassingly true: as she'd grown older and her bedtime got later, I was too shattered to sit for twenty minutes reading a story at the end of the day – a classic example of knowing what's right, but not actually doing it. We therefore agreed to import a tape player into my daughter's bedroom and build up a library of good 'talking books'. Sometimes I would still read to her, sometimes she listened to one of her collection instead, and often I enjoyed just sitting, sharing Alan Bennett's rendition of *Winnie the Pooh* as she drifted off to sleep.

This is one sort of technology that may therefore have a place in older children's bedrooms. If you're not able to read to children yourself, letting them listen to a good book, well read on CD or tape, seems to me a much sounder way of helping them settle down for sleep than the fret and fizz of television. (Talking books are also a boon and a blessing on long car journeys.)

The joy of txt

As children grow older, another factor begins to bother parents: emails and texting. Will children's use of careless, unpunctuated, abbreviated language on chat-room message boards and mobile phone texts infect their schoolwork? Will using and responding to smiley faces and other icons interfere with their ability to read and write? As a specialist in educational linguistics, I think this is a massive distraction from the real problems, described above. In fact, txt is the least of our worries.

As long as children have well-developed listening and language skills by the time they reach school, there's no reason why they shouldn't learn to read and write (see Chapter 7). And as long as they can read and write properly when necessary, there's no reason not to use their own personal style of writing in their spare time. It's normal for human beings to adjust the way they use language depending on whom they're addressing and the message they're conveying. For instance, we speak to children differently from the way we'd speak to the boss, and we express ourselves differently depending on whether our message is serious or flippant, casual or official.

Young people have always had their own specialised slang languages – largely unintelligible and therefore threatening to adults – which help them proclaim their identity. During the last century most slang was spoken, so when, thanks to technology, a written slang appeared, it seemed even more threatening to the older generation. However, in the past, when letter-writing was fashionable, chatty letter-writers often adopted their own types of speed-writing. I once had the opportunity to look at Queen Victoria's childhood letters (of which she wrote a great many) and was fascinated to find them riddled with strange personal abbreviations and misspellings – it almost looked like 'txt'. Queen Victoria had no difficulty in swapping from that to the language of state when she needed to. And, as cognitive psychologist Steven Pinker once pointed out, 'The telegraph didn't lead people to omit prepositions from their speech or end every sentence with STOP.'

Marketing gurus refer to the language of text as 'TweenSpeak' because it peaks among tweenagers (the eight to fourteen age group). It's different from previous slangs in being a global phenomenon, uniting young people across geographical boundaries. Like many aspects of technological culture, therefore, it may well prove important in children's development as future inhabitants of the global village.

*

There's no doubt that the older children are, the more beneficial technology can be for widening horizons and developing knowledge and vocabulary. Nevertheless too much viewing, or too long on the PlayStation, mobile or Internet are still not recommended – suggested time limits for various ages are given in Chapter 9, but parents should use common sense in applying these in their own children's circumstances. Chapter 9 also points out the importance of monitoring what children watch on TV or do on their computers – and shared experiences of technology can, of course, be another focus for conversation.

There's no need to worry that reducing their time online will mean they'll be left behind on the technology front: contemporary children easily learn the 'media literacy' skills required to navigate around computers – these skills are designed to be intuitive, so can be picked up by trial and error. But to ensure successful development of 'old-fashioned' language, listening and literacy skills on which depend the capacity to think, analyse, explore and express ideas – not to mention important aspects of emotional and social development – children need *real* interactive communication and *real* talk. At the moment, too much technology is dumbing our children down.

DETOXING COMMUNICATION

Babies and toddlers

- More than anything else, your child needs the time and interest of a loving adult. Do everything you can to ensure this is available constantly in the first eighteen months of life, and frequently and regularly thereafter. Social, emotional and intellectual development are rooted in early attachment and later opportunities for interactive talk.

- Limit electronic noise from TV, radio, CDs, etc.

- Talk to your baby as often as possible – when you're playing, when you're out and about, as you do household chores. Make eye contact, smile, and just chat about what you're doing. When you point and talk about something, make sure your child can see where you're pointing.

- Try to ensure that when you're chatting, your baby can see your face, smile and eyes. If possible, find a buggy that allows your baby to face you.

- Don't be worried about using 'parentese' – the sort of exaggerated, musical pronunciation that most adults find themselves automatically adopting when talking to a very young child. It helps children discriminate the key sounds of the language, which will come in useful when they begin to speak themselves (and later when they learn to read – see Chapter 7).

- Whenever you have time, sing nursery songs and lullabies, recite rhythmic rhymes and chants, use repetitive games like Pat-a-cake, tickling rhymes and number chants – this too lays sound foundations for language and literacy.

- To develop your child's attention skills, play games involving pleasurable anticipation (such as 'This little piggy' and 'Round and round the garden, like a teddy bear') and later play Ready Steady Go games, where they have to wait for a signal.

- Listen carefully when your child responds to what you have said, and try always to reply in some way. As children begin to speak, repeat and expand on their words. If they say something incorrectly, say it back the right way. Praise your child for using new words correctly.

- Provide opportunities for children to initiate talk, and respond to their verbal and non-verbal communications.
- If possible, don't let the under-threes watch TV or video for more than an hour a day.

Three-year olds and upwards

- When sharing precious time with your child, try to minimise interruptions from communication technology. Switch off the mobile, put the phone on answer machine, resist the temptation to check the email — you would do this for an important person at work, and who is more important than your child?
- When sharing time with children, try to escape the need to rush and multi-task. Slow down to a more 'human' pace. Do not rush a child who is talking, and don't look away.
- Limit TV time for older children, keep to shows designed for your child's age group and if possible watch with them.
- Use TV as a focus for talk — if you watch together, you can chat about the characters, what they did, why they did it, and so on.
- Encourage your child to speak directly to other adults and children (translate if their language is unclear, but don't talk *for* them).
- Continue to sing with children as they grow older, encourage action songs and dances, and model listening to music. If your child shows an interest in music, encourage it — it's one of the greatest humanising forces there is.
- Ensure that there are regular 'ring-fenced family times' such as mealtimes, shared activities and bedtime routines, when there is plenty of space for talk.
- Look for ways of 'opening up' your child's language through speculative language and tentative questions, thus developing 'sustained shared thinking'. Avoid closing down your child's language with 'closed' questions to which there is only one right answer.
- Encourage children to talk about their own experiences, past, present and future, and model how to listen attentively (see also 'How to Help Your Child at School', Chapter 7).

- Share family history and lore, tell about what you did 'when you were little' and reminisce about your child's experiences – as well as providing good conversational fodder, this develops a sense of identity and self-esteem.
- Read and/or tell stories every day, whatever the age of your child. With younger children, share a cuddle as you read favourite books repeatedly.
- As children get older, go on reading to them, even when they can read themselves. On long car journeys, listen together to talking books, and when they get too old for a bedtime story, let older children listen to talking books as they go to sleep.

HOW TO TEACH THEM TO TALK IT OVER

Communication is the best way to avoid misunderstandings. Encouraging children to talk things through helps them solve their problems, understand other people's point of view, avoid conflicts and prevent disagreements escalating into fights.

- Acknowledge children's feelings, and give them time to talk through what worries them, rather than immediately offering solutions or opinions (see Faber and Mazlish, page 132).
- Be a good role model: always try to talk through issues to be sure you understand your child's (and other family members') point of view. This does *not* mean allowing yourself to be drawn into an argument (see Chapter 10: 'Detoxing Behaviour').
- Model how to listen, and to repeat back what someone else has said to be sure you've understood.
- Teach children a four-point 'conflict resolution' technique for resolving their arguments. Model this yourself, and whenever a problem arises help them go through the routine. It does actually work.

When someone upsets you so much you want to start a fight, stop and:

    1. state what they've done to make you upset or angry

    2. explain how it's made you feel and why (this will usually be because you are *hurt* or *afraid* of further consequences)

    3. say what you'd like the other person to do to help sort it out

    4. ask for an acknowledgement that the other person has understood

The other party should be helped to listen and show they've understood, then engage in discussion/negotiation about how to solve the problem.

HOW TO GET THE TV OUT OF THE BEDROOM

The best way to keep technological items out of bedrooms is never to let them in. If you're not already convinced about the importance of removing a bedroom TV, read Chapters 8 and 9.

- Make it a family rule that no one has a TV in their room (at least until they are in their teens). If children younger than that already have TVs, plan a campaign to get them out.
- If possible, choose a time when the transition will be easy, e.g. immediately after returning from a holiday when children watched little TV.
- Before removing the TV, plan plenty of activities that your child will enjoy more than sitting alone in the bedroom. See for instance:

  – 'How to Avoid Couch Potato Syndrome', pages 70–73
  – 'Detoxing Family Life', pages 159–162
  – 'How to Detox a TV Addict', pages 274–275

- Talk to your child about the fact that the bedroom TV will be removed, and when. Explain clearly why life will be better without it, e.g.:

  – there will be more time for talking, playing, having fun with parents and others
  – the family will be able to share time together (including family viewing)
  – it will help your child sleep better and do better at school.

- Listen to any problems your child voices and respond as positively as possible. But don't get into an argument. If necessary, say you've learned that bedroom TV can be harmful, you love your child and are protecting him/her from harm.
- Place a 'family TV' in a comfortable family space in the home.
- Make sure you have a pleasant bedtime routine in place (see Chapter 3), involving a bedtime story. For older children, you may wish to provide a CD or tape player so they can listen to talking books.

- Accept that you and other adults will have to be more selective about your viewing when your child is present. Agree strategies for choosing what you'll watch, allow everyone a say and expect everyone to compromise to some extent. As always, adult role models count for a lot.
- When you remove the bedroom TV, ensure you and others are available to talk, play, have fun with your child (for instance, ask friends around to play).
- As time goes on, expect your child to play more independently and need less company – see 'How to Encourage Creative Play' (pages 247–248) and 'How to Detox a TV Addict'.

PARENT POWER: GUIDELINES ON TECHNOLOGY AND TALK

Our technological culture has expanded so rapidly that many parents aren't aware of its increasing ill effects on communication within families. Just as for sleep issues, it would be helpful to have national guidelines delivered through schools and health services, to support parents in promoting children's well-being, for instance:

- the importance of talking to children from birth
- how songs, rhymes and moving to music help children's later learning
- why and how to remove TV and other technology from bedrooms
- the importance of developing children's speaking and listening skills in school, as well as literacy skills.

Request such guidelines for your child's school and ask that the Parent Teacher Association lobbies for national guidelines and parents' classes about talking and listening to children.

Further reading

Professor James Law, *Johnson's Learning to Talk: A Practical Guide for Parents* (Dorling Kindersley, 2004)

Dr Richard C. Woolfson, *Small Talk: From First Gestures to Simple Sentences* (Hamlyn, 2002)

Philip Sheppard, *Music Makes Your Child Smarter: How Music Helps Every Child's Development* (Artemis Editions, 2005)

Adele Faber and Elaine Mazlish, *How to Talk so Kids Will Listen and Listen so Kids Will Talk* (Piccadilly Press, 2001)

Useful websites

www.talktoyourbaby.org.uk
Talk to Me! Campaign: **www.basic-skills.co.uk**

Mind the gap

The chorus of concern from teachers in disadvantaged areas about children's level of language competence is now so loud that I could fill this section a hundred times over with their stories. Only yesterday, as I arrived at a school to address a meeting about 'talking to your child', I noticed one mother – who didn't attend – sitting in a car outside. She was in the front seat, iPod earphones in place, and her baby was strapped, facing away from her and keening quietly to itself, in the back. But there are also statistics on the subject – some of the most depressing statistics I've ever read.

About a decade ago, two American researchers, Betty Hart and Todd Risley, followed three groups of children through the early years of childhood, from carefully selected 'professional', 'working-class' and 'welfare' families. They regularly tape-recorded hour-long periods of interaction between adults and children in their homes, analysed the findings and extrapolated how many different words the various children had heard, in conversations with adults, by the age of four. On average, it appeared a professional's child has heard around 50 million words, a working-class child 30 million and a welfare child a meagre 12 million. To ram home the alarming difference in language exposure, they found that, by the age of three, the average vocabulary level of professional children was higher than that of the *parents* in the welfare group.

However, Hart and Risley didn't just measure the number of words children heard and spoke. They also recorded differences in the way children were spoken to, and the extent to which parents explained things, gave choices or listened to what they had to say. By the age of three, professional children had heard about 700,000 encouragements and only 80,000 discouragements. In contrast, the welfare child had been encouraged only 60,000 times and discouraged 120,000. Working-class children were somewhere in the middle.

All this backs up teachers' anecdotal evidence about the way parents in poor areas talk to children at the school gate at the end of the day. All too often, instead of a cheerful greeting or enquiry about how the day's gone, the first the first words these children hear are dismissive and apparently uncaring. When the child presents mum with a picture or something else made in class, it's received not with thanks or praise but with lack of interest or, even worse, a put-down.

Hart and Risley, with their vast experience of parent-child interaction, make it clear the unkindness isn't intentional. These parents love their children just as much as anyone else. They're simply reflecting back their experience of the way people speak to them (disadvantaged parents have seldom received much praise or spoken gratitude themselves, either as children or adults), just as their lack of vocabulary reflects their own impoverished exposure to language.

Right from the earliest stages, attachment is also affected by parents' lack of understanding and personal experience. One mother, asked about how much she talked to her six-month-old child replied that she was 'waiting till he talks to me' and another said she *would* like to cuddle her baby but was frightened it would 'spoil' him. It's all too easy to see how children raised in such circumstances become unresponsive themselves, and – if you subscribe to Peter Hobson's theory – fail to acquire the insights that will help them learn once they reach school.

Add to all this the fact that parents at the bottom of the social heap are often so preoccupied with questions of basic survival – especially if most of the money that comes their way disappears into the hands of the local drug baron or pub – that sociable chitchat with a child is an unthinkable waste of time. The constant quacking of television in the home, as mentioned Chapter 3's 'Mind the gap', contributes to the problem – why bother talking when TV fills the airways with noise?

Yet poverty does not inevitably lead into a downward cycle of discouragement, impoverished language and failure. Research from thirty or more years ago suggests that, until social and cultural change began to create barriers between parents and their children, songs, rhymes, cuddles and 'sustained shared thinking' were just as likely to occur in poorer homes as in wealthy ones. (From a personal perspective, I'm sure my own success in the education system was underpinned by the time, love and attention bestowed by my grandmother, who was poor as a church mouse and barely literate.)

If the technological miracles of the modern world could be rallied to support and inform all parents about how real-life interaction enhances children's development (along with the benefits of real food, play and rest), we could break the vicious cycle of social deprivation that undermines our society. But if TV and other technological paraphernalia merely fill homes with noise and distraction, creating an artificial barrier to communication between the generations, the experience of the children at the bottom of the social heap will become ever more toxic.

CHAPTER FIVE

WE ARE FAMILY

The clear message of the previous four chapters is that, for healthy development in body and mind, children need love, stability, attention … and time. Raising children – even a single child – isn't something you can do in the odd few minutes here and there. Across the animal kingdom, where the young of a species require careful or prolonged rearing, the parents tend to stay together to share the burden – and many species rear their young in packs for extra support. Over the millennia, homo sapiens has developed a similar support system for rearing our young – families, based on parent-child relationships, are supported by their wider community through social, religious and legal frameworks.

The family has had many incarnations over the ages, but most of us tend to identify with the nuclear family of the mid-twentieth century (husband, wife, two point four children). However, as couples increasingly choose to cohabit rather than marry, and more marriages end in divorce, the stereotypical nuclear family hasn't so much changed as dissolved. Social scientists today talk about 'family units' or 'networks', taking a multitude of forms. The adults involved may be single or married parents, step-parents, ex-partners, same-sex partners, friends or cohabitees; the children may be siblings, half-siblings or step-siblings; there may also be grandparents, step-grandparents, ex-grandparents and a range of other friends and relations that would do justice to Winnie the Pooh's friend Rabbit.

This means an infinite number of possible families, each with its own very specific dynamics.

Revolution, relationships and roles

Changes in the way families are structured necessarily impact on the way children are reared, and these changes seem at first sight so profound that it's scary. But human beings are flexible creatures who have weathered many revolutions; there's no reason why we shouldn't eventually come through this one too. In a 2004 evaluation of the family in Britain for the Gulbenkian Foundation, social scientist Fiona Williams looked on the bright side, towards a future of 'democratic relationships' where partners are bound not by 'obligation and duty' but by independent choice. If humanity can manage this, democratic relationships could be just the thing for rearing balanced, civilised children.

Unfortunately, Utopia is still a long way off. At present, millions of disparate (often very confused) contemporary families seem to be trying to sort out the business of twenty-first-century child-rearing from scratch, to fit their own individual circumstances – circumstances which are themselves often subject to sudden change. What's more, they're struggling to do this within the maelstrom of contemporary life, where the rapid pace of technology means human beings are constantly running to keep up with machines. Families live – to quote the ancient Chinese curse – in extremely interesting times.

The driving force of all this social change has been the revolution in the status of women – a revolution that started in the early twentieth century, picked up speed in the sixties, then accelerated wildly with the electric speed of the last three decades. Aided and abetted by computers and the media, a majority of women have progressed from helpmates and homemakers to independent earners in not much more than a generation. Sexual equality was inevitable as developed nations embraced a widening ideal of democracy, but it was also inevitable that there'd be difficulties adjusting, especially when it all happened so fast. One of the biggest questions facing all parents today is: how do we define the roles and responsibilities of mothers and fathers within the rapidly shifting kaleidoscope of the twenty-first-century family?

In the past, for obvious biological reasons, bringing up children was largely 'women's work'. Because they did it at home, unpaid, along with the cooking and the cleaning, nobody saw child-rearing as particularly important. On the other hand, the father's role was clearly vital. From primitive hunter-gatherer to the archetypal breadwinner of the 1950s, hanging up his hat with a cry of 'Honey, I'm home', he was the protector and provider. His relationship with his children was often distant and centred on the aspect of 'discipline', but his bread-winning work outside the home gave him far greater status in the family than his wife. Whatever you think of the social and economic inequalities in this arrangement, at least roles were relatively clear-cut.

Equality of opportunity and women's increased economic inde-pendence blew the traditional roles apart. When there's only one parent in a family, or when both parents are out at work, who is the nurturer and who is the provider? And as we change the way we view human behaviour and gender differences – men *can* change nappies, women *can* dominate the boardroom – old stereotypes no longer apply. Yet in biological terms, the hormonal differences associated with the two evolutionary roles are still there. Our DNA determines that, on the whole, women still feel the need to nurture and men to provide and protect. Interesting times indeed.

The mommy wars

Let's look at mothers first. The opening battles of the mommy wars were fought mainly in the US during the late twentieth century, but hostilities still linger on. Rallying the troops on one side is the women's movement, anxious to consolidate their sex's newfound freedom. Since the 1980s they've gathered increasing support from two unlikely allies – big business and national governments, who've worked out that getting women into work means more consumers, more taxpayers and a massive boost to the economy.

On the opposite side of the battlefield are the champions of the traditional family. They urge a return to 'old-fashioned values' by pleading the case of the child ... and, as an incidental aside, the return of woman to the home front and the right of man to retain the role of primary provider. Often the forces of organised religion have joined in on this side of the debate, making it even more difficult to see the wood for the ideological trees.

As the 'mommy wars' rage, women – keen to savour their sex's hard-won freedom but genetically programmed to be nurturers – have struggled in the real world to sort out their new maternal role. Battalions of women of child-bearing age who marched off to work, hopeful that working conditions would change to accommodate their other job as mothers, were seriously disappointed. On the whole, conditions of paid employment are even less family-friendly today than they were in the days when Honey stayed at home.

Technological developments, globalisation and the growth of a round-the-clock consumer society have spawned a long-hours culture that affects both men and women. Despite legislation on working hours and lip service from business leaders about 'work-life balance', employees often feel obliged to stay at their desks well beyond their official hours of employment ... and, thanks to the wonders of technology, are not even free from work demands at home. A 2005 report from the Economic and Social Research Council recorded that many women now have 'a resigned understanding' that asking for shorter hours, flexible working patterns, maternity leave or part-time work is simply not acceptable in the culture of most organisations.

So there have been many casualties in the mommy wars, and there are likely to be many more. At the more privileged end of the social scale are mothers who try to 'have it all' to the point of exhaustion. They struggle to prove that women are the equals of men by holding down a demanding job and keeping the home fires burning, while determinedly presenting a controlled, carefully made-up face to the world. It's no coincidence that one of the best-selling cosmetic products of the early twenty-first century is a light-reflecting liquid that conceals dark circles beneath the eyes. Allison Pearson has catalogued the misery behind the make-up in her novel I Don't Know How She Does It, and concluded, along with a growing number of educated women, that 'having it all' is not a viable option.

Some women opt for Plan B, concentrating on a career in their twenties and early thirties, saving motherhood for later in life when, hopefully, they have sufficient funds to support a period of full-time domesticity. Sadly, this can lead to bitter distress if the woman fails to conceive and, with time no longer on her side, the possibility of motherhood recedes – by the age of forty, a third of women are infertile. (IVF treatment might help ... but that's another – very long – story). Even where Plan B works, psychologists point out that motherhood often comes as a terrible shock to someone used to the order and predictability of a successful career – as a Plan B mother, I can vouch for this.

At the other end of the social scale, there are massed ranks of women now raising children alone who have no option but to 'do it all' while actually having very little. They work long hours for low pay, trying to keep home and family together, with neither time nor money left over for fripperies like make-up, novels or life plans. The tragedy of the 'pink medicine' babies, reported in Jody Heyman's book The Widening Gap, sums them up – mothers who are so desperate not to lose their job that they dose sick children with painkillers to mask a high fever, so they can leave them in daycare while they go to work. One can't begin to imagine the anguish of a mother who has to desert a sick child in order to earn enough to feed and clothe it.

The mother of all dilemmas

There is also, of course, the anguish of the children. It's easy with hindsight to recognise that they've been the worst casualties in the mommy wars, but it would be wrong to conclude that working women of the last twenty-five years were intentionally uncaring. They were propelled out of the home by a cultural tsunami – carried into work on a tide of democratic ideals. Reassured by tales of celebrity mums who apparently proved you could have it all, conned into believing that 'quality time' was an adequate substitute for parental attention, women really believed that a child is just one more ball in the modern mother's juggling act.

But the damage has been done. The withdrawal of mothers from the home left a yawning gap that was quickly filled by the products of technology. With no one around to sing, chat and listen to them, children learned instead to gaze mindlessly at the TV. In the absence of mum, cooking regular meals and encouraging families to eat together, the food industry plied our children with processed junk. Since there were no adults at home to supervise play, or to provide 'eyes on the street' so they could play outside, children turned instead to sedentary electronic entertainment. And if parents were too tired after a day's work to supervise regular bedtime routines, the electronic entertainment fizzed on late into the night, rendering them ever more difficult to control. The results, in terms of disaffected, disengaged and self-destructive young people, are all around us.

The hugely important lesson the developed world has to learn from the great sociological experiment of the last quarter-century is that bringing up children is not some sort of part-time hobby. It's a real job: skilled, full-time and personally demanding. Owing to women's low status in the past, this traditional aspect of 'women's work' has never been properly valued – and much of the developed world still finds it difficult to grasp its significance. Whether performed by mother, father, paid carers, or a combination of them all, the way we bring up children matters – we cannot expect our young to civilise themselves.

In the words of one well-known working mother, Madonna, 'contemporary women now struggle with the polarity between work and family'. Which should they put first – the biological drive towards motherhood (and the responsibilities this brings in terms of mothering) or the socio-economic drive towards work and status? There is, of course, no simple answer to the question – it has to be solved by each individual mother, preferably in consultation with her partner (see next section) and in full knowledge of the childcare options available (see Chapter 6). But as it becomes increasingly clear that for a woman to have it all – all at one time – is not an option, the obvious solution in a democratic relationship is, of course, to share it all.

What are fathers for?

Changes for fathers over the last generation have been every bit as profound as those for mothers. While the novelty of women's changing status has taken centre stage, homage is due to those men who supported and worked for such democratising change. It was clearly not in their immediate interests to give up the traditional status as the lone family breadwinners. This was particularly painful where women's entry into the labour market coincided with a decline in heavy industry and therefore male unemployment.

On the home front as well the role of the father has been seriously eroded. As they watched women apparently assume the roles of both breadwinner and nurturer, many men began to wonder what was left for them to do. In a 2004 UK survey, fathers confessed to feeling sidelined, depressed and pessimistic about their parenting skills, and stressed by the conflicting demands of work and home. In her 2005 book The Future of Men, Marian Salzman records that the changes 'appear to be having a negative effect on the male psyche, leaving modern men hesitant, disorientated and, in many cases, more than a little depressed', and sociologist Laurie Taylor has suggested that fathers, once mediators between the home and the wider world, are redundant now that women go out to work and children interface constantly with the world via the TV and computer screens.

But even though men and women are now equally knowledgeable about the world, children are not: parents know considerably more about life and life skills than their offspring, and it's still their job to teach them the ropes. All the aspects of child-rearing described in this book can be performed by either mothers or fathers – and often have been performed by enlightened fathers in the past. If economic responsibilities are shared, these tasks can be shared too, much to children's benefit.

Psychologists point out that father-child relationships are different from those of mothers and children. They tend to be rather 'blokeish' – involving more joking, teasing, tickling, physical play and shared outdoor interests such as football and fishing. Men bounce babies boisterously on their knees, swing toddlers up on to their shoulders, encourage children to ever braver displays on play equipment – often to the horror of their female partners, whose genetic make-up inclines against risk-taking or rough and tumble. By being more adventurous about games than women, men encourage their children to be more daring – perhaps fathers' uncertainty about their role helps account for our generally overprotective attitude to children in the early twenty-first century?

Fathers' influence is clearly important for boys – for whom they will always be the most important role model – and many research projects catalogue the problems of boys brought up without the benefit of a father figure. Perhaps the most startling statistic is that in the United States 70 per cent of violent male delinquents and criminals were reared without fathers (see also Mind the gap, page 167). But their influence is also important for girls, who grow in self-esteem by sharing their father's time and interests (as a daughter who was initiated at the age of eight into the mysteries of cricket, I can personally vouch for the beneficial effect on self-confidence of a father's interest – without it, I doubt I'd have the brass neck to attempt this book).

The growing body of research connecting paternal involvement in child-rearing with educational achievement, social behaviour and long-term mental health testifies to the fact that fathers are far from redundant. And involvement is not difficult. The best sort of fathering simply involves taking an interest in your children, spending time in their company and letting them join in with whatever you're doing. In this respect, being a father – like being a mother – is utterly 'natural'. No special skills, qualities or equipment are required, just plenty of time and loving attention.

Old and new dads

The other traditional paternal role is as the dispenser of discipline. Most contemporary societies are confused about this aspect of child-rearing, to the extent that fathers often feel marginalised – indeed, these days the word 'abusive' attaches itself so easily to the word 'father' that many have felt it safer to opt out of the discipline equation altogether. Mothers have therefore increasingly taken on the task of children's social and moral education. After a lifetime in education, however, I believe the disappearance of the conventional father figure in helping their offspring recognise the difference between right and wrong is a tragic one, both for families and society.

I'm not advocating the 'Wait till your father gets home' approach to discipline, in which the father's part was to dispense fear, trembling and, all too often, physical pain. But I do believe men are sometimes better placed than women to bring a dispassionate eye to their children's behaviour. 'Mother love' – the hormonally charged instinct to protect one's young from any sort of distress – is traditionally both blind and passionate: in the heat of the moment a woman is programmed to take her children's part, like a tigress defending her cubs. And a woman at the end of her tether due to chronic overwork is probably even less able to take a rational view of her children's behaviour.

If mothers sometimes allow the tigress instinct to cloud their judgement, fathers may be able to take a more detached view, balancing their children's needs against those of the whole family and of society in general. All too often, this ability to see the wider issues seems to be missing today, and when parents take an our-child-can-do-no-wrong line they do the child, the family and society great damage. The parental negotiation involved in developing social and moral guidelines for a family – and then applying them – isn't easy, but it is essential. Indeed, it's the essence of a truly 'democratic relationship'. The experts' advice on this aspect of child-rearing is covered in Chapter 10.

As the traditional image of the father receded, there was an attempt by the media to fill the gap with the concept of a New Dad – a sensitive and nurturing chap, usually represented by soft-focus pictures of celebrity fathers gently cradling their young. Like most media confections, it failed to catch on with the target audience: in the UK a 'New Dad' magazine didn't survive beyond the first edition, and similar publications in America went belly-up after a couple of issues. On the other hand, New Mums often found the sentimental image of a feminised father very appealing. Indeed, a 2005 survey suggested many working women would appreciate a complete role reversal: a Stepford Husband, waiting at home with the supper on, while they held the economic reins.

But in the long march towards democratic relationships, Stepford Husbands – like Stepford Wives – are not an option. Equality does not mean emasculation for men any more than it means defeminisation for women: the day we no longer cry 'Vive la différence' is the day the species starts to die out. There's no reason why men shouldn't look after children (just as there's no reason why women shouldn't go out to work), but they don't have to sacrifice their identity to do so. What parents should be looking for as the social revolutionary dust settles are ways of sharing the responsibilities and rewards of bringing up children that capitalise on the strengths of fathers *and* mothers. And government and employers should be looking for ways of making it easier for both sexes to spend time at home with their children.

How technology comes between parents and children

Technology has, however, presented humanity with another hurdle to overcome in the process of rethinking work and family commitments, one that may be more difficult for men than for women. All the prescriptions for successful parenting come back to two key words – time and attention – the two things adults born in the latter part of the twentieth century find it most difficult to spare.

It's not surprising: people reared in an era of labour-saving devices are conditioned to expect simple and instant solutions to domestic issues – food comes pre-packaged, oven-ready and microwaveable; machines remove dirt from clothes, carpets and crockery; almost every problem can be solved by turning a dial or flicking a switch. To fill in the time this saves, personalised entertainment is instantly available at all hours of the day and night. For anyone raised in such a quick-fix world, the tiring and often tedious business of looking after small children can seem positively primitive.

At work too, time is of the essence, and the capacity to process information quickly is often highly valued. Working on a computer involves diving in and out of different programs and windows, stopping to deal with phone calls and check emails, juggling a dozen different mental operations a minute. In his book *The New Brain*, neurologist Richard Restak calls attention deficit the 'paradigmatic disorder of our times', as the constant rapid processing of information affects the internal wiring of our brains.

The quick-fire world of modern technology is in direct contrast to the slow process of dealing with biological development. Looking after a small child means putting time on hold to concentrate on his or her human (and, for many adults, often interminable) needs. Playing endless games of peek-a-boo, telling a favourite bedtime story for the forty-third time, walking slowly through the park with a short-legged infant staggering along beside you, letting your child 'help' wash the car while making a sodden mess of the garden borders – all these are in 'slow time'.

If part of one's life demands a degree of attention deficit and the other demands lengthy, time-consuming attention, there is a clear conflict of mental interest. So as well as struggling with new family structures and confusion about their personal role, many contemporary parents find their attitude to their children deeply perplexing. On the one hand, they love them (nature sees to that – and love for one's children is a particularly deep and powerful love), but on the other, they may find themselves bored and irritated by the business of looking after them.

This phenomenon isn't often mentioned in polite circles, as it seems shameful to dislike spending time with one's children. But if it is a problem, parents must acknowledge, confront and deal with it. Otherwise, another complex emotion enters the familial mix: guilt. And guilt leads to all sorts of strange behaviour (see 'Money Can't Buy Me Love', page 184).

For fathers, attention deficit often sets in not long after a baby is born. The harassed new mother bustles the father away, leaving him feeling sidelined and resentful. Without the benefit of a bodyful of female hormones, he may also be somewhat wary of his mewling, puking offspring, and secretly grateful to be let off the hook. Concentrating on breadwinning is a useful displacement activity, and much less messy and confusing than what's going on at home. Unfortunately, once a father has backed off like this, it can be difficult to find a way back into family 'slow time'.

This isn't to say that mothers don't suffer from attention deficit too. As we saw in Chapter 4, even those who've chosen to stay at home are often distracted from their children by the technological marvels that dominate our lives today. And working mothers often find it as difficult as their partners to switch from a work mentality to the tempo of home.

It's now abundantly clear that if the gap left by preoccupied parents is filled by the fruits of technology, toxic childhood syndrome begins to take hold. Then, as their offspring grow ever more distractible, impulsive, egocentric and difficult to manage, there's even more incentive for parents to find alternative, more congenial company. Like sociologist Arlie Russell Hochschild, author of *The Time Bind*, I suspect one explanation for the long-hours culture is an unspoken wish on behalf of many parents to escape from bewildering and unfulfilling family life to the 'reliable orderliness, harmony and managed cheer of work'. Toxic childhood syndrome puts all parents in danger of drifting into the macho workaholism of Japanese salarymen, for whom company culture is often stronger than family ties, and family-friendly legislation has so far made little difference to insane working hours.

Work does indeed provide many obvious and immediate rewards: social status, mental stimulation, adult company and, of course, regular payment, which for most of us is an important measure of our worth. The rewards of raising children are less worldly, there's no salary cheque at the end of the month and you don't know how well you've done until a couple of decades into the job. It's easy to see how contemporary culture lures parents of both sexes into focusing on short-term breadwinning for their children, at the expense of long-term nurturing. But if a family is to flourish, the members of that family have to enjoy each other's company, or the whole thing is likely to fall apart.

Happily ever after ... ?

Campaigners for 'old-fashioned family values', clinging to the belief that a woman's place is in the home, work on the assumption of an indissoluble union between man and wife. But twenty-first-century marriages dissolve with remarkable ease – the Nobel Prizewinning economist Gary Becker has described contemporary marriage as 'a contract which ends when either party has a better option'. Another commentator remarked wearily that marriage was once a sacrament, then a legal contract, and is now merely an 'arrangement' ... and in a recent survey most young British women believed that getting a joint mortgage on a home is now a bigger commitment than marriage.

In the USA these days, around half of all marriages end in divorce and secular European countries like UK and Germany are not far behind. In Japan, where traditional male and female roles were more deeply embedded in the culture, the drive towards sexual equality has been slower than in the West – but the influence of the global village means that there too women are becoming increasingly independent ... and divorce is now on the increase. Japanese economist Hiroshi Ono puts it succinctly, 'Lower dependency allows greater voice, and lowers the cost of exiting a marriage.'

Attitudes to divorce have also changed enormously. Even twenty years ago it was viewed as a major catastrophe in the lives of those involved, but today there's no social stigma. A friend of mine cites Charles and Diana's failed marriage as the turning point: once that 'fairytale' turned out to be a sham, and fell apart in full public view, the mystique of marriage disappeared for ever. If princes and princesses don't make the effort to live happily ever after, why should anyone else?

So family breakdown has now become commonplace – even a form of entertainment. Celebrity marriages are picked over by the press, with particular delight when they fall apart, and family traumas are played out every day in television soaps, dramas and documentaries.

With the honourable exception of Marge and Homer Simpson, we now expect all TV relationships to come under ever more startling pressures until they eventually crumble. John Baker, a judge in the UK family courts, puts it thus, 'Family breakdown – driven by the needs and relationships of the adults involved – has come to be regarded as the norm, to be accepted without criticism by the majority.' In democratic relationships, guilt-free divorce may be a good thing for the adults involved, but its effects on the children of a marriage are seldom considered.

Children's part in divorce is kept pretty secret. Newspapers and magazines dishing the dirt on celebrity divorces don't include interviews with the children involved – it would be an infringement of privacy – so we don't hear their point of view. TV shows and films about divorce seldom dwell on children's role, because they're awkward, unpredictable things to have around the studio. Anyway, an adult audience wants to empathise with the adults' point of view. Even in real life, even in the courts, the question of divorce has, over the last twenty-five years, seldom been viewed from the child's perspective.

Yet where children are involved, the break-up of a family unit has consequences far beyond those envisaged by their parents. Beside the emotional ordeal of witnessing parental trauma and losing daily contact with one of the defining pillars of their existence, children have to cope with anxiety-inducing life changes – maybe a new home, a new school, sharing a house with a parent's new partner ... or even bedrooms with step-siblings or half-siblings. If they end up living with a single parent, it usually means considerably reduced circumstances. For an under-ten, such shifts can be as significant as moving to Mars.

Breaking up is hard to do

The emotional repercussions of parental separation can significantly affect the course of children's social and intellectual development. In a comprehensive 2001 survey of the impact of divorce, children with divorced parents were shown to perform significantly worse on academic tests than others, and displayed 'more conduct problems, poorer psychological adjustment, lower self-esteem scores and weaker social relationships' – that is, tears and tantrums, regression to immature behaviour, and the all-too familiar symptoms of distractibility, impulsiveness, egocentricity and lack of concern for others. Yet still society views the breakdown of marriages as a largely adult concern.

While researching this issue, I phoned a helpline to ask about advice on minimising the effects of divorce on children. 'Oh, they weather it really well these days,' said the woman brightly. 'It's quite normal really – lots of their friends will have gone through it.' When I expressed disbelief, and cited evidence from law journals and transcripts of children's comments, she explained that these were extreme cases: 'Where the divorce is well managed, children suffer very little. It's just a fact of life for them.'

There is indeed recent research showing that, as divorce has become socially acceptable, children seem to suffer less trauma than in the past. However, while it's undoubtedly easier to be one of a crowd than a lone outcast, this doesn't mean the emotional pain of parents' separation is any the less. When a marriage is breaking up, most adults are so busy dealing with their own problems that, as long as the children aren't causing a fuss, it's easier to assume they're OK. And children do soldier on to avoid upsetting their parents – from a child's point of view one of the most important people in the world is leaving home; if they're not careful the other might clear off too.

Teachers, being outside the family loop but close to the children, are often more aware of the emotional toll than parents. One recently told me about a little boy in her class of five-year-olds. 'His dad works nights, so Adam doesn't see him much during the week and he wasn't aware Dad had left till a few days after the event. I don't think anyone's really explained. Yesterday I saw him sitting at his desk with two big tears running down his cheeks. He's now absolutely terrified of upsetting me in class – being really good, but in a worrying way – I think he's frightened I'll go too.'

Research also shows that children's insecurity and distress often begin years before the divorce as the parental relationship gradually breaks down. Charlotte, aged twelve, gave this interview to a Sunday newspaper: 'Mum and Dad were arguing for ages before they split up: they used to throw things at each other and that made my brother and me frightened and we used to cry ... I think it would have helped if we could have all sat down together and talked about how life was going to be once Dad had moved out, but he and Mum either fought or didn't talk at all ... I really wish we could go back to how it used to be. Everything seemed so easy then, and it all seems so complicated now.'

Children's pain continues if the divorce is acrimonious, especially if custody becomes an issue: some find themselves being passed back and forth like a parcel, others suffer because of lack of contact with one parent. In the USA, where shared custody is common, air stewardesses are well used to looking after small passengers winging their lonely way back and forth between parents; in Japan, where shared custody is rare, newspapers are often full of lurid tales of abduction. And emotional wounds from childhood often fester for years. Statistics show that children of divorced parents are more likely than others to become depressed, drug or drink dependent and involved in crime; they're also more likely to have unhappy marriages themselves.

Minimising the trauma

The advice on minimising trauma is fairly obvious (see summary on page 163). One key aspect is to ensure opportunities for children to talk about what's happening, and listen to their point of view. However, parents aren't always the best listeners – as we've seen, children often fear worrying them further or hurting their feelings. A group of British family law experts observed sadly in a summary of the problems that 'some children are only left with "talking to teddy" when things get too much for them'. Children's counsellors may be available – and there are calls around the world for more such services – but formal provision of this kind can look like therapy, shifting the problem away from the parents and on to the children, whose burden becomes even greater. More informal confidantes – a trusted school-teacher or mentor, non-partisan family friends or relations, or even an anonymous helpline – might be preferable.

Parents are also advised to put their own feelings aside and avoid acrimony for the children's sake. As American psychologist James Kraut puts it, 'It's more important to love your children than it is to hate your ex-spouse.' Sadly, such principles are much easier to list than to follow, especially when the breakdown of the relationship has thrown both spouses into emotional turmoil. It also requires remarkable restraint to ensure that children aren't torn in their allegiances. Not only must both parties resist the temptation to dole out blame, they also have to steer clear of self-justification – one of the hardest things for a bruised human being to achieve. This is probably why Charles and Diana, like many other celebrity divorcees, didn't set a particularly good example – much to the delight of the popular press. However, if parents can be helped to focus on the present and future needs of their children, it does deflect attention from their own grievances. There is a welcome movement internationally in legal circles to provide conciliation and counselling services rather than the old-fashioned confrontational approach to divorce.

More encouragement in this direction through social pressures could also be helpful to all parties – and the media could play an important part in changing social mores. Their present tendency to represent the breakdown of celebrity marriages as a sort of gladi-atorial combat takes no account of the significance of the celebrities' roles as parents. If newspapers could report divorces more in sorrow than exultation, it would help concentrate everyone's minds on the human costs. Divorce may be becoming commonplace but breaking up hasn't got any less hard to do.

Once a marriage is over, parents' new relationships often take centre stage. In the throes of a new romantic entanglement, it's difficult for a parent or a new partner to focus on 'the needs of the children'. But the introduction of another adult into a child's life – let alone a step-parent or ready-made step-family – can be deeply threatening and unsettling. It's an invasion of emotional territory that needs planning with almost military efficiency. Parents who don't think it through, or misjudge children's initial politeness as acceptance, are often amazed at the strength and bitterness of the eventual reaction to their new partner.

There's plenty of detailed advice available to parents on helping children through divorce and remarriage in books and on websites (see page 166), but sadly by the time most people access it, the damage has already begun. When a marriage is crumbling or a new relationship is in its infancy, no one can expect to be emotionally balanced. Perhaps the best way to detoxify children's experience would be to ensure parents know how best to mitigate any ill-effects *before* they actually start to happen.

Children in the centre

The advice to 'focus on the needs of the children' is not, however, to deny the significance of adult relationships, or indeed the right of every adult to have a life and strive for happiness and self-realisation. Parents shouldn't be focusing on the needs of their children every living minute of the day. Indeed, those who do so run the risk of 'over-parenting' – and flamboyant self-denial can imbue their offspring with a lifetime's guilt or create a self-obsessed little monster. The Swedish psychologist Anna Wahlgren (whose bestselling books on child-rearing have, sadly, not been translated into English) makes a useful distinction when she says children should not be the centre of their parents' world, they should be 'in the centre'.

I love that preposition 'in'. It shows there's room for a number of people and interests in the centre of any adult's life. As long as the focus of attention swivels regularly on to the children and their needs, grown-ups can seek fulfilment for themselves as well as tending to their offspring. The key is finding the right balance – which will change from day to day – and being sensitive to the feelings of children about situations that involve them (not merely assuming they feel what you want them to feel).

These situations usually revolve around family life. If, as seems likely, marriage is of dwindling significance – long term as an institution or short term in the case of particular couples – it's the family, in all its contemporary incarnations, that must be preserved and strengthened if children are to thrive. Forging a strong sense of family, with successful child-rearing as its primary purpose, is therefore the major task for twenty-first-century parents.

The key figures in this task, married or not, are biological mothers and fathers. In terms of producing children, this is still the major partnership (and is likely to remain so, despite ingenious technological alternatives). But as time goes on, other adults may be pulled into the family circle – most frequently step-parents, but also other family members, friends or employees such as nannies and au pairs (who 'live as family'). There may also be another, overlapping circle belonging to an ex-partner.

Whatever the mixture, it's critical that all adult members of a family circle (or, after divorce, circles) accept responsibility for children's welfare – putting them in the centre of family life. For a biological parent putting the child's interests in the centre of this circle comes fairly naturally (as it often does for adoptive parents, who have invested a great deal of emotional energy in the quest for a child), but step-parents and other adults can find it more of an effort to focus on children's needs, especially if the children concerned are acting up because they're emotionally disturbed. Anyone taking on the role of 'adult in charge' within a family should think long and hard about it, and prepare themselves well by consulting books, websites or counselling services.

Forging a family

In order to forge a viable family, the 'adults in charge' have to be physically present for a reasonable amount of time every week. This means sorting out their work-life balance (see Chapter 6) so that, even if they work full-time, they still spend plenty of time at home. A recent snippet of Internet wisdom put the case rather well: 'If you died tomorrow, the company that employs you would fill your place within a week or so; your family would miss you for ever.' Indeed, in many cases they're missing you already, and toxic childhood is the result.

All the experts I've met and read on the subject of family welfare and social cohesion condemn the long-hours culture and commend flexible working practices. Families don't flourish unless their members spend time together, so it really is time that governments, businesses and individual human beings got their act together on this one – as the journalist Richard Reeves puts it, if our culture is to have a future we need to create family-friendly economies, not economy-friendly families.

When families don't spend enough time in each other's company, special events such as Christmas, special celebrations or holidays are often a terrible disappointment. In a 2005 UK survey, 75 per cent of parents said they found family holidays stressful, even though they were supposed to be a precious opportunity to spend more 'quality time' with their children. As social psychologist Pat Spungin says, if parents and children don't spend time together on a regular basis, 'the pressure on everyone to be having a perfect time and the feeling this is a one-off chance can permeate every aspect of the holiday to increase overall stress levels'.

Given that time is available, much of the experts' advice for creating strong families applies to everyone involved, whether they're biologically related or not. For instance, families need to develop their identity as a group, which means shared interests and activities (see the lists on pages 159–160). Adults also need time to bond with children one-to-one – while of course avoiding any suggestion of favouritism between siblings and/or step-siblings.

This one-to-one time doesn't have to be spent doing anything special – indeed, one of the most important parental tasks is to pass on simple life skills to the next generation, just by involving them in day-to-day tasks. The list of skills on page 162 is a good starting point – let your child watch and chat as you do something; then treat them as a valued apprentice until one day they can do it on their own. There's no rush to achieve, no competition, no prizes – it's just a question of taking your time over the years, gradually initiating your child into adult skills. Involving children in a hobby, sport or other interest can also be fulfilling for both generations. Whether it's sewing or cinema-going, fishing or supporting a football team, parents who pass on their passions to their children always have a point of communication, even during the difficult years of adolescence.

There's another element of balance here. Spending time with children doesn't mean having to be with them interminably – especially as the children grow older, and their social circle widens. But when adults *are* in the bosom of the family, we should be free to engage with children rather than wishing them out of the way. That means switching off mobile phones, ignoring the email, and concentrating on the chosen family activity, or just chatting with and listening to the children. It's shifting from the rapid pace of everyday life to 'slow time', and it's not only good for your family, it's good for your health.

To ensure time spent together is as pleasant an experience as possible, families need carefully formulated policies on issues like discipline, mealtime behaviour, bedtimes, and so on. American researchers Betty Hart and Todd Risley, who analysed 42 US families over two and a half years, concluded that 'what made a family normal was its stable and predictable ways of interacting'. Very young children obviously should have little input into family policies – adults are in charge because they know what's good for them – but as children grow older and wiser, there's room for increased negotiation. At all stages, adults have to agree on a reasonable policy, then keep up a united front (trying never to row in front of the children) and act as role models for the sorts of behaviour they want to see. There's further discussion of parenting in Chapter 10.

For adults who are not biologically related to children in their family, one frequently given piece of advice is to acknowledge the fact that you're not a blood relation. The inevitable stepchild's cry of 'You're not my mum/dad!' can be countered immediately with 'You're right. I could never even try to replace your mum/dad. But I'm the adult in charge at the moment, so what I say goes.' Experts generally agree that biological parents should take the lead in discipline, making it clear that other 'adults in charge' are their trusted lieutenants.

Now that many children divide their time between two family homes, it helps if basic rules for behaviour, bedtime and so on are consistent; if they aren't, acceptable boundaries in your own home must be very clearly drawn. Schedules and arrangements for visits are important to children, so it helps if they're easily manageable – if they're not, it behoves adults to put themselves out so children are not let down.

*

That is what forging a family is all about: adults putting themselves out so children's developmental needs are met. In the revolutionary whirlwind of the last twenty-five years, the focus has been firmly on the needs of adults – the changes in their roles and the resultant dramas in their relationships. The Archbishop of Canterbury summed up our current problems in a speech in 2005: 'Children are so caught up in the energy of adult dramas that they do not have the space, the period of latency, in which to be securely children ... We have to accept that growing up is about taking on the task of forming other human lives.'

The family – love it or hate it – is where the grown-up generation forms the generation to come. It's where parents, and other adults-in-charge, develop children's sense of self, security and self-esteem, their ability to get along with other people, their knowledge about life and life skills, and an inner code of conduct to guide and protect them when we're no longer around. So far the human race hasn't come up with any better way of passing on these essential elements of our culture. The family is where, in the words of the old adage, we give our children 'roots to grow and wings to fly'.

DETOXING FAMILY LIFE

- Recognise that child-rearing (and home-making) is not a hobby but a full-time job. If you aren't able to do it, or can only do part of it, you'll need to pay someone else to cover for your absence – see Chapter 6. But the two people most committed to any child's welfare are the parents, so take on as much responsibility as possible yourself.
- Break free from the traditional view of low-status nurturing and high-status breadwinning. Rearing children is important, and good childcare will cost you, in terms of either time or money.
- Forging a family is a joint responsibility. Discuss the balance of breadwinning versus child-rearing between yourself and your partner, and keep discussing, and continually adjusting, as circumstances change. Ensure both parents read this list, or compile one of your own.
- Recognise that men and women bring different strengths (and weaknesses) to child-rearing, and children need a balance of both. Learn the art of compromise.
- Recognise the supreme importance of *time* in bringing up children – the younger the child, the more 'slow time' you need. When with your children, find ways of switching from the rapid tempo of daily life into the slower, more natural tempo of child-rearing (e.g. switch off the computer, mobile phone, TV and learn to enjoy their absence).
- Families need to spend time together. Don't let breadwinning activities prevent you from being with your children, for instance:

  – family mealtimes (see Chapter 1)
  – family outings, such as visiting friends and relations, walking the dog, shopping, going to the park, cinema, swimming pool (see Chapter 2)
  – family viewing: sitting down together to watch a favourite TV show or a film
  – shared bedtime routines in which mum and dad can take part (see Chapter 3)
  – playing games, such as board or card games or outdoor kick-abouts
  – family holidays, when you can share new experiences together.

- Try as hard as you can to keep work and family separate, so that work-based stress doesn't overflow into family time.
- Children also sometimes need the exclusive attention of individual parents, for instance:

  – a shared hobby or interest
  – time spent helping with household tasks, car maintenance, gardening, etc, which includes biting your tongue when the child's 'help' is actually a hindrance
  – time while travelling (either by foot or in the car) can be a good opportunity to chat – see it as social, not dead time
  – boys especially need to spend time with their father.

- Time spent with children need not – indeed *should* not – involve spending money. It should be about:

  – giving children attention and showing an interest in what they say
  – passing on (by example, not in a teacherish way) useful life skills, such as those listed on page 162
  – relaxing and enjoying their company
  – rewarding them with praise for good behaviour
  – modelling the manners and sorts of behaviour you want to see in them.

- If you find children's company difficult or personally unrewarding, reading up about child development – and then spotting evidence of your child's progress – can make it easier to appreciate family time. Courses such as the Positive Parenting Programme can also be helpful (see pages 293 and 305).
- However, ensure there's also time for you and your partner to spend together, e.g.

  – regular evenings out (or in) when the children are looked after by babysitters

– if possible, occasional holidays or weekends away, when the children are catered for elsewhere.

- As well as parents, children benefit hugely from spending time with other family members, such as grandparents, or other adults who know them well.
- In the words of Mary Pipher in *The Shelter of Each Other*, 'Love each other while you can.'

THIRTY-FOUR LIFE SKILLS FOR YOUR CHILD TO LEARN BY EXAMPLE BY THE AGE OF TWELVE

Start by demonstrating the skill to your child and talking about what you do. Then suggest they have a go, while you stand by offering advice (not too much) and praise (lots). Give them the opportunity to practise the skill, again with lots of encouragement, attention and praise.

Sew on a button

Use a vacuum cleaner

Change a plug

Iron a shirt

Clean and dress a wound

Change the bed

Wash a car

Find the way home (with map or A to Z)

Take phone messages

Make a hot drink

Mow a lawn

Clean a cooker hob

Change a fuse

Put out the rubbish

Wash the dishes

Use a washing machine

Use a screwdriver

Cook a meal

Handwash clothes

Use a potato peeler

Grow a plant

Unblock a sink

Use public transport

Look after a pet

Use the phone book

Go shopping (with a list)

Weed a garden

Defrost a fridge

Change a light bulb

Sort the recycling

Clean a window

Stack and empty a dishwasher

Make conversation with a guest

Give simple first aid (e.g. cuts, bruises, burns)

HOW TO MAKE BREAK-UPS AS PAINLESS AS POSSIBLE

- The two most important people in a child's life are its parents. If at all possible, it's best that parents stay together, so if your partnership falters, take action to mend it sooner rather than later. That means talking over problems and seeking help – books, websites, counselling services.
- If the partnership can't be mended, do everything you can to protect your children from the adverse effects of family breakdown, for instance:

  – make sure you're fully informed about the pitfalls through books, websites, etc, and try to plan ahead (see lists on page 166)
  – ensure children know that, even if you are quarrelling, you both have their interests at heart, you both love them, and will make sure they're OK
  – keep talking and listening to your children, and help them find other trusted adults in whom they can confide their concerns (e.g., other family members, a favourite teacher or youth worker, a specialist phone helpline)
  – ensure children feel positive towards both parents, and don't have to take sides.

- Try to ensure custody and visiting arrangements are manageable and take children's wishes into consideration. If possible, arrange to be consistent on issues such as bedtime, diet and behaviour.
- If you're a single parent, seek out trusted friends or relations to help you rear your children, especially male role models for boys. These should be long-term, constant relationships, not threatened by romantic entanglements.
- If you're a single parent embarking on a new relationship, take great care about introducing your new partner to your children. Discuss the issues with your new partner, and consult expert advice through books and websites. Beware! This issue is riven with difficulty.
- If you're about to become a step-parent, seek education. Step-parenting comes even less naturally than parenting.

BEING AN ADULT-IN-CHARGE: SOME THINGS TO TALK TO A PARTNER ABOUT

Talk to your partner about important issues in your relationship and negotiate solutions that suit you both as far as possible before they become an issue. In terms of children, this could involve:

- how many you both want, and when
- how you feel about childcare (see page 191)
- how *both* parents can make time to give children plenty of attention – around the house, in outdoor activities, at mealtimes, at bedtime
- how work patterns can be changed to ensure more family time
- ways to ensure you don't fall into 'default activities' during family time, e.g., checking email or chatting on the mobile, reading the paper or a magazine, watching TV – the sort of things that 'expand to fill the given space', but also cut you off from contact with others around you
- your expectations of your child's behaviour at each stage in development (this needs constant renegotiation as behaviour changes)
- your beliefs about right and wrong, and how you'll help your children understand these, including what to do when they step out of line (see Chapter 10)
- the sorts of regular routines and procedures you'll adopt (e.g., mealtimes, bedtimes) and how they'll be supervised
- how to distribute the chores of child-rearing on a daily basis, e.g., dealing with crying, nappy-changing, clearing up messes, organising school clothes and equipment, supervising behaviour management, etc
- how to ensure that each week you get:

  – some individual 'private time' to pursue your own interests or see friends
  – some time together, without the children.

PARENT POWER: THE FAMILY IN THE CENTRE

Just as children must be in the centre of the family, families should be in the centre of public policy. From the beginning, a major function of civilised societies was to protect the interests of law-abiding families, but in recent years politicians have often concentrated on promoting economic growth and individual human rights, leaving twenty-first-century families to sort themselves out. It's therefore up to parents to ensure that the needs of the family are returned to the heart of social and economic policy by demanding that their elected representatives work for:

- a family-friendly economy, rather than economy-friendly families
- legislation rather than lip service to protect work-life balance
- support for parents and adults-in-charge (see other Parent Power sections throughout this book)
- public policy that supports healthy child-rearing practices.

However, politicians are remarkably good at converting human ideals into mind-numbing bureaucracy, as the next two chapters show. As the social revolutionary dust settles and families become politically sexy again, the real challenge for parent power is to keep them on track.

Further reading

Mary Pipher, *The Shelter of Each Other: Rebuilding Our Families* (Ballantine Books, New York, 1997) and other titles

Noel Brook, *Back to Basics: 1001 Ideas for Strengthening Our Children and Our Families* (Champion Press, 1999)

Carl Honoré, *In Praise of Slow: How a Worldwide Movement is Challenging the Cult of Speed* (Orion, 2004)

Jill Curtis, *Find Your Way Through Divorce* (Hodder and Stoughton, 2001)

Jane Fearnley-Whittingstall, *The Good Granny Guide* (Short Books, 2005)

Flora McEvedy, *The Step-Parents' Parachute: the Four Cornerstones to Good Step-parenting* (Time Warner, 2005)

Useful websites

Parents Online: **www.parents.org.uk** (magazine format)

Family Onwards: **www.familyonwards.com** (magazine format, particularly good on divorce, second families, etc)

Parentline Plus: **www.parentlineplus.org.uk** (national charity, information plus a network of parent volunteers offering help and advice to other parents)

Mums Net: **www.mumsnet.com** (UK-based information and community network for mothers)

Fathers Direct (National Information Centre on Fatherhood): **www.fathersdirect.com**

Dads and Daughters: **www.dadsanddaughters.org** (US organisation)

Mind the gap

The Hart and Risley research quoted on page 132 shows clearly how family background affects children's life chances. If we are to help close the widening gap between rich and poor, support for child-rearing in poorer families is essential. But the knock-on effects of changes in women's status have created an extra problem: a huge increase in single-parent families. And if you're a single parent, your chances of being poor are much greater than the average. A 2003 survey found that one-third of all children living in poverty in Britain were the children of one-parent families.

Although an increasing number of fathers are now bringing up families, most single parents are women. Some are struggling to bring up their children alone as a result of divorce. Sometimes it's simply that the mother has never married – in the UK 40 per cent of all live births in 2001 were to unmarried mothers (Britain is unfortunately a world leader in this phenomenon). Whatever the circumstances, the life chances of their children are hampered by their parent's single status. No matter how hard single parents work to raise their children, child-rearing requires more time and attention than one person can reasonably give.

Children also need the balance of a maternal and paternal approach, and boys seem particularly to suffer from the lack of a father figure. A 2005 government survey in the UK found the sons of poorly educated, unemployed single mothers are more likely to have a mental health, developmental or behavioural problem between the ages of five and sixteen than any other group. Not surprising, then, that they turn to antisocial activities. American psychologist David Lykken has found that 70 per cent of young males convicted of serious crimes in the USA have been raised in fatherless families.

The other group of families over-represented among the ranks of poor are those from ethnic minorities. Many are recently arrived economic migrants or asylum seekers, anxious to make a better life for their children. In previous generations nations have benefited greatly from such injections of new blood, with the second or third generation moving steadily up the social ranks. However, our widening social gap, along with the effects of toxic childhood syndrome on many children, threatens this social mobility, creating ghettos where ethnic minority groups become increasingly inward-looking or dissatisfied at their social exclusion. This enhances the potential for racial tensions – not least because the indigenous poor are looking for someone handy to blame for their own apparently unchangeable living conditions.

In late 2005 the French politician Henri Weber explained the riots sweeping his country in these terms: 'A movement which is outside politics, that represents pure revolt ... which attacks every symbol of society it finds ... Destruction has become practically an end in itself. There is a nihilist agenda in this.' It reminded me of the words of a Liverpool nun, standing amid the burned-out ruins of her school: 'It's not personal. They just have this deep need to destroy.'

States around the world are now looking seriously at ways to improve the life chances of all children in poor families, for obvious humanitarian reasons and to avert the potential dangers. There have always been problems, as pointed out in the introductory Mind the Gap about 'the legitimacy of the state as an instrument of moral authority in the lives of children and families'. But where families feel powerless to change children's life chances themselves, surely society has a responsibility to help them counter toxic childhood syndrome?

CHAPTER SIX

WHO'S LOOKING AFTER THE CHILDREN?

However long the mommy wars rumble on, there's little doubt the results of our cultural revolution are here to stay. Family structures have changed, and working mothers are increasingly the norm, with more than half of all women in the developed world now in the workforce. In 2004 figures ranged between 80 per cent (France) and 40 per cent (Greece) and numbers are increasing all the time.

But just as mothers in their millions started streaming out to work, science began to recognise the huge contribution they'd been making in the home over all those centuries. Neuroscientists now know that a massive number of neural connections are made in a child's brain in the first three years of life, and neural networks continue to develop at an astounding rate throughout childhood, especially in the areas of the prefrontal cortex which are associated with focused concentration, planning, self-control and empathy. The transformation from helpless babe-in-arms to civilised member of society is clearly influenced by what happens to children in these pre-teenage years. So one of the biggest questions we all have to ask – as parents, and collectively as a society – is who will do the child-rearing when both parents are out at work?

For love or money ...

There are two ways to approach the question of childcare. You can concentrate on the children's point of view, considering what they need at different ages and stages. Or you can concern yourself with the economic aspect: keeping children out of harm's way so that parents can go to work. Having spent some months ploughing through the international literature on the subject, it seems to me the success of any system depends upon politicians' attention to the first perspective as well as the second.

The countries that seem to make the best fist of it are those with a long tradition of working mothers and a commitment to social provision. Many parts of mainland Europe have well-established, child-friendly systems of childcare, funded by a combination of taxes and parental contributions. A recent OECD (Organisation for Economic Co-operation and Development) review singled out Sweden and Finland for particular praise, describing 'a continuum of support for parents until children are in their teens ... flexible parental leave, high-quality childcare and reduced working hours for parents of young children'. (To a British mother who struggled in a very different system, it sounds like heaven!) Having shouldered the burden of childcare for some decades, the Swedes and Finns clearly recognise 'the invisible curriculum of child-rearing', and are prepared to invest money in getting it right.

On the other hand, in countries where women have traditionally been expected to stay at home, and their child-rearing expertise has been under-valued, there's usually a hotchpotch of provision, of variable quality. Interestingly, these include the four most economically successful countries: the USA, Japan, Germany and the UK. When the women of these nations suddenly moved wholesale into the workforce in the closing years of the last century, their governments started trying to fill the gaps in their childcare provision – with very mixed results.

Surveying the chaotic state of American provision a couple of years ago, the OECD commented dryly that the political drive seemed to be for quantity rather than quality. The review of Japan's progress pointed out that inflexible employment practices still force women to choose between motherhood and career. The UK, while praised for recent investment, was nevertheless criticised for the patchy quality and high costs of childcare, especially for poorer families. And after Germany's recent review, the minister for the family ruefully exclaimed that 'when it comes to childcare, compared to the rest of the European Union, Germany is a third-world country'.

For successful politicians in the Big Four, it seems that catering for the interests of employers and working parents is the priority. Their interest in the needs of small children is minimal. As US economist Shirley Burgraff put it, 'Children might as well come from cabbage patches as far as most political and economic theory is concerned.'

Childcare on the cheap

This isn't to deny the political and economic significance of childcare. Apart from anything else, it might help solve the economic time bomb of falling birth rates. Forced to choose between career and family, more and more women – particularly highly educated ones – are choosing not to have children at all. In Germany, for instance, many consider childlessness preferable to the choice between being a *rabenmutter* ('uncaring mother', the label for one who works) and *hausmutterchen* (dutiful stay-at-home little woman). Having someone to look after the children is also of enormous economic importance in terms of gross national product. Working women's earnings and taxes give a huge boost to the economy – indeed they've been responsible for much of the last twenty-odd years' economic growth.

And very importantly, childcare delivers a double benefit in the case of those problematical single mothers the social revolution left cluttering up state benefits systems. As well as helping them make the wondrous transformation from drain-on-the-public-purse to valued taxpayer, it brings their children – and other children from under-privileged backgrounds – under the care of the state during the working day. Just as nineteenth-century politicians spotted that universal education could remove poor children from the streets and help a few escape from poverty, their late-twentieth-century counterparts have realised that universal childcare might be the best way to address the worryingly yawning gap between the children of the poor and everyone else.

This, however, is where politicians need some understanding of what successful child-rearing actually involves. Just removing children from their homes into childcare settings won't necessarily improve their life chances – the childcare setting has to be well resourced, with trained staff who know what they're doing. In successful countries, qualifications for childcare workers are often of a high level (in Finland, for instance, you need a masters degree to teach nursery children), and long-term investment means buildings and equipment are of a high standard. On the whole, the experience of these countries does bear out the research that early input pays off – there's less ingrained poverty and able, hard-working children often take advantage of educational opportunities to escape their background.

Sadly, countries fixated exclusively on the needs of employers and working parents are unlikely to duplicate this success. If politicians pay scant attention to children's needs and everyone continues to see child-rearing as something anyone can do (something we expect to 'happen naturally') there's little chance of raising taxes to pay for it. Britain at present leads the world in efforts to provide pre-school education and childcare for all ages on the cheap. Promises of free nursery places for the youngest children and after-school care for older ones are based on the cheapest option available: maximising the use of school buildings, and using low-qualified or even unqualified staff.

Parents deciding how best to provide for their children need to bear these political and economic factors in mind. In childcare, as in just about everything else these days, you tend to get what you pay for, and the better qualified the people who look after your children, the more likely they are to look after them well.

The hot housing rat race

On the other hand, there's also a danger of paying through the nose for dubious advantages. One famous neuroscientific experiment of the 1980s showed that rats raised in interesting, stimulating environments grew up smarter than those reared in conditions of abject boredom. Among some highly competitive parents, this fed an already established appetite for 'hot housing' – providing ever greater stimulation for children from as early as possible in an attempt to enhance and accelerate their development.

There are now private nurseries in the United States where two- and three-year-olds are crammed to bursting point with supposedly brain-enriching 'sensory stimulation', and others offering courses for the under-threes in languages, mathematics, logic and music. And around the world there are CDs, videos, clubs and courses offering early enrichment in everything under the sun. Parents who want to rear the next Mozart, Picasso or Tiger Woods need only hand over their hard-earned cash and wait for a decade or so to see if it works.

In fact, it's likely that pressure to achieve too much too soon does more harm than good. There are many tales of hot-housed children who failed to live up to their potential, and others whose eventual success was off-set by emotional turmoil or social ineptitude. Researchers in Montreal in 2005 found 'maternal investment in educational performance' to be 'significantly negatively related to social adjustment' – in other words, the pushier the parents, the more likely their child is to be an unpopular social misfit.

Neither is there any actual scientific evidence that hyper-stimulation creates brighter babies. The environments that bred smart rats in the experiment were, in fact, very like a rat's normal habitat (sewers are actually quite busy and exciting places). What the experiment established was that lack of normal stimulation breeds dull, miserable rats. In the words of US neuroscientist Steve Petersen, the message to parents is simply, 'don't raise your children in a closet, starve them, or hit them over the head with a frying pan'. A recent summary of research by UK child development experts Dr Sarah-Jane Blakemore and Professor Uta Frith points out that, while deprivation is definitely bad for the brain, 'hyper-enrichment' doesn't appear to be particularly good for it, and the input children need in the first few years 'is readily available in normal environments'. For a very young child the most successful normal environment is, of course, a happy family home.

Home sweet home

For the first year or so of a child's life, familiar faces and settings are of paramount importance. This is when attachment is critical, when calming, sleeping and eating habits are established, and when the process of learning to communicate begins. The opinion of all the developmental and childcare experts I met was that – if at all possible – parental care in the family home is the best option, at least for the first eighteen months. The work of developmental psychologist John Bowlby suggests that a child's 'internal map' is largely determined by the relationships formed during this period, and other theorists (such as Hobson, cited in Chapter 4) support his case.

Evidence from neuroscience backs them up – there is an intense increase in the neural connections in the all-important prefrontal cortex between the ages of six months and two years. While human brains are extraordinarily plastic, and connections continue to be forged throughout childhood (and, indeed, throughout life), loving one-to-one care at the beginning of a child's life seems to be the most important element of all in creating a happy, balanced human being. Looking after a small child takes real commitment, and parents have more of a vested interest in summoning commitment for their own children than anyone else on earth. Mothers, being hormonally assisted, usually find baby-rearing easier than fathers – although increasingly there are fathers who heroically stay the course.

Some parents, however, find themselves unable to become full-time carers. There are financial implications in giving up part of the family income for a couple of years, which in some cases seem insuperable. Other parents discover they can't cope with the change in lifestyle – education and work experience has distanced them so far from the domestic sphere that full-time childcare, with no other adults around, plunges them into depression. As one who struggled with this problem myself, I know it's not lack of love that causes it, but the conflict between parental love and the desperate need to preserve one's sense of self. A parent tussling with personal mental instability is in no condition to tend to a baby's needs.

In these cases, it's a question of working out how best to keep financial or mental meltdown at bay while still spending as much time as possible with one's offspring. Part-time work, job-sharing, working from home or arranging flexible hours are much better than disappearing from a child's life almost completely. To fend off depression, there's also the option of seeking out other sources of adult company and intellectual stimulation, through local parents' groups and classes. The emphasis on home and family doesn't mean children should be closeted away: babies and toddlers need regular doses of fresh air, as well as opportunities to mingle with other children, which helps build immunity to childhood diseases.

From the age of about three, research is clear that children benefit from a widening of horizons, taking them away from home and family for gradually lengthening periods, and leading into increasingly structured sorts of learning. The older the child, the more time they're usually happy to spend away from home – and the more good it can do them. But even then, there's plenty of time at either end of a busy day when home and family remain important to children's development – family meals, bedtime routines, shared talk and activities continue to be important into the teenage years.

Finding a parent substitute

When parents can't be at home, one answer is to employ a substitute carer for all or part of the day. Alternatives range from live-in nannies (very expensive but hopefully well qualified), through registered child-minders (less expensive and usually in their home not yours – but generally good-quality care) to unqualified minders or au pairs (you may be lucky, but you never know). A relative is sometimes happy to take on the role, and UK research in 2005 showed that grandmothers are increasingly called upon to cover for their working children. Anecdotal evidence about grandmothers' valuable contribution as carers is easy to find, but recent research studies in the US and UK suggest family help in general may be a less successful option than other parent substitutes.

The main problem with substitute carers is that parents often find themselves struggling with jealousy if the carer is a hit with their off-spring, or panic-stricken worry if the child seems less than happy. The need to nurture one's own child is a deep one, taking many contemporary parents by surprise and sometimes leading to exaggerated emotional reactions. However, on something as important as caring for a beloved infant, it's essential that everyone involved likes and trusts each other. Apart from anything else, there has to be agreement on domestic routines and behaviour management – without this, even very young children will find it easy to play off one half of their caring community against the other. If jealousy or anxiety occur, they have to be confronted and dealt with as soon as possible. And if a child is genuinely unhappy, it's obviously essential to find out why and take immediate action.

Many parents prefer to use institutional childcare – day nurseries for babies and toddlers, day centres for pre-schoolers and primary-age children, and 'kids' clubs' to cover during school holidays. These often seem a safer option – the centres are regularly inspected, plenty of staff mean checks and balances, you don't have to share your home with them, and they're not likely to disappear suddenly and let you down. It also probably works out cheaper than high-quality care in the home, and there's no problem about hymn-sheet sharing – here the rules are written for you, and if your own system is slightly different, it doesn't matter because a daycare centre is a very different environment. The great question is: how far can an institution duplicate the security and stability of home and the sensitive, personal, human engagement of a single familiar carer?

Birth to three: the great daycare controversy

The younger the child, the more pressing that question is. A good day nursery for very young children should try to duplicate home and family as far as possible, providing a named carer with whom the parents are in regular contact, a low adult-child ratio and a comfortable domestic atmosphere. But parents can't always find (or afford) such high-quality provision, and there's a niggling body of research suggesting that more than a few hours a day of less-than-perfect institutional care causes emotional and behavioural problems for some young children. In 1997 a report for the US National Institute for Child Health and Human Development identified three risk factors for insecure attachment in children under two: more than ten hours of daycare a week in the first year, a change in the childcare arrangements in the first year, and low-quality daycare.

Despite attempts by the pro-day-nursery lobby to counter these findings, they won't go away. A 2004 review of international research sponsored by the UK government found that even with good-quality care more than about twenty hours a week for the under-twos led to 'a slight risk of increased disruptive, antisocial behaviour and children less likely to obey rules and to be less cooperative'. This risk increases after forty or more institutional hours a week – not unusual if parents are in full-time employment. In 2005, the UK Families, Children and Childcare study again showed 'a small but significant difference in a large group of children' for whom daycare led to 'withdrawn, compliant and sad' behaviour or higher levels of aggression.

The journalist Mary Eberstadt brings the issue of infant aggression to life with a review of the literature on biting in US daycare centres. Apparently, outbreaks of biting (that is babies or toddlers biting themselves, each other and their carers) is one of the chief reasons children are expelled from American daycare, and can 'sweep through a pre-school like measles'. As Eberstadt points out, most young children occasionally bite in play or because they're teething, but chronic, contagious biting, where 'randomly assembled children ... start using their teeth as weapons' is a distressingly new phenomenon.

Unfortunately, so far there's little research evidence on the emotional effects of institutional daycare, owing to the fact that emotional effects are difficult to measure. Most long-term research studies have focused instead on children's academic progress, and in this respect attending a daycare centre doesn't seem to have any adverse effects – indeed, in the case of children from poorer homes, it may even improve test scores in the early primary years. But as the evidence of increased aggression and withdrawn, sad behaviour mounts, many experts agree with British childcare guru Penelope Leach that children 'can catch up on cognitive skills later on, but they can't catch up on emotional development'. As stated earlier, my own conclusion after reviewing the huge body of international research is that 'East, West, home's best': the sweetest place for babies or young toddlers is – if at all possible – in their home, with a parent or another beloved adult.

That does, of course, assume that the home is a happy one. One of the major researchers in this field, Jay Belsky, interviewed by the American Psychology Association, went as far as any academic seems prepared to venture with this quote: 'If God gave you the choice between putting a child in a well-functioning, well-resourced family but lots of crummy childcare, or into a poorly functioning, poorly resourced family and lots of good childcare, there's no choice. You'd have to choose the former. With all the debate about childcare, I think we've lost sight of that reality. Any effect childcare has, it has against the background of the overwhelming effect of the family.'

Once children are about three, it's a different matter – research internationally suggests that by this age they generally benefit from good-quality pre-school provision for several hours a day. The period between one and three years is a grey area, depending on individual circumstances – the personalities of parents and children, and the quality of provision. But internationally the historical trend has been to start the kindergarten stage at three (apart from France, where the *écoles maternelles* begin at two).

Three to six: the quest for quality pre-school provision

At the pre-school stage another controversy raises its head: do three- to six-year-olds benefit more from a 'child-centred' approach to learning or an early start on more formal education? Early-years specialists are universally keen on child-centred methods (where learning arises out of children's play and their natural interests), while non-specialists and politicians often want to crack on with something that looks a lot more like school. Parents tend to be in two minds: on the one hand, they want their children to be happy, and small children seem happiest when playing; on the other, they're fearful that wasting time on play could mean their offspring is 'left behind' in a competitive educational culture. So what exactly is high-quality pre-school provision?

In those countries with a long tradition of pre-school education, such as the Scandinavian countries, Italy, Belgium and Switzerland, a child-centred approach is the norm. Children's play and interests are used as the starting point for talk, role-play, stories, music and art, with occasional adult-directed activities to develop listening skills, understanding of number and so on, and there's also emphasis on the importance of playing outdoors and learning from nature. Formal learning of the Three Rs is left until primary school, which doesn't start until children are six or seven.

However, in highly competitive countries (such as the USA, UK and Japan), where education systems are driven by tests, targets and concern about literacy standards, many children under six are expected to press on as soon as possible with the Three Rs of reading, writing and reckoning. This is particularly noticeable in the UK, where children have historically started formal education at an early age and, despite the efforts of early-years specialists to move towards a more play-based curriculum, the national culture still favours an early start.* Indeed, when it became politically expedient in England in the late 1990s to offer one year's free pre-school education, most of the four-year-olds concerned were simply shipped straight into primary school, and started on a primary school curriculum. This would be unthinkable in much of the world: I've heard teachers in several European countries condemn the system as 'cruel', and a Dutch headmaster simply laughed and said, 'Here on the mainland, we educators think you Anglo-Saxons are mad.'

There is in fact no evidence that an early start to formal education benefits children, and plenty suggesting that a structured child-centred approach breeds more confident, resilient, high-achieving children in the long run. All the research, including the UK's current Effective Provision of Preschool Education (EPPE) Project, points to the importance of talk arising from children's interests, outdoor play, music, song, and – at around five years of age – a playful introduction

---

*   The UK's early start actually has nothing to do with education. When the English state school system began in 1870, the starting age was set at five for two reasons: first, to get the poorest children out of their homes and off the streets as early as possible; second, because the sooner education started, the sooner it would finish – so the now-educated children of the poor could enter gainful employment. Other UK countries, and a few colonies like New Zealand and Malta, simply followed suit.

to phonics (the ways sounds are represented by symbols) rather than plunging too soon into pencil-and-paper work. And international comparisons show that, where countries invest time in these pre-literacy activities, children tend to catch up in the Three Rs – and often overtake their counterparts in early-start countries – by the time they are ten. Finland and Sweden, where formal education doesn't start till seven, are traditionally at the top of the international league for literacy attainment. They also have lower achievement gaps between rich and poor children, and between girls and boys.

What's more, a structured child-centred approach and later start to formal learning seem to produce significant benefits in terms of children's behaviour. A 2003 UK government comparison between six-year-olds in England, Denmark and Finland found the Scandinavian children had better concentration and longer attention span than the English and fewer behaviour problems.

As more and more children arrive in nursery and reception classes with poorly developed language and listening skills, and less first-hand experience than in the past (see Chapter 4), it seems only sensible to invest time in laying sound foundations for literacy and numeracy, and developing children's attention and social skills, rather than expecting them to pick up a book or wield a pencil at the earliest opportunity. Indeed, the overall message of international research seems to be that 'too much too young' is yet another ingredient in toxic childhood syndrome.

Child-centred or not, however, pre-school education usually lasts only a few hours a day and research shows that – for three- and four-year-olds at least – there's no benefit in extending these hours. The rest of the time, working parents still have to make the choice between looking after their own children, finding a parent substitute or relying on institutional care – and the decision doesn't get any easier. On a recent radio phone-in, I talked to a working mother whose pre-school children are in daycare from 8 a.m. to 6 p.m.: 'By the time I've picked them up, I haven't got time to engage with them and they're just too tired and strung out.' While on long-term sick leave she'd discovered the pleasure of looking after them herself, and was now agonising over choosing between her career and her children. The problems of filling the home-and-family gap may be less acute once children are over three, but they can be just as heart-rending for a parent.

Six to eleven: home from home?

In all developed countries, by the time children are six (or in the UK, five) they're required to attend primary school for between four and a half and seven hours a day, which means part-time childcare is now provided free of charge, courtesy of the education system. Educational issues are dealt with in Chapter 7, but for an increasing number of children, school is no longer just a place you go to learn.

Schools all over the world are now opening an hour or so before lessons start, often offering breakfast, and staying open for after-school clubs, homework clubs and other activities until around 6 p.m. In many areas, these arrangements are available not only during term time but in school holidays. On the one hand, they can bring welcome relief for working parents, who no longer have to struggle with complicated childcare arrangements – an extended school day means a safe, readily available, affordable, reliable child-minding service. On the other, how do children feel about being penned up in the same institution for up to ten hours a day, five days a week, forty-eight weeks a year?

As before, the younger the children, the more pressing the question. For a six-year-old there's a huge difference between staying on at school for a snack, clubs and extra playtime a couple of days a week, and practically living there for most of one's waking life. If parents aren't available, a home-and-family substitute, such as a child-minder or au pair, may be a better childcare option for at least part of the week than long hours in an institution. But as they grow older children need to spend less time with familiar adults and more with their peers. For the eight to twelves, well-resourced and well-organised 'extended schools' could be a blessing.

Once again, however, it's a question of quality – and quality depends on the extent to which extended schools take into account the optimal conditions for child development. At a conference in 2006, pyschologist Dr Christopher Arnold warned that this kind of institutionalised care could have unintended consequences, as 'raising children in an environment with very large numbers of children with very small numbers of adults is not emotionally healthy'. A study in the West Midlands had found that when 'wrap-around care' was offered by school staff, children perceived it as an extension of class: 'Registers were taken and they were directed by adults, what to play and when to play'.

So what exactly should wrap-around care look like? Clearly, there should be a good adult-child ratio, and preferably there should be a clear distinction between 'education' and 'childcare'. The 'caring environment' should, as far as possible be a home from home, and that means providing for all the aspects of successful child-rearing mentioned so far in this book.

Given the expert advice in Chapter 1, it goes without saying that any meals, snacks and drinks on offer should be both attractive and nutritious, there should be no access to unhealthy junk food or sugary drinks, and mealtimes should be regular, pleasant civilised affairs (not the noisy, uncomfortable chaos I see in all too many British school dining halls). From the experts in Chapter 2, we know that – as well as access to clubs for part of the time (for developing creative and imaginative talents, discovering the joys of teamwork and competitive sports), children also need opportunities for unstructured, loosely supervised play, preferably in green places. Some need to burn off more energy than others, so they'll probably need extension not only to the school day but to the school environment. Organisers should be looking at ways of moving beyond the school grounds to make use of local parks and wild spaces – this is where the specialist knowledge of playworkers would be helpful.

We also know from Chapter 3 about the importance of rest. While opportunities for a nice little nap might be limited, any after-school care should include the option of a few quiet places – for board games, reading, doing homework, or just curling up in a corner and dreaming. And from Chapter 4 (and chapters yet to come) it's clear that, while it would be easy to keep children quietly plugged into the TV, games consoles or school computers, these should be limited (and carefully monitored) just as they should at home. Children need real-life experiences and interactions, with each other and with adults who are interested in their opinions and informed about their development. An American research team summed up the challenge: 'Since so many children nowadays spend so many hours, months and years in childcare ... the environment of these institutions must be designed to be very dynamic ... First, a rich, diverse environment needs to be installed inside and outside the centre. Second, the staff needs to learn to play with the children in those environments. Third, a training program needs to be established to deepen and extend the professional skills and understanding of the type of environment.' Which brings us back where this chapter started: providing effective childcare costs money – lots of it.

Money can't buy me love

This emphasis on the costs of childcare does not mean, however, that all child-rearing problems can be solved by throwing money at them. Quality childcare outside the home is expensive: as has been pointed out in previous chapters, quality childcare in the home is costly in terms of time rather than money. But in a competitive consumer culture it's all too easy to equate spending money on children with loving them, and many contemporary children come home not to parental time and attention, but to a relentless schedule of expensive extra-curricular activities.

I witnessed a typical after-school schedule some years ago when visiting a highly educated couple in a middle-class area of England. On the day I arrived, their eight-year-old son came home to a drink and a sandwich from the au pair, then was whisked away to a Kumon maths lesson. On return, he completed his homework before setting off to swimming club; then, after a hasty family supper, he was allowed an hour on the PlayStation before bed. Other evenings, weekends and holidays were similarly filled to bursting point with extra tuition, clubs, music lessons and special outings – with no time left over for unstructured play or simply 'chilling out'. On one occasion the poor child had a few minutes spare between appointments and his mother seemed to panic: she eventually filled the gap by asking him to entertain me by turning somersaults. He was rather good at this, but then he clearly spent his life turning somersaults to please his parents.

This type of frenzied activity may seem far from the experience of the latch-key child who lets himself in, pops some processed food in the microwave and retires to a bedroom full of electronic equipment, to while away the hours in a 'virtual world'. But both scenarios are caused by the same thing: parents who work long hours and attempt to compensate for their absence (or exhausted presence) by spending money on their children. The educated middle classes justify their extra-curricular payments with the argument that they're providing 'the best possible start in life'; other parents feel their offspring have to keep up with the Joneses' children down the road in terms of electronic and designer must-haves.

Their overspending may be the result of guilt (see Chapter 5), over-protectiveness (see Chapter 2), anxiety for one's child to do well in a competitive world (see Chapter 7), a personal belief that stuff equals contentment (see Chapter 8), or a heady cocktail of all four. The world turns so quickly nowadays, and everyone's running so frantically to keep up with it, that there's no time to stop and wonder, 'Why am I doing this?' The myth of quality time and the burgeoning market in toys, activities and equipment to fill it have added to the emotionally charged brew, so that parents feel they have to earn more and more, meaning they spend less and less time at home. But the key to successful child development is presence, not presents; and children suffering from 'too muchness' can be as emotionally impoverished as those who have too little.

Of course, a few extra-curricular activities are valuable – maybe two or three hours a week, depending on children's interests (and assuming they haven't already had it up to the back teeth with organised activities as part of the extended school day). Clubs and sporting activities develop new skills, help children learn to get along with others and develop their time-management and personal organisation skills. School-age children also benefit from some time relaxing in front of the TV – if nothing else, to ensure they can keep their end up in playground conversation – or enjoying other electronic entertainment. But they also need time for the sort of casual family activities described in Chapter 5, for their own unstructured, natural play or for simply daydreaming.

Our adult preoccupations can make us unaware of these developmental needs. As Carl Honoré put it in his book In Praise of Slow, 'To an adult used to making every second count, unstructured play looks like wasted time.' I suspect the friend who asked her son to turn somersaults was terrified that, left to his own devices, he'd be bored – and she was probably right. Children whose lives are filled every moment of every day with structured activity don't learn to think for themselves or exercise their own imaginations. They become dependent on others to educate, entertain and otherwise occupy them – and, in consequence, are easily bored. They then demand more activities or more stuff to ease their boredom, and parents – under the influence of that potent cocktail of love, guilt and anxiety – fork out more and more cash in a desperate attempt to keep them happy.

*

In a world where all adults – women as well as men – expect to have opportunities for self-realisation and economic independence, the issue of childcare raises political, economic, social and emotional problems. To solve them, all adults – men as well as women – have to wise up to what looking after children involves. Child-rearing is not, as many politicians seem to think, the same as babysitting. Neither is childhood a race, in which the chances of success are improved by hot housing, an early start on formal learning or endless 'enrichment'. Caring for young children involves expertise which was, in the past, handed down through the female line, but today has often been forgotten. While genetic inheritance and hormones mean human beings almost inevitably love their children, our species seems increasingly uncertain how best to look after them or to ensure they're well looked after.

This problem is compounded, in the most competitive countries of the developed world, by a confused attitude to love and money. Parents who don't see the point of seeking out and paying for high-quality daycare are nevertheless prepared to work day and night to afford expensive extra-curricular activities or gifts of technological paraphernalia. Society has conditioned us all to believe that money, hard work and consumer durables can solve most problems. But the problems of babies who bite, pre-schoolers struggling to write before they can talk, and children corralled for several hours with unqualified minders round the edges of every school day will not be assuaged by purchase of the latest technological gadgets. As the twenty-first century progresses, the problem of who's looking after the children isn't going to go away.

DETOXING CHILDCARE

- Make sure you're clear about the difference between childcare and education. In the early years, learning is largely informal, but once children reach the age of six education becomes increasingly formal. It's useful to think of formal learning as being like children's 'work' (requiring mental effort and discipline), while childcare, with its opportunities for child-centred informal learning, is more like 'family time'.
- Good childcare should, therefore, reproduce as far as possible the conditions we'd expect in a happy family home.
- Plan for childcare well in advance – don't leave it till the last minute and thus end up compromising on quality.

Birth to three

- In the early years children's main requirements are consistent one-to-one personal relationships and familiar surroundings. The possible options are:

  – care by parent(s) or other committed family members (youthful enough to cater for the needs of a small baby)
  – a substitute carer in your own or their home, such as a nanny, childminder or unqualified minder (the higher the carer's qualifications the more likely they are to be effective)
  – a day nursery which provides one-to-one care with a named carer in a highly domesticated setting.

- Avoid:

  – little contact with parents
  – frequent changes of carer
  – poor-quality childcare
  – institutional care for more than a few hours a day.

- Look for childcare that can provide:

– the sort of child-rearing practices described in Chapters 1 to 4

– as seamless as possible a transition between childcare and parents

– reliability and carer(s) with whom you feel comfortable

– opportunities for your child to mix with others while feeling safe in the care of a beloved adult.

Three to six

- By this stage children need plenty of opportunities to explore and learn, along with the chance to meet and play with other children, so pre-school is important.

- Quality pre-school should provide:

  – child-centred activities arising out of the children's own interests interspersed with adult-directed sessions to lay solid foundations for 'school learning' (the latter increasing in significance as time goes on)

  – plenty of outdoor play, music, art and 'sustained shared thinking' (see page 118)

  – about three hours a day of this sort of activity for children up to four years old, up to six hours thereafter.

- During the rest of the day, children still need the more familial type of childcare described in 'Birth to Three' above. The options are:

  – a day nursery in which pre-school activities are interspersed with 'family-like' mealtimes, rests, quiet time, unstructured play and so on

  – part-time attendance at a pre-school, with other appropriate childcare around the edges.

- Avoid:

  – little contact with parents

  – frequent changes of care arrangements

  – poor-quality pre-school provision or childcare

  – too formal an approach to learning before the age of six.

- Look for a good balance between exciting pre-school provision and the home comforts listed in the 'Birth to Three' bullet points.

Six to twelve

- During this period, children should grow in independence so the need for home and family gradually lessens. However, just like adults, they need respite from 'work' in the hours around the school day (and the younger they are, the more that respite should resemble a happy family home).
- Childcare options around the school day and during school holidays are:

  – family or substitute carers as described above
  – institutionalised care in an 'extended school' or similar provision.

- Good institutionalised care should provide:

  – quality supervision, incorporating the sorts of attitude to eating habits, play, outdoor activity and child–adult interaction described in Chapters 1 to 4, albeit adapted to fit a larger group of children
  – organised activities and clubs
  – opportunities for unstructured play, reading and quiet relaxation
  – the right for children to choose their own balance of organised and unstructured activities.

- The older the child, the longer and more frequently they are likely to benefit from being in good institutionalised care. However, all children still need plenty of time at home with their own family (see Chapter 5).

THE WORK-CHILDCARE BALANCE

- Discuss childcare with your partner – preferably before you have children – bearing in mind:

  - the available maternal and paternal leave arrangements, including benefits
  - your *real* financial needs (i.e., living costs, as opposed to 'lifestyle choices')
  - your interest in/ability to look after a baby (you may find this changes, for better or worse, when the baby arrives)
  - the effects on your respective careers of taking time off – and whether you want a child enough to risk these effects.*

  There's more discussion of the economic issues behind child-rearing in Chapter 10 and the 'Conclusion: Detoxing Childhood'.

- Bear in mind that raising a child involves time, effort and attention, and if you can't or aren't prepared to provide these you have two options:

  - pay someone else to do it as well as possible on your behalf (but still making sure you put in enough time to 'forge a family' – see Chapter 5)
  - don't have children – just get on with enjoying life as a non-parent.

- The options available in terms of caring for a child at home are:

  - one parent takes full-time responsibility for childcare, the other for bread-winning
  - one or both parents reduce working hours to allow for childcare.

- Reduced working hours could involve:

  - part-time work (reducing the days worked each week, or hours each day)
  - job-sharing (e.g., do you work with/know other parents who might like to share?)
  - working from home (choosing hours to fit around childcare).

---

* However, bear in mind that the effects of taking time off are not necessarily negative. Some people end up with a completely new, more interesting career.

- Childcare options available while you're at work are outlined in 'Detoxing Childcare'. But remember that these options can themselves be time-consuming and effortful in terms of:

  – arrangements for dropping off and collecting children
  – communicating and liaising with carers to ensure your child is happy
  – providing and keeping special equipment and clothing in good repair
  – any parental 'duties' expected (as one mother put it, 'You're usually required to keep up your end of the grunt work, regardless of whether you work outside the home')
  – dealing with emergencies, e.g., if travel arrangements break down.

- Remember that children thrive on consistency and regularity. The younger the child, the more damaging it is to chop and change arrangements, so:

  – put in plenty of groundwork on providing the best possible option from the beginning
  – spend time devising efficient emergency systems, including more than one trusty 'safety net' should your arrangements go awry.

- Review your arrangements frequently. Are both partners happy with the way things are? Does your child seem happy?

PARENT POWER: CHANGING THE WORLD

Most parents are so busy coping with their own lives there seems to be no time to exercise parent power to improve the work-life balance. But even in the midst of the parental juggling act, there are some simple steps that could improve life for you, and for future generations.

- Talk to other parents (and anyone else who'll listen) about the particular problems you're encountering with work–life balance. As well as helping you develop your own social network, this is a good way of discovering what's available and going on locally. But don't just moan – talk about what can be done to make things better.

- Don't be put off by other parents' apparent competence and organisation. Everyone puts on a front, and every parent I've ever met turned out to be struggling just as hard as me, no matter how swanlike and serene they appeared on the surface. But people always like to be asked for advice, so that's a good way to introduce yourself.

- For further information and advice, consult the web – it's amazing what you can find out with half an hour's Googling – the BBC's parenting website has much helpful advice and opportunities to chat. But *don't* get stuck on the net when you're supposed to be sharing time with your child (see Chapter 4), and don't use net-based contacts as a substitute for meeting real people.

- Use casual chats and virtual leads to develop real-life contacts with people who share your concerns and interests. Real-life contacts are good for you and your child (see Chapter 10), even if you don't solve the immediate problem.

- Don't be put off going to more formal meetings – PTAs, parent groups, pressure groups for change. You don't have to get involved if you don't want to – but if you don't go you'll never find out what's available. Nobody ever changed anything by sitting around bemoaning the status quo.

- At work, ask about family-friendly alternatives to full-time commitment. But don't enrage the non-parents by expecting special treatment – you chose to be a parent, so can't expect the rest of the world to pay your way. But everyone benefits from flexible work structures that respect employees' right to a life beyond the office.

- When local and national elections come round, make it clear (by emailing, writing to or buttonholing candidates) that your vote will be influenced by policies on:

  – effective childcare provision, at each of the three age ranges in this chapter
  – work–life balance, including flexible working hours and parental leave.

- If you're the sort of person who likes to get involved, this really is your chance. As a parent, you have inside, expert knowledge on one of the most significant issues of our generation: use it to help build a better world.

Further reading

For parents of children from birth to three years old:
Sue Gerhardt, *Why Love Matters: How Affection Shapes a Baby's Brain* (Brunner-Routledge, 2004)

For parents of three to six-year olds:
Diane Rich and others, *First hand experience – what matters to children* (Rich Learning Opportunities, 2005)
Ros Bayley and Lynn Broadbent, *Flying Start with Literacy* (Network Educational Press Ltd, 2005)

Useful websites

For details on childcare options see national websites:
Daycare Trust: **www.daycaretrust.org.uk**
National Network for Childcare: **www.nncc.org**
Child Care Link: **www.childcarelink.gov.uk**
For excellent leaflets on early education for three to six-year olds see **www.early-education.org.uk**

Mind the gap

In the 1960s, the US government launched a programme called Headstart, aimed at providing early childcare support for 'at risk' families and trying to prevent social problems before they began. Long-term research has suggested that for every dollar invested in effective early-years provision, seven dollars are saved in terms of lower crime, better jobs and improved educational outcomes. But that word 'effective' is significant. As US economist Steven Levitt says, state-provided childcare is unlikely to make much impact if, 'instead of spending the day with his own undereducated, overworked mother, the ... child spends his day with someone else's undereducated, overworked mother. (And a whole roomful of needy children.)'

One of the flagship enterprises of the UK's Labour government is based on Headstart. The Sure Start movement now provides day centres and children's services to children from birth to three in poor areas of England. Sadly, an early assessment found no differences in language, behaviour or overall development between poor children in Sure Start and non-Sure Start areas – but it did appear that Sure Start mothers were 'warmer' in their treatment of their children, using less negative criticism and more affection. As usual, the likelihood of long-term success will depend on levels of investment and staff training. There are outstanding examples of work around the country, such as the Pen Green Centre in Northamptonshire and the Thomas Coram Centre in London, but these successful initiatives are highly dependent on their staff knowing how to play the system (public and private) to fund their work.

Once children are three, research shows clearly that effective pre-school provision can provide a 'second chance' to escape the heritage of an impoverished family background – but only if their pre-schools are well run and resourced. The long-term harm caused by over-formal pre-school practice is much greater for children from poorer homes. The High/Scope Foundation in the USA followed the progress of a group of pre-school pupils from the late 1960s, and found that those who attended a formal pre-school were much more likely to have social problems thirty years down the line. These long-term problems include trouble holding down a job, difficulties with personal relationships and a significantly greater chance of involvement in crime.

Finally, as children grow older, where do you suppose an 'extended school day' is more likely to be a life-enhancing experience? In a middle-class area, where school grounds are extensive and parental pressure ensures exciting, varied, well-resourced provision? Or in an inner city school with ancient buildings, limited play areas, little parental involvement and 'someone else's undereducated overworked mother' keeping an eye on the children?

Inadequate childcare, at any age, has a greater negative impact on children from poor families than on those from more privileged backgrounds. On the other hand, the experience of countries like Finland, Norway and Sweden shows clearly that investment in quality provision (and education) for the first ten years of all children's lives benefits everyone. It means less mental instability, less crime, less antisocial behaviour and less handing on of a chaotic, dishevelled lifestyle to future generations. If we are to close the widening gap, the best investment we can make is high quality care for *all* our children.

CHAPTER SEVEN

THE BEST DAYS OF THEIR LIVES

Children start learning from the moment they're born. By trial and error they learn to control their limbs, sit up, walk, talk, run and jump. They learn through experience what a vast variety of things look, sound, feel, smell and taste like. They watch adults performing daily tasks, such as buttoning up a coat, and as their own physical dexterity grows they start to copy them, then practise the activity until it becomes second nature. They watch natural events, such as water running down a slope, and make deductions about how the world works – some of which, of course, are wildly wrong ... but surprisingly many turn out to be right. Neuroscientists studying children's brain development in the early years wax lyrical about all the learning they do, which for most of human history we've taken entirely for granted.

And almost all this learning is entirely voluntary, for the sheer pleasure of doing it. There are a few social skills adults insist on – such as toilet training, saying 'please' and 'thank you' and table manners. But children learn these skills quickly too if the adults give lots of praise and compliments on how 'grown up' they're being. On the whole, children want to learn, and parents and other primary care-givers are pretty good at gauging what can be expected of them. Even when, at around three years old, children go to pre-school, the routine is usually much the same – learning develops out of their interests and pre-school teachers take their developmental level into account.

And then they start school.

Shades of the prison house ...

When children are about six years old, countries across the developed world require them to sign up for formal education. For too many children nowadays, Wordsworth's unenthusiastic description:

> Shades of the prison-house begin to close
> Upon the growing boy

sums up what learning feels like when it ceases to be voluntary and is instead determined by the demands of the curriculum. What's more, in large classes – typically thirty or more in state primary schools – a single teacher isn't usually in a position to take the developmental level of individual children into account.

Nevertheless, society needs schools to help create citizens who'll keep the contemporary cultural show on the road, and primary education has the task of laying the foundations for lifelong learning. This means developing children's motivation to learn, their ability to work, both independently and with others, and – very importantly – their skills in the Three Rs. If children are bright-eyed, bushy-tailed and up to speed in reading, writing and basic maths by the end of their primary years, they should be able to take full advantage of secondary education and hopefully go on to be successful, hard-working adults.

After more than a hundred years of state-aided elementary education, you'd think the nations of the developed world would be able to deliver most children into their teens happy, motivated and literate. However, schools have been battered as much as other institutions by the winds of tumultuous social and technological change. Over the last couple of decades, toxic childhood syndrome has made children harder to teach and more difficult to control. Parents, anxious about their offspring's prospects in an increasingly competitive world and worried by reports of falling standards, bullying and disrupted classes, are less confident about schools' effectiveness. And governments around the world, responding to these changes in the only way they know how, have taken ever greater control over the way schools are run.

One unfortunate result of government involvement in education is mushrooming bureaucracy. Each year sees more systems, regulations and targets imposed, and more requests for records, statistics and test results, spawning a mountain of paperwork. The more teachers are preoccupied with tending to this bureaucracy, the less time and energy they have for teaching, and the less children's individual needs can be taken into account.

Another problem is politicians' need for quick results to impress the voters and statistical evidence of improvement. This has led schools into a tests-and-targets culture with a fierce focus on standards of achievement. Elementary schools in the USA, for instance, are dominated by the No Child Left Behind legislation, while in the UK millions of pounds have been poured into 'National Strategies' for literacy and numeracy. Parents generally welcome the focus on the Three Rs, since they know how important these basic skills are to their children. But there's a serious danger that this focus can grow too narrow and, if so, it can damage children's chances rather than improving them.

Why reading is important in a multimedia age

There's no doubt that the Three Rs of reading, writing and reckoning are the bedrock of education, with reading arguably the most important R. Even in a multimedia world, where entertainment and information are increasingly visual, the ability to read is essential in every walk of life. But reading brings with it many extra advantages. The very process of learning to read, 'the getting of literacy', is a hugely important part of children's intellectual and social development.

For a start, learning to read actually improves children's thinking skills. Written language is more complex and sophisticated than the everyday language of speech, so reading leads to a significant expansion of children's ideas, vocabulary and the capacity to express themselves. The second R – writing – also helps, because learning to write involves slowing down the thought processes, choosing the best words and expressions to communicate an idea. Since language and thought are closely intertwined, this increased word power leads to increased brain power – it's long been recognised that, when children become literate, there's a knock-on effect in terms of IQ.

Literacy also affects children's emotional and social development. The symbolic system by which we represent language is a human invention – a complex early technology whereby squiggles on a page are converted by the human brain into meaningful words. Learning to read and write doesn't come naturally like learning to walk, talk and so on, and each new generation has to acquire the skills by conscious application. This is a long, painstaking process (most adults have forgotten quite how difficult it is), but as children gradually become literate there's a steady growth of connections in the prefrontal cortex of their brains, the area associated with focused concentration, planning, self-control and decision-making.

Thus 'the getting of literacy' creates enriched neural networks in children's brains, which may well be significant in the development of civilised behaviour. I don't think it's any coincidence that written language has proved a key element in all successful civilisations and that universal literacy appears essential to the success of democratic systems. As the American writer Neil Postman put it, 'Print means a slowed down mind ... The written, and then the printed word brought a new kind of social organisation to civilisation. It brought logic, science, education, civilité.' However, Postman also points out that 'electronics speeds up the mind', and the long slow process of acquiring literacy is more difficult for children living in a world that travels at electric speed.

True literacy therefore requires motivation and plenty of practice, and this is where a narrow focus on test results can be damaging. The superficial skills children need for scoring points on multiple choice tests aren't anywhere near as enriching and civilising as genuine reading for pleasure – they merely skim the surface of literacy. In this respect, J.K. Rowling has probably done more for the children of the developed world than the entire twenty-first-century educational establishment. Nurturing children's motivation to learn and their enjoyment of reading is every bit as important as teaching them the underpinning skills.

Nevertheless, they won't get anywhere without those skills ... and a significant number of children still don't manage to learn them. To some extent this is because the early stages of 'the getting of literacy' involve application and perseverance, so teachers have to convince children to slow down their minds and attend to complex symbolic information on a page. This may be difficult if formal reading instruction begins too early, or at any age if the children concerned are suffering from toxic childhood syndrome. But there are other reasons why children sometimes fail to acquire basic reading skills, associated with the vexed educational question of 'phonics'.

Why Johnny still can't read ... and how he might

As well as bureaucracy, primary education is often bedevilled by the fads and fashions of academic theory. For over a hundred years, academics have wrangled over the best way to teach reading: phonics (showing children that the sounds 'c', 'a', 't' go together to make *cat*) or fun (getting children hooked on reading so they want to suss out the phonics for themselves). Schools have been pulled back and forth, and for a prolonged period towards the end of the last century, phonics went completely out of fashion.

Fortunately, there is currently agreement that, in an alphabetic language such as English, phonics teaching is essential. Without some grasp of phonics, children are unlikely to read at all, let alone get hooked on it. However, despite this triumph of common sense, many children are still finding reading difficult: teachers teach phonics, but some children don't catch on. Recent research suggests that this – like so many other developmental problems – could be the result of nature or nurture.

For children to take advantage of phonics teaching, they have to be able to distinguish the individual speech sounds (phonemes) of their native language, an ability acquired long before they start school, during the first year or so of life. Research has shown that newborn babies are equipped to recognise and produce the phonemes of any language, but – as they listen to the adults in their lives – they narrow it down to the speech sounds of the language they'll need. (This is why Chinese people find it so difficult not only to pronounce but also to hear the sound 'r'. It doesn't exist in Chinese, so in very early childhood they excise it from their phonemic repertoire.) If phonemic awareness isn't acquired naturally at this very early stage, it can be very difficult for children to develop it later.

Scientists have now pinpointed the sections of the brain involved in processing speech sounds, and it's clear that for some children genetic factors make it difficult (in extreme cases perhaps impossible) to discriminate certain phonemes. In this case, personal biology holds the child back.

Other children may have poor phonemic awareness because, even though they are neurologically OK, they simply don't get enough exposure to language in the early years. This is one reason why earlier chapters have stressed the significance of a child's constant interaction with a primary caregiver in the first eighteen months and the importance of talking, singing and rhyming with very small children. At present, many children's poor phonemic awareness may be due to lack of adult time and attention in their earliest years.

Once they reach school age, if children have trouble discriminating speech sounds – whether through nurture, nature or a combination of both – they are less well equipped to read than their peers. Researchers are now looking at ways to identify which sounds they can't distinguish (it seems to vary from child to child) and train them in recognising these sounds. This is an exciting development, because it could mean a 'cure' for dyslexia. But the problem facing schools and researchers is that learning to process speech sounds is only one tiny facet of human development, and one tiny facet of reading. If overexcited educational experts start bombarding small children with phonological training schedules without attending to the wider picture, they could end up doing more harm than good (see Chapter 6: 'The Quest for Quality Pre-School Education'). It's probably going to take some time to find the most effective type of intervention.

Meanwhile, there's plenty parents and carers can do to prevent problems *before* they begin. For the overwhelming majority of children, the age-old wisdom quoted in Chapter 4 can open up the relevant neural pathways quite naturally long before anyone even thinks about school. Songs, rhymes, laughter and conversation with a loved one are far more effective ways of preparing a child to read than a phonological training schedule.

The educational rat race

While the importance of the Three Rs can't be overemphasised, focusing on them too narrowly doesn't help children in the long run. One ill-effect is the 'too much too young' syndrome described in Chapter 6. It may make sense to adults to think 'there's a lot to learn, so the sooner they get on with it the better' or 'if some children can start reading at the age of four, we can expect them all to manage it', but children are all different and develop at different rates, and the younger they are the more significant these differences are. Every developmental psychologist I've spoken to agrees that formal learning is best left till children are at least six years old, when the differences have begun to even out and most are sufficiently mature to cope with abstract ideas.

This doesn't mean holding back those children who show precocious ability in reading, writing or numbers. Holding children back would be as cruel and counter-productive as forcing them to struggle with skills that are beyond them. But a child can continue to enjoy mastery in one area of the curriculum while simultaneously being encouraged to develop abilities in other areas. Early readers, for instance, often benefit from attention to social skills, physical co-ordination and control, music and creative arts, concepts of number or learning how things work.

Sadly, parents and teachers in the UK and USA have allowed themselves to be drawn into an educational rat race, modelled on the competitive ethos of big business, and focused in the early years on literacy. In a cut-throat world, parents are understandably worried that their child may be 'left behind', but all the research cited in Chapter 6 suggests this is another example of contemporary cultural influences blinding adults to children's biological needs – like letting them feed almost exclusively on junk food or stay inside developing square eyeballs when they'd be better off playing in the fresh air.

We wouldn't dream of suggesting twelve-year-olds should learn to drive (even though technically most of them probably could) because we know that emotionally they're not ready for the responsibility of being in charge of a car. Similarly, we shouldn't force unwilling four- and five-year-olds to struggle with skills most would learn easily a couple of years later. Russian researcher Galina Dolya believes this early pressure feeds emotional and behavioural difficulties. 'A child who's accelerated is more likely to experience frustration and burn-out,' she says. Certainly, in US and UK primary schools, teachers are reporting more violence and aggression than ever before in their youngest children, with some of the most violent offenders being only five, six and seven years old.

Apart from emotional repercussions (which are sometimes immediate, sometimes not apparent for many years), many children in early-start countries now fall at the first fence in the literacy stakes, leading to long-term difficulties with reading and writing. As Marion Dowling, president of Early Education, warns, 'If young children have

knowledge and skills forced on them, they'll withdraw their dis-
position to learn. It's much more difficult to rekindle that desire later.'
This is particularly the case with boys, for whom the skills underpinning literacy develop more slowly than girls. Time, money and
effort then have to be invested in 'catch-up' programmes, which,
sadly, do not seem to work. Japanese politicians who reacted to a
recent fall in literacy standards with calls for 'children to study harder
from the time when they are small' should note the current drop-out
rate among five-year-olds in England.

Winners and losers

Another ill-effect of a narrow, standards-driven agenda is the proliferation of tests. Schools must, of course, be accountable and
occasional national tests are essential to keep tabs on children's
progress, but if testing assumes too much importance it becomes an
end in itself. In both the USA and UK high-stakes testing throughout
the primary years (win or lose, pass or fail) is, in the words of
Professor Joe Frost of the University of Texas, turning schools into
'factories that sort both children and teachers into "winners" and
"losers" and grade children like chickens on the assembly line'.

Unfortunately, once labelled 'losers', many children never recover.
Thomas Jefferson once described childhood as a time when 'the
imagination is warm, and impressions are permanent'. Thus the most
likely result of early failure is summed up by that other American
aphorist, Homer Simpson: 'Kids, you tried your hardest and you failed
miserably. The lesson is: don't try.'

No one could dispute that, in a competitive world, children need to
learn about winning and losing. Traditionally, schools have provided
opportunities for this in the form of competitive events, from sports
days, team games and swimming galas to art competitions, quizzes
and spelling bees. The greater the range, the more chance that every
child can find an activity in which to excel, and thus experience the

delights of success. To be of any value these activities should, of course, be truly competitive, not watered-down events where everyone gets a prize. If the lesson is how to cope with triumph and disaster, there must be the possibility of both, and schools where sports day means the indiscriminate award of winners' ribbons and certificates clearly miss the point.

The difference between competitive events and high-stakes testing is that sports, games, galas and quizzes are 'play'. However much play matters while you're doing it, everyone knows it's just a game, not life and death. Learning how to read, write and reckon is not a game: even the youngest child can sense from parents' and teachers' attitudes to these skills that acquiring them is a matter of serious import. Learning the Three Rs is not an appropriate vehicle for learning about winning and losing. Indeed, this is an area of educational life where all must have prizes – when children leave primary school illiterate or innumerate, society as a whole is the long-term loser.

The more emphasis we put on tests in primary school, the more we ratchet up the stress on young children. Indeed, when serious testing starts as young as six or seven, even the 'winners' may suffer. For some, the pressure to keep up their high scores becomes oppressive, and by the time they reach their teens they're showing signs of wear and tear (depression, substance abuse, self-harm, eating disorders ...). The teachers I meet from prestigious preparatory schools are often deeply worried about the effects of pressure to achieve on some of the children they teach.

To produce citizens who can cope with whatever life throws at them, primary schools must be places where children aren't afraid to try – where, like every successful scientist and entrepreneur, they can discover that failure is a necessary staging point on the route to success. This doesn't mean teachers should let them off with less than their best, praise them indiscriminately or suggest that correctness doesn't matter. But it does mean that the younger the children, the more sensitive adults must be to their different needs, talents and stages of development, and throughout the primary years learning should be as much fun as possible, with the emphasis on celebrating strengths and helping overcome weaknesses. As a society, we also have to recognise that characteristics such as social competence, perseverance and self-control, which can't be measured by pencil-and-paper tests, are in the long run just as important as academic achievement.

Thinking in blinkers

High-stakes testing can also blind teachers, parents and children to the importance of a wide and balanced curriculum. When schools are judged almost exclusively on their test results, and especially when teachers' status and earnings depend on those results, they inevitably begin to focus on the narrow range of skills to be tested in end-of-year exams. 'Teaching to the test' (training children in tricks and techniques to earn marks rather than helping them understand and enjoy the subject) becomes the order of the day, and creativity and the development of enquiring minds fall to the bottom of the educational priority list. All too often in schools today, when a new topic crops up, able children ask 'Is this on the test?' and lose interest if it isn't. This is the sort of mindset that led Einstein to remark, 'It's a miracle that curiosity survives formal education.' A test-based primary-school system trains children to think in blinkers.

Take reading, for example. In 2004, the UK government trumpeted that eleven-year olds in England (the nation that undergoes the most tests in the world) had moved up to third place in an international comparison of reading scores; they were less keen to mention that those same children languished at the bottom of the league for enjoyment of reading. Schools may have reinstated phonics, but in doing so they seem to have lost sight of the fun.

As mentioned earlier, reading is one of those skills, like riding a bicycle, that's developed through repeated practice ... and to ensure

enough practice, children must want to do it. The truth is that the pro-
tagonists on both sides of the 'phonics versus fun' reading wars were
partly right. The challenge for teachers is to establish the right
balance between teaching the skills and developing a love of learning,
but an obsessive testing regime inevitably tips that balance too far in
the direction of the skills. Training children to tick the right boxes in a
national reading test is a short-term measure that pushes up test
scores – all too often, the 'literacy skills' children demonstrate on the
test seem to evaporate a few weeks later. Inspiring them to become
genuine, committed, enthusiastic readers takes more time and effort,
isn't easy to measure, but bears much more significant fruit in the
long run.

Japan, famed for its highly competitive testing regime long before
the trend hit the West, decided some years ago that the high levels of
stress this caused students were proving counter-productive – in 1998
Prime Minister Ryutaro Hashimoto explained, 'Our children are truly
suffering, crying out for help.' So as the USA and UK embarked on the
high-stakes testing route, Japan was busily dismantling it. Now, just
as Japanese schools have introduced a new primary curriculum
emphasising curiosity and creativity, panic about falling reading
standards may lead to another U-turn – the blinkers may be on the way
back. Yet as Mr Hashimoto pointed out in his speech, the real problem
behind declining standards is the effects of social and cultural change
– and an overcompetitive, tests-and-targets educational regime
simply adds to children's problems.

The great e-learning revolution

One much-vaunted means of engaging children's attention, while at
the same time developing their skills, is to make more use of new
technology. There's no question that in a multimedia age it's foolish
to ignore the strengths of e-learning resources – video can transport a
class through time and space, facts are readily available on the

Internet, and computer graphics can brighten up dull educational chores. But, as usual in education, it's important not to get carried away. Electronic teaching can enrich real-life learning, but it can't be a substitute. Inside as well as outside school, children need human interaction and hands-on activities more than second-hand experiences on screen. This is acknowledged by e-learning visionaries such as Seymour Papert, who have always recommended the use of technology to enhance first-hand experience.

When used merely to support a narrow, standards-driven school curriculum, there is scant evidence of computers making much difference to educational achievement. Investment by schools in computers and other electronic paraphernalia – at least 55 billion dollars in the USA in the 1990s alone – has made no noticeable impact and, despite the blandishments of software manufacturers and the optimism of politicians, standards have not soared. Researchers at Munich University in 2004 analysed the results of an international study of computer use and found that, 'the evidence suggests that computer use in schools does not seem to contribute substantially to pupils' learning of basic skills such as maths or reading'.

On the other hand, technology *can* make learners lazy. Back in the early 1990s, English primary schools introduced calculators, on the principle that contemporary children needed to know how to use them, and within five years they had to be withdrawn, because children around the country were forgetting how to add and subtract. Technology can also be a powerful distraction from more useful occupations. The plummeting literacy scores in Japan have been linked to children's declining interest in reading – more than half have no reading habit at all, while time spent on computer games, Internet chatting and other electronic gadgets has soared.

The Munich researchers' conclusion was that using home computers for learning improved school performance, but using them for games and gossip had the opposite effect; in school, occasional access to computers led to a slight improvement, but frequent access (several times a week) was linked to even worse performance than no access at all. All this leads to the common sense conclusion voiced by IT expert Greg Pearson – unless you're using computers knowledgeably for a specific purpose, they can be 'a waste of time and energy much more easily than they can be useful'.

Parents and teachers

It's clear that what happens at home profoundly affects children's ability to learn at school. Where home and school work in harmony, children have a much better chance of success. While researching this book, therefore, I asked teachers what they thought made good parents, and asked parents what they looked for in a teacher.

The teachers' verdict was that the best parents are supportive, well organised and interested in their children's work – but have realistic expectations and don't push too hard. They make sure their children eat well, exercise enough, and have plenty of sleep. They get them to school on time (complete with all the necessary sports equipment and so on) and collect them promptly at the end of the day. They chat with their children about their day, praise achievements and supervise any work that has to be done at home. (They do not do the homework for them.) They turn up to parents' evenings and other school functions – especially performances in which their child has a part, however minuscule – and keep in regular touch about their children's progress and welfare. Apparently, there aren't many of these paragons about – most parents are now so busy juggling jobs, children and domestic responsibilities that being supportive to school is fairly low down their list of priorities.

According to parents, the ideal teacher is in short supply too. This is someone who's confident and approachable, keeps them well informed (but not constantly bombarded with newsletters and forms to sign), has a sensible and clear homework schedule (including plenty of notice of when it's to be handed in) and runs an orderly classroom where belongings don't go missing and children know what's going on. He or she has strong discipline skills while still maintaining a good relationship with the children, and ensures their child is happy in class but also working hard and getting good results. However, most teachers are so busy with bureaucracy, the quest for better test results and stemming the rising tide of indiscipline that keeping parents informed and catered for is the last thing on their minds.

This all seems a terrible shame since the two wish lists, when combined, look like a recipe for happy, high-achieving children. A few honest exchanges of views between the two groups could benefit a school and its pupils more than several shelf-fuls of government initiatives. But Hilary Wilce, a journalist who writes an educational agony column for a UK national newspaper, reckons there's a crucial reason why parents and teachers don't find it easy to communicate: 'Teachers and parents come from different corners, and have different goals. Parents want red-carpet treatment for their children; teachers want to keep their classroom show on the road. Parents get frustrated when schools don't take them seriously; schools get hostile and defensive when parents make demands they think unreasonable.' So all too often parents avoid schools and schools avoid parents.

This means that, when something goes wrong and parent and teacher meet to sort it out, emotions can get in the way of reason. Parents often feel nervous about disagreeing with the teacher, fearing it may rebound on their child. If they're also upset about the problem in hand, they can arrive at the school feeling aggressive, defensive, anxious or tongue-tied. Teachers are usually in a similarly stressed condition – due perhaps to insecurity, inexperience in dealing with parents or fear of confrontation. Hilary Wilce believes this clash can only be solved by more understanding on both sides – training for new teachers in how to build links with parents, and more encouragement for parents to be involved with the school.

The most successful schools do seem able to provide opportunities for comfortable interaction between parents and teachers, in which they focus on common goals. And since both parties have a vested interest in the welfare and progress of children, these are many. There are suggestions throughout this book for ways schools can support parents in detoxifying children's lives and many of these suggestions would provide opportunities for parents and teachers to come together for a common purpose, rather than languishing in Hilary Wilce's opposing corners. As will be argued in Chapter 10, everyone would benefit from the forging of an 'adult alliance' to counter toxic childhood syndrome.

Bullying tactics

A worrying example of parents and teachers failing to see each other's point of view is the growing problem of bullying. Parents often feel schools could be doing more to protect their children from bullying, while teachers reckon some behaviour now labelled as bullying is actually just the cut-and-thrust of playground politics, and that overzealous interference can do more harm than good.

Bullying is defined on a UK government website as 'teasing and name-calling, threats and physical violence, damage to property, deliberately leaving children out of social activities, spreading rumours or upsetting mobile-phone or email messages'. With boys, it often involves violence; in girls it's more likely to be psychological, which can be just as damaging. A parent whose child comes home complaining of being bullied is understandably concerned, and can reasonably expect the school to take action.

However, small examples of the activities listed above happen every day in every playground in the world – and until children are born fully civilised they'll continue to happen. There's a difference between full-blown bullying and playground spats, occasional spiteful behaviour or infant fallings out. Resilient children deal with such episodes themselves and learning to sort them out is an important part of every child's social education. All children benefit from talking things over with trusted adults to work out the best ways of dealing with playground incidents, but, as pointed out in Chapter 2, too much policing of play can create both bullies and victims, rather than helping children develop social skills for themselves.

Real bullying, on the other hand, is extreme or prolonged damaging behaviour, vindictive enough to deprive victims of the capacity to defend themselves. As one teacher described it to me, 'A spat's like the flicker of a candle, bullying's a continuous burn.' All children need protection from true bullying, and every school needs a clear, no-nonsense anti-bullying policy (with unpleasant consequences for the bullies – see next section) brought rapidly into force when incidents occur. Given that such policies are in place, and their children are well-informed about the best way to deal with bullies (see website addresses on page 224), parents have to trust teachers to decide whether an incident is a flicker or part of a first-degree burn.

The cultural factors described in Chapter 2 have made both parents and children inceasingly anxious. Media reports of the occasional tragic consequences of bullying, or of faddish policies that let bullies off the hook (such as the 'no blame' strategy recently trialled in some English schools) fan the flames of this anxiety. Many parents are less inclined to accept a school's assessment than in the past. This, in turn, puts schools on the defensive about parental complaints. And, as has been argued above, this breakdown of trust between partners in the child-rearing enterprise has long-term implications for children and society that are every bit as worrying as the bullying itself.

Dealing with discipline

No child is born a bully, just as no child is born a nasty little brat. Some poor souls may be genetically predestined to lag behind in the development stakes, in which case they need extra help to fit into normal social patterns. But the majority of children brought up in a peaceful, prosperous country should, by the time they're six or so, be able to settle down and take full advantage of school.

So why are so many of them turning brattish? Let me count the ways: diet, lack of sleep or outdoor play, inadequate attachment or language, family problems, early failure at school, lack of motivation, a playground culture in which it's cool to be badly behaved (see Chapter 8), the influence of TV and computer violence (Chapter 9) … the cocktail will be different in every case, but its origins are in a culture that has forgotten the essential elements of successful child-rearing.

And once bad behaviour at school begins, it adds considerably to the toxic mix. A few misbehaving children in a class means the teacher becomes preoccupied with the business of crowd control. There's less time and energy available for producing motivating lessons, and the education of every child in the class suffers. There are now many schools around the developed world where education is the least of the teachers' worries – they spend their days desperately trying to hold back a tide of low-level disruption, refusal to follow instructions and, increasingly, physical violence to classmates and teachers.

The issue of discipline is as confusing for teachers these days as it is for parents. During the twentieth century the educational establishment, like the rest of Western society, swung from traditional authoritarian attitudes to much more liberal views on behaviour, with increasing focus on the rights of the individual. Concern for children's rights, culminating in 1989 in the United Nations Convention on the Rights of the Child, has led some educational policymakers to reject the notion of punishment when children break rules or breach the boundaries of acceptable behaviour, resulting in fads like the 'no blame' bullying policy mentioned earlier. Teachers, who have to try and maintain order on the ground, are often unconvinced by the 'behaviour modification strategies' foisted on them by national or local advisers.

The problem is compounded by the general erosion of respect for authority over the last few decades. But in order to control a group of thirty or so children, teachers must have authority. Research on parenting quoted on pages 281–284 suggests the most effective parental style is 'authoritative', where warmth and respect for a child's point of view are balanced by the need to maintain firm boundaries for behaviour. Teachers too have to strive for an authoritative balance. If they're too indulgent, their class will run rings around them; if they're authoritarian, their pupils are likely to erupt into bad behaviour as soon as they turn their backs.

In a morally relative society, it can be difficult for any adult to feel authoritative. It's particularly hard for a teacher, attempting to balance the interests of thirty or so children in a class. It's therefore important that schools have clearly agreed rules, to which everyone involved – children, teachers, parents, school community – are happy to subscribe. The authoritative teacher then does everything possible to respect individual children's viewpoints, while imposing and maintaining the rules in a firm but friendly fashion.

But when children flout the rules, the teacher has to be able to impose some kind of sanction, both to maintain authority and to demonstrate to all pupils that antisocial behaviour has unpleasant consequences. When dealing with children en masse, justice has to be seen to be done – if they get away with bad behaviour, it simply encourages them (and others) to push the boundaries further. Teachers usually have a sliding scale of punishments, culminating in removing the offender from the class. This demonstrates to everyone that breaking the rules, and thus ignoring one's responsibility to the group, can ultimately result in social exclusion.

In the case of the very youngest offenders, research suggests it may be possible to improve behaviour through kindness. There's now a movement in the UK to provide 'nurture groups' where trained staff work with small groups of emotionally disturbed young children to teach them social skills in less formal, more domestic settings. The children's reward for learning self-control is to be considered 'grown up' enough to return to their class.

These nurturing tactics are, however, less likely to make an impact as children grow older. Most teachers I've talked to feel that by the time children are nearing double figures, it's too late to treat misbehaviour (especially bullying) with overt kindness. The older the child, the tougher the love has to be. What's more, to encourage the others, shame has to be part of the deal. Whatever the sanction is, everyone involved in the social life of the school – teachers, parents and children – has to consider it unpleasant, or it won't have any effect. Whether the miscreant has privileges removed, is sent to a 'sin bin' until prepared to toe the line or, in the worst scenario, excluded from school altogether, there's no getting away from the fact that punishment (even if it's for *your* child) isn't pleasant.

For well-balanced and happy children, however, tough measures are seldom necessary. So rather than battling with a rising tide of bad behaviour, it makes sense for adults to work together to stop the rot before it begins, which means tackling the causes of toxic childhood syndrome both at home and at school.

*

Ensuring that all children win the must-have prizes upon which successful citizenship depends – motivation to learn, the Three Rs and the ability to get along with others – has never been easy, but aspects of contemporary culture, and the effects of that culture on children, now make the task more challenging than ever. In the circumstances, teachers and parents – the two groups with the interests of schoolchildren most at heart – would gain immensely from joining forces to tackle toxic childhood syndrome. Yet the social and cultural environment in which the syndrome flourishes has made this 'adult alliance' increasingly difficult.

While the responsibility for reinvigorating the educational adult alliance rests with schools, it also relies on parents recognising that 'red carpet treatment' for their own child at the expense of others isn't on the cards. A fiercely competitive culture isn't appropriate for the under-tens – childhood is *not* a race – but neither should children be coddled, cosseted and shielded from the consequences of their actions. The capacity to co-exist with others (which is arguably in the long run the greatest of the must-have primary prizes) relies on children learning within a safe environment how to deal with success and failure, how to cope with playground politics and how to balance their own rights as individuals with their social responsibilities to others. Schools must be supported by society (and parents have to trust them) to ensure these lessons are learned.

It's in the interests of parents, teachers and society as a whole to work for a primary education system that prepares *all* children for successful citizenship ... and to ensure that it isn't derailed by educational fads and fashions, time-wasting bureaucracy or misguided political tinkering.

DETOXING EDUCATION FOR YOUR CHILD

- Recognise from the beginning that primary education is not a race.
- Remember that the children who do well in the long run are those who

  – enjoy learning for its own sake, not just to get stars or high marks
  – are motivated to learn and don't give up easily
  – get on with other children and with their teacher, and can work well with others.

- Accept that children develop at different rates. A child who's doing wonderfully today may slow off tomorrow; a slow starter may eventually overtake everyone.
- Give heartfelt praise for your child's achievements, especially evidence of hard work and effort. Show your delight when things go well.
- *But* don't overdo the praise – if you go into raptures about everything your child does, your praise won't carry much weight when it's really justified.
- If you think your child isn't achieving as well as he or she could, keep critical comments to a minimum – discuss what's going wrong and look for ways to help.
- *But* try not to pile on the pressure. If your expectations are too high, it can damage your child's chances of success.
- The single most important way parents can help children do well is through talking with them, and encouraging them to talk. As well as the suggestions in Chapter 4, ask about your child's day at school in ways that encourage talk, for instance, 'What was the best thing that happened today, then?' 'How's that story going, the one the teacher's reading you?' 'What's this Roman project all about?' The more interest you show and the more you actively listen to their responses, the more children are likely to talk.
- Make sure your child knows what bullying is (and isn't) and how to deal with it, including reporting straight back to you and/or a teacher. There's good advice on websites such as those listed on page 224.

- Make every attempt to attend school events, no matter how dreary you find them – just by being there you demonstrate your love and support for your child, and you also send a message of support to the school. If you can't make it, explain why to your child, and try to send a substitute (for instance a grandparent, childminder or family friend).

- Keep an intelligent eye on the news about education, and make sure you know your school's take on it. But don't be swayed by excessive claims about particular educational strategies – there are no magic bullets in education, because it depends so much on the personalities of the teachers and children involved. What works for one particular class with one particular teacher may well be a complete fiasco in the classroom down the road.

HOW TO DETOX THE PARENT-SCHOOL RELATIONSHIP

- Choose a school by reading the prospectus, arranging a visit, chatting with other parents in the area – for instance, is this a school that encourages the development of 'the whole child' – not just focusing on tests? (Interestingly, schools that provide a wide and exciting curriculum often do particularly well in tests too.)

- When your child starts school, make sure you know the organisational ropes, in terms of expectations about homework, arrangements for taking children to school, collecting them and so on. Integrate these into family routines so they become second nature.

- Keep a folder for the prospectus and any other communications about school procedures and so on, and check it once in a while. It can also be useful for keeping your child's school reports and any special commendations or certificates.

- Always make an effort to turn up to parent-teacher interviews. If you can't make it, write to ask if it's possible to arrange an appointment at an alternative time. Teachers are often rushed off their feet and can't always stop for a chat about a child without notice.

- Try to be positive about school when talking about it to your child – parental attitudes rub off on children, and the more positive their attitude to school, the better they'll do. So:

  – if you had bad experiences of school yourself, don't let them influence you
  – look for things to praise about the school and your child's teacher, and hold your tongue if possible about anything that annoys you
  – don't gossip carelessly with other parents in front of your children.

- But don't lie to your child if anything's amiss. Children know when you're telling the truth. They also need to know that if anything is troubling them, they can speak openly to you about it.

- Take opportunities to get to know other parents, but beware of school-gate gossip – it's easy for rumours and misunderstandings to get out of hand. The best policy is probably 'hear no evil, see no evil, speak no evil'.

- If you're able to support the Parent Teacher Association, meetings and functions, do so. Apart from being an opportunity to exercise parent power, it's a chance to meet teachers informally and get to know the parents of your child's classmates.

Dealing with problems at school

- If something goes wrong for your child at school, help them talk it through. Try to work out what's actually happened, and help your child find a way to deal with it (see Chapter 4).
- If your child's in trouble, try to be dispassionate – don't automatically leap to his or her defence. Try to see both sides of the argument. Loving your child doesn't mean assuming he or she can do no wrong.
- On the other hand, no one knows your child, or cares about his or her welfare, as much as you. If, on serious reflection, you believe the school is wrong, you must act.
- On such occasions, don't rush in to complain in an angry or upset state of mind. Try to keep calm and use the correct channels to put across your point of view.
- Make sure you are completely aware of school rules and discipline procedures and who to contact in particular circumstances (this is where that folder with the prospectus, etc comes into its own). Don't be tempted to go 'straight to the top' as this can escalate problems rather than solving them.
- It's a good idea to write a letter about the problem first, keeping it as calm and reasonable as possible. It helps you sort out what's gone on, and you can also be sure the main facts are clearly stated (and that you don't forget any in the heat of the moment).
- Before going to any meetings, think about what outcome you would like to see – do you know what you want the school to do to sort out the issue?
- Putting things in writing from the start is also useful if it's necessary to take the case further – i.e., to school governors or county/city authorities.

PARENT POWER: WORKING WITH THE SCHOOL

As one who's been both a parent and a teacher, I know that parent–teacher liaison is one of the toughest nuts to crack, but when communication is good everyone benefits – especially the children. Many of the present difficulties in schools are compounded by lack of understanding on both sides. For instance, the parents I speak to think schools cause the educational rat race, while teachers often blame the parents. Since both schools and parents want to raise happy healthy children, it's vital to break through such pointless prejudices.

- Try in any way you can to open up lines of communication through official channels – parents' meetings, PTAs, boards of governors – and raise issues that concern you about children's welfare. When I talk in schools about the ill-effects of testing and targets, I'm amazed by the number of parents who've clearly been worried about this issue, but didn't like to say.

- The thought of school social occasions may be ghastly, but the only way to improve them is to join in. Turn up, smile, socialise, network ... and talk about your concerns. Try to avoid outright criticism – you'll get much further by looking for positive ways forward.

- Use school-gate conversations and out-of-school contact with other parents to develop positive, can-do attitudes to parent–school liaison. If you can find one way of working with the school on a particular issue, opportunities for further collaboration are very likely to arise.

- Do you have a talent (arts? sciences? practical skills?) and some spare time to help make the curriculum (or after-school clubs) come alive? Non-working parents and grandparents could be a huge resource in this respect, and there's great satisfaction to be had in passing on one's enthusiasm to another generation.

Further reading

Bill Lucas and Alistair Smith, *Help Your Child to Succeed: the Essential Guide for Parents* (Network Educational Press Ltd, 2002)

Hilary Wilce, *Help Your Child Succeed at School* (Piatkus, 2004)

Adele Faber and Elaine Mazlish, *How to Talk So Kids Can Learn: at Home and in School* (Piccadilly Press, 2003)

Noel Janis-Norton, *Could Do Better: how parents can help their child succeed at school* (Barrington Stoke, 2005)

Useful websites

Websites for help with bullying: **www.bullying.co.uk**; **www.kidscape.org.uk**; **www.parentlineplus.org.uk**

The Advisory Centre for Education: **www.ace-ed.org.uk** (independent information and advice)

Advice on education law: **www.childrenslegalcentre.com**

The official government website for education in England: **www.dfes.gov.uk**

Mind the gap

One of the aims of a state-sponsored educational system is to provide a 'level playing field' – a certain level of basic education available to all children. Another is to provide an opportunity for children from different backgrounds to mingle, and so promote greater social cohesion. The last primary class I taught back in the early 1980s included children from a wide range of backgrounds – from professional families to those of unskilled workers. They all rubbed along together, and I think both children and their parents benefited from the opportunities this gave to mix with people from different backgrounds.

However, when people lose faith in a system, those who can afford it move out. Despite rising fees, private education is flourishing – nearly 10 per cent of children are now educated outside the state system in the US and UK. Indeed, part of the reason many parents have to work so hard is that they're paying exorbitant school fees. Where they stay within the system, better-off parents are adept at manoeuvring to get their children into 'good' schools. Their support then makes the good schools better, while the less popular ones sink lower down the heap, leading to a two-tier system where some schools, especially in the inner cities, are in a desperate plight. As the effects of toxic childhood syndrome worsen, discipline problems spiral out of control, and it's sometimes hardly possible to educate children at all.

Primary teachers around the world continue to hold the line, but they haven't been helped by politicians insisting that fierce and early concentration on the Three Rs is enough to overcome disadvantaged children's problems – a contention which, in the light of research quoted so far in this book, is clearly nonsense. The UK Education Secretary has finally been forced to admit that 'we must treat seriously the possibility that – despite all our efforts – who your parents are still affects attainment as much in 2005 as it did in 1998.' Well done, that girl! But obsessive attention to tests and targets caused by political tinkering has now further hindered poor children's chances, by bringing an ever more competitive edge to the educational process. The children who suffer most from this winners-and-losers approach are the very ones we're trying so hard not to leave behind.

Extricating primary education from this rat race isn't going to be easy. Now it's seen in such intensely competitive terms, better-off parents are understandably keen to ensure their own children are among the winners, so they don't worry unduly when poorer children fall by the wayside. But they *will* worry, a decade or so down the line, when those infant 'losers' are transformed into disaffected youths hanging threateningly around the mall, teenage mums devouring taxpayers' money, or criminals who don't see why they should give a damn about the welfare of the moneyed classes. Whether we like it or not, the widening gap affects us all – and it's in everyone's interest to have a state education system that works, for rich and poor alike.

CHAPTER EIGHT

THE WORD ON THE STREET

'It takes a whole village to educate a child' as Hillary Clinton reminded us in the 1990s. Children's development is affected not only by their parents, but by other members of the family, friends and figures in the local community. Indeed, the neuroscientist Steven Pinker argues that the influence of this wider community is more important than that of parents themselves.

The village the children of the developed world now inhabit is the electronic village of mass communications and entertainment. Many of them spend at least as much of their leisure time on screen-based activities as they do with the real people in their lives. So what children watch on TV, film and DVD and what they do on computers and console games clearly affects their development. The main issues arising from their direct interaction with electronic media are dealt with in the next chapter. However, there's another, highly insidious way in which these media affect children's lives, through the influence of marketing on their play, their friendships and their culture.

Peer pressure has always been an important part of growing up, but in previous generations, children's games and playground inter-actions were largely their own private concern. Fads and crazes would come and go, often related to the adult world, but very much under children's control. But in recent decades, as screen-based activity has grown, what happens in the playground has increasingly moved under the control of the marketing industry. Most parents seem unaware – or are in denial – that behind the TV programmes and computer games keeping their children entertained lurks an army of anonymous manipulators – marketing executives and child psychologists employed by big business to capture the hearts and minds of the next generation of consumers. These very powerful 'electronic villagers' now have a huge impact on the culture of childhood and the way children relate to each other.

From creative play to 'toy consumption'

One obvious aspect of this cultural change is the changing nature of toys. Psychologists explain that, especially in the case of very young children, the simpler the item, the more likely it is to stimulate creative play. A cloth thrown over a table can create a den, an empty box can be transformed through the imagination into a car, a boat, anything in the world ... or, indeed, the universe. Symbolic play of this kind has been significant throughout history in developing children's imagination and problem-solving skills. Similarly, children's natural creative drive can be satisfied using simple materials – sand, water, paper, coloured pencils, a dressing-up box of cast-off clothes, household junk for making models ...

The problem is that old clothes and household junk are free, and free stuff has no place in a highly developed consumer culture. Toy companies have therefore devised ever more brightly coloured sophisticated substitutes (often labelled 'educational') that parents can pay for. And advertisers have devoted much time, money and energy to convincing children that these substitutes will make them happy. Sadly, since many of these toys leave little to the imagination, parents around the world have noticed that – once the excitement of acquisition has worn off – children don't seem to play as much as they used to.

In the last couple of decades, there's been a further, even more worrying move towards more technologically based play: a growing number of toys are merely a stepping stone from one screen-based activity to another – part of an all-embracing multimedia experience that usually starts with a film or TV show. Films aimed at children are now designed from the outset to optimise merchandising opportunities, including toys (dolls, models, etc), paraphernalia (pencil cases, lunch boxes, clothing and so on) and website and console games. Children's TV shows come complete with the same range of consumer products. The toys that marketeers encourage children to covet are no longer levers to their own creativity, but bridges from one type of passive, sedentary entertainment to another.

Marketing guru Martin Lindstrom points out that this trend has always been fiercest in Japan, where technology took hold of the public imagination particularly early – and with minimal government interference – so that electronic games and toys have been fully integrated with movie and TV merchandising since the 1970s. Nowadays, almost all Japanese products are linked in this way, and Japanese children are more addicted to screens than any others in the world. As mentioned in the last chapter, by the end of the twentieth century, authorities in Japan had become alarmed at the lack of creativity in their younger generation – a classic case of reaping what you sow. Sadly, at present the entire developed world is sowing the same imagination-rotting, creativity-dumbing whirlwind.

Strangers on screen

Another worrying feature of contemporary play – covered in Chapter 2 – is that it seldom takes place outdoors, and one of the main reasons for the retreat inside is 'stranger danger'. Yet the same parents who are desperate to protect their children from strangers outside their home are happy to leave even the youngest in the care of strangers on screen for hours on end. And these strangers, or the promoters behind them, usually have something to sell.

We are all, whatever our age, constantly manipulated by the mass media, but most adults are savvy enough to recognise the manipulation, understand the differences between real and make-believe, enjoy our viewing and make rational decisions based on what we see. Children are not. The younger they are, the more the distinction between TV and reality is blurred. Responsible programme-makers realise this and take it into account – but marketing agencies are not renowned for responsible behaviour. Their interest in children is to sell more stuff. And as well as the adverts around the edges of TV programmes, marketeers increasingly reach out to children via the Internet, console games, mobile phones and – through sponsorship and product placement – many other aspects of their daily life.

Children today are growing up in what US psychiatrist Susan Linn calls 'a marketing maelstrom'. The average child in the US, UK and Australia sees between 20,000 and 40,000 TV commercials a year. Research has shown that up to the age of about eight, children are not aware of marketeers' intent – they see adverts merely as an enjoyable form of entertainment and information. Indeed, they have to be eleven or twelve before they can articulate a critical understanding of marketing messages and by this age many have been effectively brainwashed. For this reason, Sweden has banned TV marketing to children until twelve, and countries across the developed world are becoming increasingly uneasy about its effects.

In the past, advertisements aimed at children related mainly to childish things – toys, chocolate bars, breakfast cereals – and were relatively low-budget affairs. Over the last twenty years there's been a huge change. In his 1992 book *Kids as Customers*, US marketing strategist James McNeal alerted big business to the potential of the children's market: 'Kids are the most unsophisticated of all consumers; they have the least and therefore want the most. Consequently, they are in a perfect position to be taken.' Marketing departments and advertising agencies now devote massive budgets to children, especially to the group labelled 'tweens' (eight- to fourteen-year-olds).

Most adults are scarcely aware of this bombardment – sophisticated marketing techniques aimed at pre-teens simply don't impinge on adult lives – and their own memories of ads are from another, more innocent age. But as Susan Linn says, 'Comparing the advertisements of three decades ago to the commercialism that permeates our children's world is like comparing a BB gun to a smart bomb ... the explosion of marketing aimed at children today is precisely targeted, refined by scientific method and honed by child psychologists – in short, it is more pervasive and intrusive than ever.'

Children as customers

There are several reasons for marketeers' change of pitch. The first is that contemporary children have increasing amounts of money to spend, and increasing access to their parents' disposable income. Marketeers now specifically target 'guilt money' – pocket money and presents doled out by parents who are worried that long hours at work keep them away from their children. Conveniently for the marketeers, the absence of parents at home means children spend more time watching TV, so there's plenty of opportunity to groom young consumers.

In fact, the long-hours culture creates a perfect circle for selling more stuff:

- Children are unhappy because of parental absence.
- Advertisements offer happiness through purchase of products.
- Children besiege parents with requests for said products and guilt-stricken parents throw money at the problem.
- The purchase makes children and parents happy for a nano-second ...
- ... Then unhappiness returns because presents are no substitute for presence, and the cycle goes on.

Children want ever more stuff, and parents have to earn more money to pay for it. Done deal.

Another factor in the change of emphasis has been the discovery that this 'pester power' works not only for children's products but for everything families buy – from cars, holidays and entertainment to food, household items and even cleaning products. As avid TV watchers, children are able to pass on marketing messages to parents, and as avid consumers they're quick to pick up on what's in and what's out. So the marketing industry has recruited children to work on their behalf, and 'nag-factor' now features in all major campaigns for family purchases. US market research shows that 67 per cent of car purchases are influenced by children while – as indicated in Chapter 1 – the younger generation has considerable input into family food shopping. In one consumer report, 100 per cent of parents of two to five-year olds agreed that their children have a major influence on their food and snack purchases. Indeed, pester power has become essential to marketing – a US study showed that sales of a product declined by a third if children didn't ask for it, even more in the case of toys and entertainment.

A third reason for targeting the young – and perhaps the most sinister of all – is to initiate them as early as possible into the cult of the brand. In a cut-throat consumer culture, brand awareness and brand loyalty are priceless assets, so the marketeers' aim is to ensnare consumers while 'the imagination is warm and impressions are permanent'. They devote millions to impressing children that a particular brand of fizzy drink, snack food, clothing, transport, entertainment or whatever will make their lives more complete than all the competing brands.

The marketing industry now works on the principle that brand loyalty can be encouraged in children as young as two through exposure to brand logos and mascots on screen and on products they enjoy. Three-year olds can be influenced to ask for brands by name. By three and a half children are ripe for the picking. At this age, they can be convinced that certain brands transmit certain qualities to the purchaser, so the marketing strategy moves from awareness-raising to creating dependence on the particular brand they're pushing.

Put bluntly, this means that big business now engages in complex mind games with children. Given the tender age of the quarry, this seems an unequal contest – amounting more or less to mass brainwashing. Marketeers argue that children are increasingly consumer savvy, but they're unlikely to be as savvy as adults armed with multi-million-pound budgets and the latest psychological weapons. As Nancy Shalek, president of a major US advertising agency, once explained to colleagues: 'Advertising at its best is making people feel that without their product, you're a loser. Kids are very sensitive to that ... You open up emotional vulnerabilities and it's very easy to do with kids because they're the most emotionally vulnerable.'

Sugar and spice ...

In targeting children, advertisers are acutely aware of gender differences. While many parents in the late twentieth century tried earnestly to protect their children from gender bias, the forces of worldwide marketing had other ideas. They immediately appreciated the claims of evolutionary biologists that the male and female of the species have different attitudes and interests. And by targeting the differences, they emphasise and encourage them, which makes the two markets even easier to analyse for the future.

Girls are, on the whole, inclined towards nurturing. They're interested in other people and have well-developed powers of empathy (the downside of which, as many parents know, is a finely honed capacity for manipulation). Marketing forces have chosen pink to symbolise these female qualities, and the psyches of small girls are addressed through a cloud of pink smog, in which swim a vast array of collectible dolls, small furry animals and grooming products. (Grooming is of great evolutionary significance. In the remote past, young human females probably bonded by picking fleas out of each other's fur; their modern counterparts delight in fixing each other's hair, but the manufacturers lure them into fixing Barbie's instead.) Though less interested in technology than boys, girls can be attracted to the computer by websites such as Barbie's EverythingGirl site – all-singing, all-dancing pink girly glamour – and Hello Kitty's chummy home page.

The cloying schmaltziness of girl-orientated marketing leads most parents to withdraw in distaste, hoping their daughters will soon grow out of it. But this early initiation into pinkness is just the beginning. Another strong evolutionary yearning present in all young children is the need to belong to the group, which opens up social and emotional vulnerabilities ideal for market exploitation.

Over the last twenty years, brands have become immensely important for establishing children's credentials in the playground. An eleven-year-old girl interviewed in Martin Lindstrom's book BRANDchild puts it this way: 'I love brands ... Brands not only tell me who I am, but also protect me from problems with the others in my class.' Increasingly, children are learning to judge themselves and others in terms of what they eat, drink, wear or own. As one UK teacher told me, 'Even the youngest can recognise the labels – the kids that wear supermarket clothes or bring own-brand crisps in their lunch boxes are looked down on, the ones with the right labels are cool.'

... and all things nice

Marketeers spend fortunes trying to ensure that their brand is the cool brand, the one that offers most belonging, most protection. A major weapon in their marketing armoury, particularly effective for girls, is the KAGOY strategy (Kids Are Getting Older Younger). Little girls have always wanted to be grown-up like their mothers – to dress like adults, wear make-up, appear sophisticated. To begin with, they aspire to be Disney heroines – all billowing ballgowns and fairy palaces – so there are, of course, plenty of dolls and accessories to feed this dream ... but the KAGOY strategy leads them rapidly to an appreciation of contemporary fashion and style. Girly magazines, websites and TV programmes nurture this interest, and the possibilities for consumption become limitless.

Manufacturers have therefore pushed KAGOY further and further down the age range, turning the tiniest of tots into fashion victims. Whole stores are devoted to trendy clothes for toddlers and many parents fork out a fortune on designer outfits. Selling adult fashion trends to children inevitably leads to the premature sexualisation of little girls, with five- and six-year-olds arriving at school in sexy thongs and lacy bras, and pre-teens plastering themselves with make-up to attract 'boyz'. Whether this sexualisation damages little girls at the time hasn't been established, but there's no doubt that, across the developed world, teenage girls are becoming sexually active at an increasingly early age.

The collateral effects are also worrying – when children dressed up like dockside tarts throng the streets, it's scarcely surprising that paedophilia thrives (see Chapter 9). And as parents became more paranoid about paedophiles, social attitudes to children have changed. When I was teaching thirty years ago, it was natural to comfort distressed youngsters by sitting them on your knee or putting an arm around their shoulders – try that on today and you'd be hauled up before the sexual offences police before you could say 'Lolita'.

Alongside a preoccupation with fashion goes a preoccupation with body image. Beset on all sides by images of physical perfection (which, in contemporary terms, means stick-thin with improbable Barbie breasts), girls trying to fit into the mould of 'cool' are subject to horrendous pressure. A report from the Social Issues Research Centre in Oxford found female dissatisfaction with their appearance begins early: 'Human infants begin to recognise themselves in mirrors at about two years old and female humans begin to dislike what they see only a few years later.' In a recent survey nearly three-quarters of seven-year-olds said they want to be slimmer because they believe it will make them more popular. It's ironic that many of these children probably *are* overweight due to junk-food marketing. Sadly, many parents feed junk food with one hand and body-image paranoia with the other – in 2005 health spas for pre-teens became the latest UK craze ('Sometimes I don't feel comfortable about my body and the spa helps me,' said one little girl, who goes to the spa with her mum). Little wonder eating disorders are rife across the developed world.

Slugs and snails ...

Marketing to boys exploits the same human vulnerabilities, but with a masculine slant. Collectibles for boys are quirky as opposed to pink, and generally linked to conflict, hierarchies or mechanics. Pokémon, Yu-Gi-Oh!, DragonBall Z, Medabots and Cardcaptors all satisfy the infant yearning to collect while simultaneously appealing to the competitive instinct of the human male. This competitive instinct is known among marketeers as 'mastery' or 'dominion', and involves appealing to little boys' inbuilt desire for 'power, force, mastery, domination, control ... '

For some boys the 'dominion instinct' leads to the sports field – and the opportunity to burn off aggression through activity. But why bother with all that effort and team building when there are now many sedentary ways of achieving the same end? Boys are naturally drawn to technology, and console and website games provide opportunities to score without the effort of physical activity or social interaction. Slogans such as Xbox's 'Life is short, play more' and Nintendo's 'Life's a game' link the idea of 'play' and 'games' with the products of technology. Most children today associate these words not with outdoor play or sport but with virtual, indoor experiences.

Gaming enthusiasts argue that the best computer games can increase players' IQ, perseverance and concentration, but most games for the under-tens involve little more than a few undemanding choices, coupled with mouse control and hand-eye coordination. In fact, in the case of many boys, the appeal of the games is not only the challenge but the thrill of forbidden violence. Marketeers know that, although most parents disapprove, the young male psyche is deeply attracted to violence, aggression and war. In most countries the law stops them from selling these things directly to children but there have always been ways round the law – including some that allow children to demonstrate another sort of 'mastery'.

An astounding number of pre-teens claim in surveys to have played violent games such as *Mortal Kombat* and *Grand Theft Auto III*. Since these are 18+ products, I'd always taken these claims as bravado – till my daughter came home from babysitting in a respectable British home with the news that her young charges (boys aged six and nine) were playing *GTA III* all evening. When she asked where they'd got it, they grinned and said that mum had bought it for them. So I asked my twenty-year-old researcher to give me a demonstration of *GTA III* and was taken aback by the realistic and gratuitous violence. The player is encouraged to steal cars, massacre pedestrians, and engage in other random violent crimes, including beating passers-by into pools of blood with a baseball bat. Since the graphics are extremely realistic, the feeling that you're actually beating someone to a pulp is quite strong. Although my researcher thought this no big deal (he's highly educated with a keen sense of irony), to someone who knows about children's social and emotional development the game definitely merits its 18+ rating. I was recounting this story to a friend and mother of a ten-year-old, when I noticed her become rather agitated. Eventually she admitted she'd got her son a copy too, 'because all his friends have it' – as a PlayStation virgin she had no idea what the game involved.

... and puppy dogs' tails

The yearning for acceptance by the group is just as strong in boys as in girls, and the reliance on brands to make them acceptable may be even greater – in a recent survey, 75 per cent of boys said they like to wear clothes with popular labels, as opposed to 67 per cent of girls. However, the definition of 'cool' is different. For marketing aimed at males, cool has 'edge' – it's often humorous, sometimes rather callous, usually anti-authority – and conning a copy of *Grand Theft Auto III* from a mother who'd ban it if she knew the contents is a very good example. Part of the appeal of machismo and violence for many small boys is that it appals the women in their lives, so there's considerable peer pressure for boys to act and talk big, play smart and put one over on the womenfolk.

Successful marketing of 'cool' involves lots of examples of just this sort of behaviour. It's usually funny because ironic humour helps to slip products past the post-modern parent, but by pandering to children's enthusiasm for backchat, sneakiness and challenging authority, it sends a message of endorsement – even encouragement – for breaking parental rules. As contemporary parents often themselves want to appear cool and edgy, they're often happy to be carried along with the joke – until it's too late to reverse their children's anti-authority attitudes. The children's channel Nickelodeon (slogan: Kids rule) has a particular fondness for this type of cool, which it claims is empowering for children.

The potential ill-effects of on-screen violence have been widely discussed (see Chapter 9), but there's been little attention to the long-term effects of encouraging an ironic, adult-mocking, anti-authority attitude in young children. Boys especially are very open to messages that, as sociologist Juliet Schor puts it, 'Adults enforce a repressive and joyless world in contrast to what kids and products do when they're left in peace.' Parental exhortations to eat greens, complete homework, finish chores and get a good night's sleep are much less attractive than assurances that 'Life's a game'. Schor suggests that the long-term effect of drip-feeding children – especially boys – with 'edgy cool' messages is to drive a wedge between them and the adults in their lives. I'd go further. The messages that marketing feeds daily to our children now amount to a gradual, oh-so-ironic subversion of civilised values.

Of course, there has always been a subversive, anti-authority children's culture, which in many ways is healthy and a vital part of the 'real play' I've been recommending throughout this book. Every teacher knows that playgrounds are full of games, stories and rhymes that celebrate the gross, the ghoulish and the scatalogical – and usually we turn a blind eye to it, because children are like that and, above all, 'boys will be boys'. But a children's culture is not the same as an unholy alliance between children and the forces of international marketing. In the words of Professor Mark Crispin Miller of New York University, 'It's part of the official advertising world view that your parents are creeps, teachers are weirdos and idiots, authority figures are laughable, nobody can really understand kids except the corporate sponsor.' By openly encouraging and validating the subversive side of childhood, marketeers are unleashing forces it's becoming increasingly difficult to control.

For instance, one decivilising effect of edgy cool is its contribution to the anti-education ethos currently destroying many children's lives – especially boys. When boys fail to prosper in a high-stakes testing regime, many choose to ignore school values and espouse an alternative playground culture. In *The Economics of Acting White*, Harvard economist Roland G. Fryer tells how a high-achieving boy moving into a new area fell foul of this culture: 'I became a target ... I got all As and was hated for it; I spoke correctly and was called a punk. I had to learn a new language simply to deal with the threats.' The nine-year-old boys in this story were black American, but that same anti-establishment, anti-educational culture can be found in playgrounds in less-advantaged areas around the developed world, whatever the colour of the children concerned. Indeed, it is increasingly finding its way into the leafy suburbs. It's difficult for parents or teachers to motivate children to try hard at school if the prevailing pre-teen culture – summed up in everything they wear, eat and do with their spare time – is anti-effort, anti-authority and anti-academic.

It's the economy, stupid

A teacher I interviewed in Spain in late 2004 put it this way: 'Sometimes it seems that what we're trying to teach the children in school is at odds with everything they're learning outside.' It seemed to her that honesty, conscientiousness, hard work and concern for others were no longer valued in the world beyond school, and children defined their worth not by any moral standards, but by what they owned and their social kudos with their peers. When I argued that most parents, like me, still believed in the virtues she'd listed, she replied, 'Maybe – but they're not passing them on to their children. They're just buying them off.'

Discussing her words with parents over the last year, it's been disturbing how many feel powerless to assert these 'old-fashioned values' in the face of cultural influences. Most believe that possessions shouldn't hold such importance in their children's lives, but beset by a combination of pester power and the very reasonable desire to protect their offspring from social exclusion, they see no option but to hand over money to purchase a place in the in-group. Only the most strong-minded can resist the excuse that 'everyone else does it, so you can't let your child be the odd one out'.

I've also encountered a few parents who don't see it as a problem. They feel that in a consumer culture, love really does equal stuff – indeed, they're keen to push their offspring up the social ladder by investing in even bigger and better brands – thus upping the ante of infant aspiration. They don't particularly disapprove of their daughters' obsession with appearance or their sons' burgeoning insolence, believing these qualities will serve them well in a competitive world.

Perhaps they're right. There's always the possibility that, as human beings evolve, values evolve with them and that, very soon, 'It's the economy, stupid' will prove to be the ultimate truth. Perhaps, as the consumer culture spreads across the globe, what you look like and own will be more important than what you are. And as mothers and fathers demonstrate their love for their children by giving them more and more stuff, money will eventually become the new currency of love ... ?

In his book BRAND*child*, Martin Lindstrom looks forward to this brave new world. He explains that 'as formal religion in the Western world continues to erode, brands move in to fill the vacuum'. Children are apparently destined to be the main evangelists in this process, since marketeers will increasingly seek to 'make children stakeholders of the company and so part of the company's destiny'. If Lindstrom's right, and marketing continues to follow current trends, the next generation can look forward to a future based on superficial appearances, disrespect, hedonism and instant gratification. Somehow, I don't think that's going to be enough to keep a complex technological culture afloat.

Heroes and villains

Another significant factor in contemporary children's lives that's been increasingly corrupted is the role model. Human beings learn largely by imitation, and in the early years they imitate parents and other family members. As time goes by, teachers or older children can also become important role models – as can admirable personalities from history, TV and other media. These role models from the wider world have always affected children's behaviour and aspirations.

When 5,000 parents were asked which fictional character they felt most influenced the way their children behaved, top of the list, rather depressingly, was Bart Simpson. Bart's most famous quote, according to *The Simpsons* quotes website, is 'I'm through with working; working is for chumps'. (Response from Homer: 'Son, I'm proud of you. I was twice your age before I figured that one out.')

I have to admit to loving *The Simpsons* and sniggering along with jokes like that. The trouble is, while adults appreciate ironic humour, children under the age of about eight take such statements literally, and even for many older pre-teens satire remains a mystery. We have no idea how many Bart Simpson act-a-likes have actually swallowed his philosophy whole. Possibly quite a few, because in the same survey 79 per cent of parents said their child was often badly behaved and 68 per cent reckoned the present generation was the worst behaved in history.

There are also many real-life role models: sportsmen and women, popular musicians, TV stars (especially child actors) and, in a celebrity culture, reality-TV contestants whose main talent is attention-seeking. I recently visited a school in a part of inner-city London that bred one of the 'stars' of *Big Brother*, and the teachers told me how difficult it now is to motivate children who expect to become famous overnight without effort or qualifications ('like Jade did').

Sadly, all we can expect many contemporary role models to model are foul language, a sleazy lifestyle, cheating (on the sports field and in their private lives), and the pursuit of money above all else. Maybe the people who make it big in a competitive culture aren't really the sort of people we want our children to look up to. Even those who lead comparatively blameless private and public lives are seldom without commercial associations: anyone perceived as cool by children is immediately jumped on by the marketeers and used to sell more stuff.

There is little parents can do to counter the influence of such role models: they're out there and children are inevitably exposed to them. What's more, even traditional institutions now seem to accept them, warts and all. Susan Linn tells the story of the mother of a seven-year-old girl who rang her school to complain at the use of a scantily clad image of Britney Spears (whose lifestyle at the time was becoming increasingly seedy) in a healthy food promotion. The school authorities could not see her problem. They did, however, offer to mitigate her concern by colouring in Britney's midriff with black marker pen. In a world gone so entirely mad, parents' only immediate line of defence is to establish better role models at home, and to establish them early.

Mind you, this is a very powerful course of action, since children are at their most impressionable between birth and about eight. That's why the Jesuits famously said, 'Give me a child till he is eight years old and he is mine for ever', and it's why advertisers are so anxious to capture this age group's brand loyalty. If parents spend time with their children, imbuing them with the values they believe will serve them best, and modelling those values themselves, the chances of Bart or Britney making a significant impact at a later date are much reduced.

*

During research for this chapter I've been shocked by the extent to which children's play and culture has been invaded by consumerism. Peer pressure, subtly directed by the forces of mass marketing, has even begun to undermine the relationship between children and the adults who care for them. Playgrounds have become places where creativity means re-enacting last night's TV show and 'cool', in the form of branded products and clothes, is the accepted route to social success.

Yet we know – and psychologists continually reaffirm – that this is not the route to happiness. Researchers in Australia found that happy youngsters reckon they feel good as a result of healthy attitudes and the satisfaction of pursuing worthwhile goals, whatever the outcome might be. On the other hand, depressed children are more likely to believe happiness comes from fame, money and looking good. So girls won't build self-esteem by matching themselves against impossible images of physical 'perfection', and boys won't develop strength of character from anti-adult backchat, bullying or swaggering about like Rambo. What they will gain from exposure to an increasingly aggressive consumer culture is intensification of the three major characteristics of toxic childhood syndrome: distractibility, impulsivity and self-obsession.

It's up to the real-life adults in children's lives to mount an offensive against the current excesses of consumer culture. Providing time, loving attention and sound role models for one's own children is an excellent start, but the playground culture won't change until marketing forces are reined in. At present, all children – no matter how well brought up at home – have to withstand the fashion-victim ethos of the playground. A ban on advertising to children, as in Sweden, may be one way forward. We should also be looking at what Ed Mayo of the National Consumer Council calls 'the bandit country of the Internet'. But we can't wait for governments, in thrall to big business, to come up with such suggestions themselves. They'll only do so if parents exercise their democratic power and work together to rid the electronic village of those who would manipulate their children's minds.

DETOXING THE CONSUMER CULTURE

- Monitor what children watch on TV, films and DVD – keep home entertainment in a shared area of the house and watch with them as often as possible.
- Keep an eye on ads and marketing, watch out for trends and be aware of the ways marketeers target children.
- Limit young children's viewing to non-commercial stations, such as CBeebies, or selected DVDs and videos.
- When they begin to watch commercial stations, play 'Spot the advertisements' to help them learn the difference between entertainment and marketing.
- Talk to your child about advertising, products and brands. Watch adverts together and discuss how the marketeers target people's hopes, fears and needs. Discuss

  – how pictures, music, slogans and so on can affect the way you feel and your attitude to the product being advertised
  – how well products they've tried live up to advertising promises
  – whether the families in the ads correspond to real life (are they like real people?)
  – how far stuff can bring contentment, and what else is important
  – what key advertising words like *freedom, choice, love, natural, exciting* really mean.

- When watching ads with your children, play 'What aren't they telling us?' (what facts about the product might be missed out and why?), e.g., when an ad says a food product is 'low in fat', does it fail to mention other calorific ingredients, such as sugar?
- Video their favourite programmes and teach your child how to fast-forward during ads.
- Do some consumer testing with your child and friends. Try 'blind tests' of food and drinks (e.g., baked beans, cereals, ketchup, soft drinks, colas) mixing

famous brand products and supermarket own labels. Can they tell the difference and how much does advertising influence their guesses?

- Don't give in to pester power. The earlier in a child's life you make a stand on this the better – but whatever the age, once you've decided, be firm. If you stick with it, your child will eventually realise it's not on.
- Have clear, fair guidelines on money and spending. Decide what you will/won't pay for on a regular basis, then agree on levels of pocket money – if children want something extra to what you provide, teach them to save for it or wait for birthday/Christmas/other regular present-giving time.
- Involve children in making consumer decisions that use marketing information wisely, along with other considerations:

  – let them help make shopping lists and discuss food choices (see Chapter 1)
  – discuss other family purchases (cars, holidays, etc.), listen respectfully to their contributions and involve them in reasoned choices.

- Limit exposure to consumer culture by doing other things with your children, such as family outings, activities and hobbies, making things and so on (see next section).

HOW TO ENCOURAGE CREATIVE PLAY

Babies and toddlers

- Very young children don't need encouragement to use their imagination – parents have to be discouraged from stopping them! Create safe environments where they can move and experiment, both inside and out.
- Make a box or basket of interesting but safe items, such as wooden spoons, large pine cones and shells, crackly packaging, discarded lids or boxes, bits of fabric, ribbon or fur. Let your child select items and watch what they do – join in, taking the lead from your child.
- Read and talk about picture books with your child – this will provide lots of ideas for play. Shared TV will give ideas as well.
- Give your toddler cheap items and let them experiment indoors, e.g.:

  – a large empty box can become a car, boat, space rocket
  – a cloth or sheet can become a den, a bed for dolls or soft toys, a hiding place
  – pots and pans can be filled and emptied, banged to make music, piled up, knocked down, carried about.

- Choose somewhere you can make a mess (outdoors? a tiled area?) and on different occasions let your child play with sand, water, mud, paint, bubbles, clay, cooking ingredients, snow, any interesting things from the natural and man-made world. Provide lots of sticks and spoons for mixing and containers for filling and emptying, and stay close by on safety watch.
- Let children know that you really value these activities.
- Ensure that other adults who look after your child know you value these activities too.

Older children

- Children will play at what they have experienced. The rich experiences offered to them will inform their play and explorations of the world. Going to places, even familiar everyday places very near to them, meeting people, exploring the world around them all provide fuel for play.

- Older children still enjoy messing and discovering with all the equipment listed above. Just leave them to it and see what they do. Continue to let children know that you really value these activities and ensure that other adults who look after your child know this too.

- Carry on sharing books together and chatting about the ideas they inspire.

- Provide household junk and packaging, along with glue, sticking tape and paint, and encourage children to make models and equipment for their play. Don't expect it to be impressive – it's the making that counts, not the product.

- Show how to make a den by throwing a cloth or sheet over a table. Encourage children to look for other ways of making dens, houses, castles, forts, mountains, planets, etc.

- Provide paper, paint, crayons, felt pens, glue, coloured scraps, glitter and suggest making greetings cards, posters for family events, books, albums, or just pictures 'out of your head'.

- Play some music (not just what's in the charts) – listen to it, move to it, try making it with anything around.

- Go out collecting – leaves, stones, shells, cones, insects, worms, tadpoles … (if it's alive, look after it and watch it grow).

- Provide a box of old clothes, shoes, hats, beads, ribbons, fabrics, etc for dressing-up games. Add to this with cheap exotic purchases from second-hand shops.

- Buy a cat-litter tray and encourage your child to make 'small worlds' (farms, islands, alien planets, dinosaur world, etc) inspired by your reading or talk. Or help make a doll's house from boxes stuck together, creating the furniture from matchboxes.

- Children love cooking or making mixtures and potions in bottles and jars from household items. Let them become chefs, scientists, inventors, witches or wizards – but keep an eye on safety.

- Don't feel you always have to provide playthings. It's good for older children to think up activities and play for themselves.

DETOXING ROLE MODELS

- Make sure you, your partner and other adults in charge are the sort of role models you want your child to copy.
- As children acquire heroes beyond the family, talk to them about the good qualities these heroes show. Discuss any aspects of the character your child may not understand (such as: why is it all right for Spiderman to fight people sometimes?).
- Keep an eye on the TV characters children admire – if they start imitating their speech or behaviour, talk about the character and why they like them. Don't be afraid to discourage your child if they've chosen an inappropriate hero.
- Similarly, when children show an interest in pop stars and other celebrities, talk and listen to your child's opinions. Encourage careful thought about people's worth. What characteristics does your child think are really important? And do these characters live up to their standards?
- If you're a single mother, do everything you can to provide a suitable male role model for your child (such as a family member, a male friend, a youth group leader) – someone who'll spend time with him and be there to give advice and support.

PARENT POWER – PUTTING THE MARKETEERS IN THEIR PLACE

Despite warnings that the content of this chapter is 'frightening', I've resisted advice to tone it down because I believe the impact of aggressive marketing on children *is* frightening and the only way to stop it is parent power. If you agree, the obvious step is to work with other parents to stem the tide.

- Talk to other parents about the effects of advertising on children.
- Log on to some of the websites below. If you agree with them, get involved. Just adding your name to a petition will help, but actually getting together with other people who feel strongly about the issue helps most. Pooling ideas, working together and networking are the best ways to promote change.
- Read up on the issue – the books recommended below by Juliet Schor and Susan Linn provide suggestions for bringing this issue to public attention.
- Let your child's school know of your views and wishes.
- Make your feelings known to all the politicians who represent you. When they're looking for re-election, ask what they're doing about aggressive marketing to children. In the meantime, you could write and ask them to lend their support to moves such as banning advertising to the under-twelves.
- The main point is to speak up. If parents don't speak up for the welfare of children – all children – who will?

Further reading

Diane Rich, Denise Casanova, Annabelle Dixon, Mary Jane Drummond, Andrea Durrant, Cathy Myer, *First Hand Experiences: What Matters to Children* (Rich Learning Opportunities, 2005)
Juliet Schor *Born to Buy* (Simon & Schuster, 2004)
Susan Linn, *Consuming Kids: the Hostile Takeover of Childhood* (The New Press, 2004)

Useful websites

The Compass think tank is running a UK campaign against the commercialisation of childhood:
www.compassline.org.uk/campaigns.asp
Media Smart (a media literacy project, initially focusing on advertising):
www.mediasmart.org.uk
Advertising Standards Authority (for complaints about the content of adverts): **www.asa.org.uk**
Sustain: the alliance for food and farming, which runs a campaign to protect children from junk food advertising and promotion:
www.childrensfoodcampaign.co.uk
The National Consumer Council (for information about consumer protection, including the *Shopping Generation* report on children):
www.ncc.org.uk
US campaign for a commercial-free childhood:
www.commercialexploitation.com
US campaign about children and the media:
www.childrennow.org/issues/media/index.html

Mind the gap

A happy childhood shouldn't depend on money, and in the past – before the market took over children's lives – it didn't. As one who grew up contentedly playing with cardboard boxes and dressing-up clothes, I can vouch for this. But when 'what you are is what you own', poverty is personal. Camilla Batmang-helidjh, who has devoted her life to working with poor children in Southwark, London, says that 'the poverty in Britain is worse than poor countries because it's so isolating. The discrepancy is staring you in the face all the time – on TV, in the shops.' Children learn very early to associate lack of money with lack of dignity.

The post-industrial democratic dream, in which dignity and respect do not rely on the circumstances of one's birth, is based on the assumption that ability and hard work offer an escape route from poverty. But as opportunities for play decline (*real* play: on the sports field, in the playground or the imagination), children's natural abilities are less likely to emerge – and a narrow, restrictive educational system is less likely to nurture them. And when the marketeers who've hijacked peer pressure endorse the pursuit of cool – edgy, ironic, anti-authority – it's hard for any child to escape the message that 'working is for chumps'.

Instead, the most vulnerable children learn to look for fairytale endings, to hope – even expect – that fame and fortune will tumble from the heavens, as it did for Jade and Chantelle. This makes them particularly vulnerable to the implicit message of celebrity culture: 'Seek attention – by whatever means – and it shall be thine.' If their parents are unable to provide positive role-models at home, and the traditional social role models (teachers, religious leaders, law enforcers) are undermined, the behaviour of those strangers on screen is the only guidance around.

The assault on childhood by the forces of marketing over recent decades has thus undermined the egalitarian ethos upon which democracy depends. Along with other aspects of toxic childhood, it has contributed significantly to the decline of social mobility in the world's richest nations. If we wish to reinstate the principle of equality of opportunity, we have to change the culture in which all children grow up. We have to protect them – if necessary, by the force of law – from an increasingly aggressive marketing industry.

CHAPTER NINE

THE ELECTRONIC VILLAGE

It's now over half a century since families began the move into Marshall McLuhan's electronic, global village. But for most of that time people have had a simple way of returning to real-time reality: it was called the 'off switch'. It's only in the last couple of decades that electric speed has overtaken real time, as technology has invaded every aspect of our life and work. PCs, the Internet, the web and mobile phones mean the electronic village is around us 24/7, whether we like it or not. There doesn't seem to be an 'off switch' any more, just a welter of remote controls.

On the whole, most adults seem happy enough in the electronic village – we may have to run twice as fast to stay in the same place, but it's an infinitely more interesting, comfortable and entertaining place than the world our parents and grandparents inhabited. Perhaps McLuhan's dream is coming true? Old geographical and national boundaries do seem to be dissolving: young Britons feel as close to *Friends* and *Neighbours* in New York and Melbourne as those in their own street, and the world community reacts as one to sporting triumphs and natural disasters. Television has already helped bring about the change in women's status: if it continues to challenge ancient prejudices it could also help overcome racism, homophobia and other social evils. Maybe the global village will eventually become a truly democratic community, where everyone has the chance of self-realisation (without interfering with the self-realisation of others).

Clearly, however, this utopian vision depends on everyone sticking to democratic principles. And that depends on each new generation of children being able to think, learn and behave well enough to get themselves an education and keep the component parts of the village working. For that, as *Toxic Childhood* has shown, they need genuine human nurture, which must proceed at biological, not electric speed. Children need the security of a real human family, opportunities to experience and learn about the world at first hand, real friends and neighbours, and human values that will help them resist the siren calls of the market. For that to happen, we have to round up the remote controls and reinvent the 'off switch'.

The electronic babysitter

TV watching now begins not long after birth. It's been commonplace in Japan since the 1980s, when research found four- and five-month-old babies happily watching more than an hour's TV a day (the set was usually in the room in which they slept, and positioned so they could see it from their cradle). A Japanese educational programme, *With Mother*, became the first broadcasting tailored to the under-twos, and although it was more than a decade before English-speaking programme-makers explored this market, *Teletubbies* eventually opened the floodgates.

The main concern about the ready availability of TV for tots is that it's all too easy to use it as an electronic babysitter. Remember the rats in Chapter 6 that became smarter through living in an interactive 'enriched environment', while rats that sat around with nothing to do became duller by the minute? One of the authors of that study, Dr Marian Cleeves Diamond, once made a guest appearance at a US conference about television and young children to point out that the dull sedentary rats didn't get any cleverer if they were allowed to watch the enriched rats running around having fun. She pointed out that, in order to learn, 'It is important to interact with the objects, to explore, to investigate, both physically and mentally.' Children learn by doing, not watching, just as (as described in Chapter 4) they acquire language skills by interacting with real speakers, not through exposure to screen-based ones.

Another worry is the possible involvement of early exposure to TV in attention deficit. In 2004, research by paediatrician Dimitri Christakis suggested that with each additional hour of TV per day that a child watches before the age of four, the risk of attention problems by age seven increases by 9 per cent. Christakis believes the rapidly shifting images on TV condition the developing brain to expect a higher level of stimulation than that available in real life. A modicum of TV should presumably do little harm, but if, as market researcher Rosemary Duff of ChildWise claims, 'Parents are happy to plonk them down in front of a specialist channel ... for hours,' the contribution of television to toxic childhood syndrome could be considerable.

The American Academy of Pediatrics therefore recommends that children under two shouldn't watch TV at all, but television is such a part of the furniture in twenty-first-century homes that this suggestion seems hopelessly unrealistic. Besides, there's also evidence that good educational TV can create a talking point between parent and child, and stimulate babies and toddlers to activity by copying the actions they see on screen. Once they're talking, the fun of television can interest children in words. And, as mentioned in Chapter 4, once children have started speaking, repeated viewing of favourite programmes or videos can add to their vocabulary.

Responsible programme-makers try to ensure their output does as little damage and as much good as possible. CBeebies, the BBC channel for pre-school children, is public service broadcasting pledged to entertain and educate – and the only part of the BBC that now takes pride in the nickname 'Aunty'. They avoid cartoons and 'montage telly' (cutting rapidly from shot to shot, as on many US children's channels), instead aiming for gentle pacing, language appropriate to the age group and plenty of real-life presenters, speaking directly to their young viewers. Clare Elstow, head of CBeebies, says children are engaged by the friendly faces and apparent eye contact, and older toddlers are more likely to pick up language from TV if they can see real lips moving as the words come out.

The key in the first few years seems to be to choose wisely – one of the main findings of research is that viewing should be age-appropriate – to watch alongside children as much as possible and talk about what you see, and to keep viewing down to sensible levels. The same advice holds good for all the other technological toys aimed at very young children. Many of these simply pander to the hot-housing impulse described in Chapter 6 (titles like *Baby Einstein* send a shiver down my spine!) and parents would probably be better spending their money on a few good picture books. And while 'non-educational' websites, DVDs and lapware computer games can be fun, and can stimulate interaction between parent and child, they should be an occasional addition to the age-old human repertoire of cuddling, playing, singing, storytelling, and just 'hanging out' with a baby or toddler. In the first few years, genuine interactive first-hand experiences are much more important than technological toys. In the words of Dr David Walsh of the National Institute on Media and the Family, 'If we orient our kids to screens so early in their lives, we risk making media their automatic default activity.'

The splintering family

In the early years, parents have control over their children's interaction with the electronic village. As children grow older, however, many of them are left to roam it at will. In terms of television, viewing patterns have changed considerably since the growth of cable, satellite and digital broadcasting in the 1980s. Until then there was a fairly restricted range of children's television – most TV programmes were aimed at adults, with children joining them in the early evening to watch as a family. TV viewing was, for most parents and children (and indeed the community around them), a shared experience, often the focus of conversation the next day.

The growth of specialist channels aimed directly at children – Nickelodeon, Disney, Fox Kids, CBBC, Toonami – has meant a constant diet of tailor-made programming is now available twenty-four hours a day. Increased choice led to family discord about control of the airways and, within the last decade, a massive increase in the number of children who have their own TVs. A US survey by the Kaiser Family Foundation found that in 2003 a quarter of children aged six and under had televisions in their bedrooms. By 2005 a UK survey claimed that among five- to sixteen-year-olds in the UK the proportion had risen as high as 80 per cent, and the rest of the industrialised world seems to be following suit.

Quite apart from the concerns voiced about bedroom TV in previous chapters, there's a huge difference between children watching television in the bosom of their family and watching it alone in their rooms, where parents can neither monitor nor mediate the content of their viewing. And it's not only television that's moved into the bedroom. A Spanish ten-year-old told me proudly about his 'virtual world' – TV, computer, games console, DVD, iPod – where he retreats after school and at weekends. His parents meanwhile lead their own virtual lives, tailored to their own interests.

Media people call this 'splintering' of the audience (children watching or playing in one room, dad watching sport in another, mum doing the email somewhere else) and it's becoming the norm across the developed world. A recent survey of 1,200 children in England found that 'a large – and rapidly growing – number of children as young as five and six now have a whole array of technology, such as their own DVD player, video recorder and MP3 player'. In Japan, where lack of space means privacy is more difficult to come by, you can now purchase MyRoom, a translucent soundproof booth to install in a corner of the living room, creating a miniature virtual world for a single family member.

Our species is by nature a social one: for most of human history we led very public lives – living, eating and even sleeping communally. Even though increasing wealth led to greater opportunities for privacy, until comparatively recently there were still many occasions when the family came together – including mealtimes, shared outings and family viewing. And it's in the family that children learn how to interact with others. This splintering is something new, and judging by the effects noted in previous chapters, it's not a healthy development.

In the last decade, Japan – practically the spiritual home of new technology – has seen the rise of a new phenomenon, known as hikikomori. Young people in their teens and twenties, especially males, are increasingly withdrawing from all human contact. It's thought that more than a million young people have locked themselves away in one room of the family home, refusing to come out, preferring instead to retreat into a virtual world. In hikikomori the natural reserve of the Japanese has been magnified into complete social isolation.

Ryu Murakami, novelist and film director, has pointed out the almost certain connection between hikikomori and 'gizmos like the new Sony PlayStation, which comes equipped with an Internet ter-minology and a DVD player ... [and] inevitably fixes people in their individual space'. But national anxiety about the phenomenon has not in any way dimmed enthusiasm for virtual existence. Psychiatrist Satoru Saito, who researches the condition, relates it to a more general withdrawal into social isolation: 'I fear Japan itself is becoming hikikomori. It is a nation that does not like to communicate. So what these young adults are doing is a mirror of what they see around them in adult society.'

We've already seen the level of playground pressure to be 'cool'. For some children, especially boys, it's easier to withdraw from the macho competitive fray into the safe haven of computer games. The more they 'play', the less socially adept they become and the greater the lure of the computer. Parents may feel their children are out of harm's way, cocooned in a virtual world, but in a pack animal like homo sapiens the long-term risks of widespread social isolation are as yet unknown.

The dark side of the village

In the meantime, there's the question of what children are watching, playing and hearing when they disappear into their technology-rich bedrooms. When parents provide them with a TV, they assume it'll be tuned to the kids' channels, those endless grinning presenters and highly coloured cartoons adults are desperate to escape from themselves. For the under-fives this may be the case, but not for long. Children are curious creatures, prone to channel hopping, and usually it's not long before they're keeping some very disturbing company.

A UK survey in 2005 found that two-thirds of children between two and twelve years old watch TV without supervision. There's also little uptake on channel-blocking devices or watershed-setting gizmos that deny access to TV after a certain time each night. According to the teachers I meet, what children tell them about their TV viewing habits would make their parents' hair stand on end.

Then there's the rest of the electronic media. Parents are often even less aware of the content of computer games, since they are probably not console-game aficionados themselves and are therefore on the other side of the 'digital divide'. They acknowledge their children's expertise and bow to their judgement in terms of purchases – hence, as described in the previous chapter, under-tens often gain access to extraordinarily violent material. On the Internet, blocking and filtering devices are not very reliable and anyway most parents are unsure how to use them: in a recent survey, even among those who use the Internet regularly only 15 per cent of parents said they knew how to install filtering software. Children are also bombarded daily with violent ideas, explicit sexual references and bad language through pop music, which they access through MTV and iPods. Again, parents are often unaware of this, because it's not the music they listen to themselves. In general, there's been a gradual escalation of gratuitous violence, antisocial behaviour and sleazy sex in the less-responsible sections of all media – and children are watching and listening to it all behind closed doors.

Psychologists believe that for children under ten much of the stuff they now view and hear is frightening, worrying and emotionally destabilising – rather like living in a mental war zone. Indeed, our children can also tune into genuine war zones, violent crimes and horrific disasters, courtesy of news broadcasts. Many pre-teens now live, to all intents and purposes, alone in a mental world that would do justice to Hieronymous Bosch. The long-term emotional toll, like the results of the divorce explosion, is yet to be discovered, but among the obvious short-term results are problems with sleep (see Chapter 3) and reluctance to play outdoors (see Chapter 2), both of which impact on learning and behaviour.

It seems that most of the developed world is in denial about the company its children are keeping. But the worst of the media is now becoming a serious child-protection issue. One obvious way to reinstate the 'off switch' is to bring technology back into family space, but this is a simplistic answer to a very complex question. The electronic media are now so omnipresent in children's lives that parents need the support of other authorities in the global village. Just as real-life villages protect law-abiding families from damaging assault, we now need a more serious approach to policing the electronic media.

A question of rights

Many parents' organisations around the developed world are now calling for greater government restrictions on what children see and hear through the media. But the subject has become entangled with a much wider debate about censorship, at the very heart of the human rights agenda. In the US, every attempt to regulate what children see and hear comes up against the First Amendment. In the rest of the world, anti-censorship campaigners cite human rights legislation. The issue of children's right to a healthy environment is thus lost in controversy about the rights of adults to read, view and listen to whatever they like.

Take violence, for example. In 2000 a number of highly influential institutions including the American Medical Association, American Psychological Association and American Academy of Pediatrics issued a joint statement: 'At this time well over 1,000 studies ... point overwhemingly to a causal connection between media violence and aggressive behaviour in children.' Given that the average American child has by the age of ten witnessed about 100,000 acts of violence and 8,000 murders, this seems a serious concern. But this concerted stand immediately drew counter-fire from anti-censorship experts around the world, rubbishing the studies cited and pointing to others proving the opposite. Parents are understandably confused by these conflicting messages – and anxious not to be killjoys if the anti-censorship lobby proves correct.

Nevertheless, if we rise above the bickering, most parents would probably agree that in real life they'd try to protect their children from viewing extreme violence. As screen images become ever more realistic, research repeatedly shows that they stimulate the same emotional centres in the brain as genuine violent experiences. What's more, videos and DVDs can be rewound, slowed down or freeze-framed and computer games played repeatedly. We are not talking about *Tom and Jerry* here, or the Roadrunner being beaten over the head with a frying pan, but about highly realistic – and, indeed, in news broadcasts completely realistic – bloody murder and mayhem. Psychologists point out that when children watch such violent material the possibility of increased aggressive behaviour is only one of a range of effects. Others are desensitisation to pain and suffering (which could contribute to the bullying explosion) and increased fear of the world around them (which makes children afraid to venture beyond the safety of their own homes). The American writer Neil Postman maintained that the most significant effect is the undermining of children's confidence in adults' ability to protect them in a violent world.

Another flashpoint in the child protection versus censorship discussion is the sexual content of many TV programmes. The effects on children of increasingly graphic sex scenes or salacious discussions (as seen daily on shows like *Jerry Springer*) are also lost in the debate about what's acceptable for adults. No one has yet proved conclusively that witnessing sexy scenarios and human sexual dramas is associated with a rise in underage sex and teenage pregnancies ... but we've already seen the effects that unmediated consumer pressure has on children. The same media that sell little girls an interest in clothes, dieting, make-up and 'boyz' also introduces them, through its regular programme content, to the fascination of sexual intrigue. Again, parents have to wonder whether they'd be happy for their children to witness these scenes in real life.

The UK forensic psychologist Professor Kevin Browne recently commented that adults should exercise 'the same care with adult media as they do with medication or chemicals around the home', since unrestricted viewing could be regarded as 'a form of emotional maltreatment of the child'. However, given the prevalence of sex and violence on TV, many parents no longer feel able to monitor what their children see and hear. Even experts like Ed Richards of the UK media regulator Ofcom agree: 'How do we think about the watershed when the ten-year-old is watching a PVR-stored 18-rated movie in the morning while the parents are out doing the shopping?' It seems that we've reached the point when adults' right to media freedom has come into direct conflict with children's right to grow up in a non-toxic environment.

Electronic friends ... and enemies

Another area of children's media activity that parents have trouble monitoring is electronic conversation. Recent UK statistics on mobile phone ownership point to about a quarter of all seven-year-olds, rising to 89 per cent of children aged between eleven and twelve. These figures have continued to grow despite strong warnings that the use of mobiles by children could increase the risk of brain disease in later life. Perhaps it's because adults are now so used to being able to contact anyone at any time of the day that they need to extend that contact to their children. When both parents are at work, the mobile phone may be one of their main points of contact between the family.

Since the brain disease warnings weren't attached to the use of mobiles for texting (and since texting is much cheaper than talking), children often now maintain their real-life friendships by the medium of texts. Increasingly too, children become involved in virtual friendships on the Internet, through chatrooms and instant messaging on websites, such as the CBBC and PlayStation sites. Children often value these types of chat as ways of making easy non-face-to-face contact (ideal if you're shy or socially isolated) and keeping in touch with friends. As they tend to be much more chat-savvy than their parents – nearly twice as many online teenagers use instant messaging as online adults – parents may feel technologically left behind.

However, as there are many dangers associated with electronic friendship, parents need to wise up about chat – perhaps by visiting some of the websites listed on page 278. For instance, as seen in the previous chapter, marketeers increasingly make contact with children via texts, Internet messaging systems and on websites. One popular way of selling 'cool' is to set up an extremely cool – and apparently genuine – weblog, which indulges in subtle product placement. News of good blogs circulates around the juvenile chat community at electric speed, so the advertiser's message is downloaded on to endless family computers – effortlessly delivering pester power into your home.

Mobile phones and the Internet are also increasingly used as a medium for bullying, so threats and nasty messages can pursue unfortunate children even beyond the safety of their own front door. In the UK, the growth in camphones and videophones led in 2005 to a craze for 'happy slapping' – sudden violent assaults by groups of youngsters on unsuspecting individuals. These are photographed or videoed (the aim being to record the victim's surprised expression) and the images circulated. There have even been episodes where children acted like paparazzi, flocking to the scene of an accident not to help but to record it on their phones – a development that brings to mind psychologists' warnings of media violence desensitising children to suffering.

Village politics

Another concern is the fact that the friends children make through virtual friendship routes may not be who they seem. A BBC booklet on safe use of the Internet looks on the sunny side with the warning: 'On the Internet, people often use nicknames, and they often pretend to be a different age or even gender: it's part of the fun' – presumably an attempt to equate Internet deceit with the 'pretend play' of children. This seems to me irresponsible. Some of the people out there masquerading under a cheery nickname have a very different idea of fun from the rest of us.

Occasional bouts of media frenzy about paedophiles using the net to 'groom' children mean parents are generally well aware of this risk. In an experiment by the technology news site ZDNet, a journalist invented 'Tina Bell' (a twelve-year-old girl living in London) and sent her into a Yahoo chatroom, where she was immediately contacted by a multitude of paedophiles. The attendant publicity led to some providers closing down chatrooms, others improving the marshalling of their sites, and plenty of advice to parents about using web-nannying services and monitoring children's computer use.

Sadly, most advice is rapidly outdated, as both children and their potential 'friends' discover innovative ways to avoid parental detection. But there are other shady characters out there besides the men in plastic macs. Children may stumble upon or (given their endless curiosity) seek out all manner of pondlife – and the pondlife is proliferating.

The unregulated nature of the Internet means people with evil intent can easily make contact with each other. In a real village, anyone who deviated from 'normal behaviour' would usually find themselves isolated. While tragic for those offering no threat to society, this state of affairs was socially constructive in the case of those who were violent or predatory. Nowadays, everyone from violent pornographers to psychopaths and terrorists can link up and organise themselves on the net. The chance to meet like-minded individuals means their deviance becomes normalised, and allows them to circulate information once difficult to come by – such as how to make bombs – or to dwell on violent or suicidal fantasies. They can also make contact with emotionally vulnerable youngsters, who – thanks to toxic childhood syndrome – are a growing breed. Within a few years, with the increasing sophistication of communications technology, startling levels of interconnectivity will be available on the average mobile phone. It's up to the law-abiding majority of electronic villagers to ensure that such generally beneficial advances don't have unintended consequences.

In the past, the inhabitants of real-life villages have collaborated to police their environment and fend off threats, particularly in terms of protecting their young from harmful influences. So far, however, the policing of the electronic village is reminiscent of the Keystone Cops pursuing wrongdoers from one dodgy Internet address to another, becoming increasingly entangled in international red tape.

It seems sensible to this old-fashioned supporter of democracy and free speech that the governments of the world should be making real efforts to protect children – and all of us – from virtual crime through the United Nations or a similar international body. There are moves afoot to protect economic interests on the net (although at the moment the UN and the US are, as usual, locked in disagreement about it) and since 2003 a Virtual Global Task Force has been working to prevent paedophile activity. So why can't we do more to close down other dangerous sites? Internet policing experts such as John Giacobbi of *Web Sheriff* suggests governments make Internet service providers and telephone companies adopt strict regulation procedures, with severe penalties for those who allow violent or depraved material to circulate via their services. To be truly effective this would require an international protocol, with sanctions imposed on rogue states – but it is possible.

However, as well as the difficulties of policing, there's the same old problem of extreme interpretations of human rights legislation and, in the USA, the First Amendment. Defenders of freedom of speech on the Internet are even more voluble than critics of media censorship, so there's a long way to go in finding a sensible balanced approach. There's also enormous reluctance among the vast majority of decent people to become involved in this debate. While parents worry about what children are seeing on TV and what they may encounter on the Internet, the fear of being thought prudish or ultra-right-wing holds most of them back from speaking up in public.

Nevertheless, as will be argued in Chapter 10, total moral relativism makes balanced child-rearing extraordinarily difficult, since it leads to a breakdown of trust and respect in society. If we believe there's a real possibility of danger to children and teenagers in the highly unregulated climate that exists in much of the electronic village, there should at least be public debate on the issues. Parent power could start that debate rolling.

And now the good news ...

Of course, children's descent into unsuitable virtual worlds is not inevitable. If parents decide to take control of the electronic media in their own homes, technology can enrich their children's lives as much as it enriches the lives of most adults. Television can be reinstated in a family space and family viewing can once again become a chance to share time and conversation, with negotiated periods for children to watch their own special programmes. If computers and console games are also positioned in a shared space in the home, everyone will know what's happening on them. Indeed, this is often an area in which children can take on the role of expert, initiating parents into their virtual interests.

While it's important to recognise the problems for child-raising that come with technology, it would be downright reprehensible to ignore the benefits. Good children's television can be a magnificent resource, touching parts of the infant consciousness that other media cannot reach. It can transport children to any part of the globe, any period of history, any realm of the imagination. TV can also help children see how other people live and understand their point of view. American psychologist Paul Bloom argues that children grow as moral beings through stories that help them take the perspective of distant others – TV can provide these stories, the opportunity to empathise with people across the global village.

What's more, it can provide these experiences in an informal, non-didactic way. Liz Cleaver, Controller of Learning and Interactive at the BBC, believes that 'what TV does best is inspire people and get them interested'. With the ever expanding capacity for interactive involvement via related websites, the potential to build on TV-inspired interest is now phenomenal. Increasingly, public service broadcasters are working alongside other agencies to develop new approaches to education – in the coming years, we may well see wonders.

This isn't to say that all encounters with TV should be educational. Today's children, like their parents, lead exhausting lives – they too have to sit in the traffic queues on the way to and from school, and deal with a world of rapid responses and constant change. A bit of mindless visual chewing gum is a great way to relax, and one could scarcely begrudge them an hour or so chilling out in front of children's programmes at the end of a hard day.

Similarly, computers and console games can be both educational and entertaining. Children who learn how to use the web for research, to word-process and desktop-publish their own work, or to create their own websites or video presentations are at a huge advantage in school and beyond. All these pursuits involve higher order thought processes and command of language and literacy skills. Some console games – the sort where you build cities or solve quests – develop thinking skills and perseverance, while webcam games involving aerobic exercise (kick-boxing or disco dancing) can be a great way of exercising indoors. And all children can benefit from the chance to enjoy web-based entertainment and make new friends on the net. The key, as always, is balance.

In their excellent book *The Media Diet for Kids* Teresa Orange and Louise O'Flynn give much helpful advice on limiting the time children spend on screen-based activities, and sensitively monitoring what they watch and do. As long as parents are aware of what their children are up to, ensuring that activities are safe and appropriate and keeping technological entertainment within safe limits, TV and computers can be an enormous force for good. But just as you wouldn't dream of entrusting your offspring to an unknown adult, it's inadvisable to deposit them alone in a room with a TV or any other magic box.

Village wisdom

There's plenty more good news in the global village, this time in terms of help for parents. As social problems – including those associated with toxic childhood syndrome – become apparent, technology provides new ways of helping to solve them. There are now a vast number of websites offering information, advice and even virtual counselling services or parenting courses – as long as you have broadband, it's never been easier to call on the instant advice of people who've been there before. As I trawled the web investigating these sites, I felt as though I was visiting a succession of 'wise men and women'. Instead of dispensing their wisdom from a cave on the edge of the village, they're now out there doing it via the Internet.

Similarly, television is regularly used to spread good ideas and useful knowledge. From chat shows to reality TV, programme-makers have looked for ways of taking on the role of village luminaries – the family doctor, the kindly schoolteacher, the moral or spiritual leader. In some ways, it's even become a substitute for the extended family – many viewers know more about the lives and loves of characters in a favourite soap than about their own family members.

In terms of childcare, as children's behaviour has deteriorated there's been plenty of TV support. There are the dispensers of wisdom on daytime chat-show sofas, regularly throwing hints and advice in parents' direction. (In France, a daily hour-long programme about raising children, *Les Maternelles*, provides a wide range of information in typically urbane French style that could act as an object lesson to programme-makers in other countries.) There are documentary-style programmes, such as the BBC's remarkable *Child of Our Times* – this series, following the lives of various children born in the year 2000, amounts to a popular course in child development and now has an interactive component available on the web through the BBC's new parenting site. The opportunity to tap into advice and video footage of parenting skills could be the twenty-first-century equivalent of learning through growing up in an extended family. And of course there are the myriad edutainment programmes such as *Supernanny*, demonstrating how despairing parents can tame their out-of-control children.

I must admit to mixed feelings about this sort of edutainment. It certainly gives useful messages about managing children's behaviour, but since it revolves around making a drama out of a crisis, there's a constant upping of the ante in terms of children's bad behaviour.

There's also usually an 'expert' imported to solve the problem – a supernanny figure or a child psychologist – who reinforces the impression of many parenting manuals that parents aren't capable of raising their children alone. As family counsellor Jill Curtis says, 'It seems in the programmes that some parents are desperate for someone to come in and be the bad guy. Why?' There's also the problem of electric speed. On TV, transformations have to happen in the half an hour or so that the programme lasts. We see only edited highlights – the reality of raising children in 'slow time' is not addressed.

*

Still, it's early days. We're all still learning. Public service broadcasters are working hard on the issues raised above, and developments in digital technology promise much more ingenious educational inter-activity in the future. And when the new media have something powerful to say, the results can be startling. The film *Super Size Me* first shown in cinemas, then on DVD, then via TV stations has, in the words of BBC documentary head Alan Hayling, 'probably made young people think about the effects of fast food more than any amount of public information'. And a TV and Internet-based campaign by celebrity chef Jamie Oliver made the UK government do a complete U-turn on the issue of school meals. Broadcasters are learning how to work in creative partnership with their audience, but that of course depends on the audience putting in their twopenn'orth too.

The great virtual battle between good and evil – the educative, mind-broadening potential of new technology versus the shadowy forces at work on the dark side of the village – has only just begun, and audience participation (especially pressure from parents' groups) will help determine the eventual outcome. In the meantime, the sooner we get those TVs and other gadgets out of children's bedrooms and back into family space, the better.

DETOXING THE ELECTRONIC VILLAGE

- As with all aspects of child-rearing, start as you mean to go on, if possible before you even have a family. Discuss your attitudes to electronic entertainment with your partner and devise policies that will work for you.
- From the point of view of children, think of strangers on screens as you would think of them in real life. Never leave your children unsupervised in the company of anyone in whom you don't have utter confidence.
- Surveys and research into TV and computers stress that the many benefits of multimedia relate only to *appropriate* material – that is programmes and soft-ware specifically designed for your child's age group.
- Don't rely on V-chips, software, etc, to protect your children from inappropriate programming. Like computer firewalls, such technology is rapidly outdated. Use it to help, by all means, but take control yourself.
- The best way to do this is to keep all electronic media in a shared part of the house, and watch/log on together as much as possible. Having to make compromises about control of the airspace means a degree of sacrifice on everyone's part, but there are hugely important benefits:

  – time is spent together rather than apart (see Chapters 4, 5 and 6)
  – you are able to monitor your child's electronic activities (see Chapters 8 and 9)
  – you are a functioning family, rather than an increasingly disparate group of individuals, splintered off into different rooms of the same house.

- While TV, the Internet and so on are wonderful resources, like anything else children can have too much of a good thing. Monitor their media diet as carefully as you monitor the food they eat.
- Don't let electronic entertainment become the 'default activity' in your home – for instance, make it a rule that no family members automatically switch on the TV or log on to a computer when they enter the family space. Ensure engagement with electronic media is always purposeful, intentional and

finite (see 'How to Detox a TV Addict' on page 274 – all these suggestions can be adopted to apply to other electronic entertainment).

- Talk to your child about the electronic media and the reasons for your decisions and rules. Ensure they know that your key concern is their welfare and well-being. Children understand 'stranger danger' and other real-life threats – help them see that electronic threats to their social, emotional and cognitive development are just as serious.

- If your child is frightened by something seen on TV, film or DVD:

  – up to the age of seven, distract them, give them a cuddle and warm reassurance
  – for eights and over, give logical explanations for why they are safe e.g.:
  * It can't happen because it's fantasy
  * It couldn't happen here/to you because ...
  * If it ever did happen, this is what we'd do ...

- In a hi-tech world, be technology-savvy. Make sure you know as much as possible about any hardware and software that comes into your home. Sometimes your child will know about it from school or friends and can initiate you into its mysteries – a great opportunity for some quality interaction. But if you aren't able to put in the time and energy to find out about an electronic product, don't buy it.

- The web is a fantastic resource for parents and children. Check out the websites below to find ways of using it positively.

- Teach children how to behave on the net, and ensure they know the dangers that are out there and how to avoid them, just as in the real world. Again, check out detailed suggestions on websites.

- Make sure your child knows never to open a suspicious email, click a suspicious hyperlink, respond to unexpected messages on mobile phones or fill in any forms on the Internet without checking with you. (Give dire warnings about viruses that knock out the system, how you could be spammed to death, etc.) Similarly, children should not give out their real addresses or phone numbers to anyone they meet in the electronic village.

- Ensure your children know that if they encounter anything in the electronic village that makes them feel uncomfortable, embarrassed or worried, they should let you know.
- Remember that all villages have their dark side, even if their PR personnel prefer to gloss over the problem. Since PR people for the electronic village now control most of the information that circulates in our world, be wary. Don't trust them to make decisions for your family – maintain that control yourself.

HOW TO DETOX A TV ADDICT

Some parents assure me the best system is to go cold turkey. Just remove the TV from the house and start life without it. If you can live without TV yourself, that would probably work a treat – but personally I enjoy my regular soap (*Coronation Street*), news programmes and documentaries. And if parents watch TV, they can scarcely ban their child from doing so.

- Look at the viewing habits of the family as a whole – it may be that you all need detoxing.
- Discuss with your child why he or she is a TV addict. Is it because there's nothing else to do? Is it a default activity and they've never thought about alternatives?
- Make sure the TV is in a shared space (see 'How to Get the TV Out of the Bedroom', p 129).
- Find ways of rationing 'electronic time' that suits your family, e.g.:

   – buy a TV guide every week, and let everyone circle the programmes they want to see (up to an agreed level), so you can just switch on when required and video any overlaps
   – have agreed time limits for viewing, playing, logging into chat each day, and stick to them – like anything else involved in child-rearing, if you are utterly consistent and determined for a week or so, this arrangement will become habitual.

- Perhaps you could have a regular 'family TV evening' when everyone settles down together with popcorn and drinks for some shared viewing of DVDs or digitally recorded programmes you all want to see.
- Make sure there are lots of real activities on offer to compete with electronic entertainment and, especially in the early stages, make time to share these. They don't have to be complicated or expensive. For instance, with your child:

   – make a pile of family photographs and sort them into albums/scrapbooks/

biographies/a collage for your child's wall (while sorting, take the opportunity to reminisce and talk)

– get out recipe books, and go through them together choosing meals you fancy cooking. Make menus for the week, take your child shopping for ingredients and do some cooking together.

– investigate your local area. Get a map, and go on expeditions to find out about all the places you don't know (however unpromising they sound). Make sure you're properly equipped – camera, notebook, food supplies – and collect information, pictures, souvenirs to make a scrapbook of your travels.

– throw a party. With your child, decide on a theme (e.g., pirates, storyland, robots) and a budget (keep it low), then enjoy planning and making costumes, decorations, food, invitations, activities – the lower your budget, the more ingenious you'll have to be. Invite a few of your child's friends and their parents, and enjoy yourselves.

See also 'How to Avoid Couch Potato Syndrome', 'Thirty-three Things a Child Should Do by the Age of Ten', 'Detoxing Communication', 'Thirty-four Life Skills for Your Child to Learn', 'How to Encourage Creative Play'.

- Demonstrate to your child that, while it's fine to occasionally slump in front of a screen and be entertained, it's much more fun to entertain yourself and others. But if you don't switch off the magic box and make the effort to do something, you'll never discover the joys of living in the real world.

PARENT POWER: POLICING THE VILLAGE

When I started researching this subject, I soon learned that Googling for information on children and the media could fill several lifetimes. I also discovered that, while there are plenty of helpful websites about Internet safety (see above), one could search for ever for a truly balanced approach to safe TV viewing. The ferocity of opinion on either side of this issue is testament to its importance – but it also deters decent non-extremist parents from speaking up, and that's bad. So here are a few modest proposals by which parents could help the move towards reasonable policing of the electronic village:

- Talk to other parents about what worries you. Make your feelings known when something disturbs you about programme content – you can find details of how to register complaints on the web, e.g., in UK www.ofcom.org.uk.
- Give your backing to calls for media education in school, to develop children's awareness of the advantages and dangers of life in the electronic village.
- Contact TV providers who offer specific packages of programmes and request a range of 'family viewing' packages (*not* mindless pap) to stop the splintering of family audiences.
- Campaign for broadcasting authorities and telecom companies to exercise tighter control over the content they make universally available. This doesn't have to be a question of censorship or denying people's right to view and say what they like. As we move into the digital age we should be aiming to make violent or sexually explicit material available only to adults on demand, rather than automatically available to everyone.
- Join the call for registration of ownership of mobile phones, as is already the case in France. If owners have to provide proof of age and identity, phones can be traced back to them so that it's easier to keep track of the images and information circulated.
- Suggest to elected representatives that specialists in child development should have greater influence in decisions on film, video and computer-game

certification; and that controls on the sale or rental of adult-rated materials to children should be tightened up.

- Work through organisations like Childnet International and CyberAngels to make the Internet safe for children.

Further reading

Teresa Orange and Louise O'Flynn, *The Media Diet for Kids* (Hay House, 2005)
Aric Sigman, *Remotely Controlled: How Television is Damaging Our Lives and What We Can Do About it* (Vermilion, 2005)

Useful websites

www.cyberangels.org (international parents organisation – very helpful)
www.chatdanger.com (magazine approach to issues, including phones, chatrooms and instant messaging)
www.kidsmart.org.uk (basic safety advice with user-friendly presentation)
www.getnetwise.org (gives list of tools for blocking websites, etc)
www.childnet-int.org (international campaign helping to make the Internet safe)
www.thegoodwebguide.co.uk (a good first port of call for reviews of websites on any subject)
www.unicef.org/magic (UNICEF MAGIC – media activities and good ideas by, with and for children)

Mind the gap

The positive side of life in the electronic village described on pages 266-270 applies mainly to wealthier families, the sort of people who would read this book, and probably have broadband access, sophisticated viewing habits and a high level of media literacy. As such parents wise up to the pros and cons of twenty-first-century technology, they take steps to protect their children from harm and ensure they reap the many benefits of life in a digital world. Meanwhile, the gap between rich and poor grows wider.

Over on the other side of the tracks, children from poor backgrounds are disadvantaged on two fronts:

- Lack of access to worthwhile digital technology in the home, so their media literacy skills are less well honed than those of children from more advantaged backgrounds
- Too wide an access to junk TV and mindless computer games, which shut down minds rather than opening them up (and, since many of these feature high levels of violence, may also cause increased levels of aggression).

Society can try to even out these disadvantages through education and access to appropriate and useful technology in after-school clubs. But if the village is inadequately policed disadvantaged children are, as usual, the most vulnerable to corruption and abuse. The current orthodoxy that it's up to parents to monitor what children see and do in the electronic village doesn't take account of those parents who either can't or won't take responsibility. There are no easy answers to this problem, but that doesn't mean we shouldn't engage with it. At present, fear of being ranked alongside prudes and the ultra-right means the decent majority prefer to turn a blind eye.

There is enormous potential in our electronic village to reach out across the widening gap and help all parents provide the best start in life for their children. But if we fail to acknowledge and deal with the growing threat to children, there is just as great a potential for damage; and the gap between those who gain from society's technological riches and those who lose will continue to widen with every passing year.

CHAPTER TEN

MANNERS MAKETH MAN

The electronic village may exert an increasing influence on children's lives, but they still have to live in the real world. Getting along in a community of real-life neighbours, shopkeepers and other random adults requires social skills that can't be learned in a virtual environment. For their first eight or so years, children are usually accompanied when out and about by parents, teachers or others in loco parentis; but as they grow older, they may increasingly wander abroad without supervision.

Civilised societies have in the past relied on an unwritten code of behaviour between children and the adults they meet outside their home. Children were expected to behave with respect towards their elders – for instance, giving up a seat on public transport, speaking when spoken to and trying, as far as possible, not to disturb adults with their play. This sort of behaviour was considered 'well mannered'. In return, most adults would keep a weather eye open for children's welfare, and even complete strangers would sometimes act in loco parentis – warning errant infants about unsafe behaviour, protecting them from obvious harm and keeping them generally on the straight and narrow. A tacitly agreed 'adult alliance' kept this cycle of trust and respect going: the whole village really did help raise the child. If children were accused of misbehaving by a neighbour, teacher or other respectable adult, most parents would take the adult's part and the children would be given short shrift.

Over the last quarter of a century, and especially in crowded inner-city areas, this unwritten code seems to have evaporated. Children in general are no longer respectful or well mannered as they were in the past. Similarly, the neighbourliness and fellow-feeling that fuelled the adult alliance has waned. Indeed, in Britain it seems almost to have disappeared – if adults see children misbehaving now, they tend to look away; and if they do intervene, they may find it is they who get short shrift. In disputes over behaviour, today's parents are much more likely to take their children's part.

This change has largely been blamed on poor parenting (and the glut of TV nanny programmes is the media's attempt to improve parenting skills) but, as I hope this book has shown, it's not that simple. Most parents are frantically doing their best in a world where the goal posts are not just moving – they've actually disappeared.

The parental balancing act

Ironically, there's now little doubt what good parenting involves. Over the last twenty-odd years, psychologists have identified the features of a variety of parenting styles, and long-term research has indicated clearly what works best for families in today's global village. Neuroscientists, studying the way children's brains develop, support the findings. The key – as usual in human behaviour – is balance.

There are four broad styles of parenting, based on the balance mothers and fathers strike between two elements: warmth and firmness. Warmth is the measure of how much love and support they give their children; firmness relates to the level of control they exercise over their children's lives.

I've already mentioned that research repeatedly shows the most effective parenting style is *authoritative*. Authoritative parents treat their children warmly, which in practical terms translates into giving them plenty of time and loving attention, listening to them and responding to their concerns and allowing some (safe) choices. But

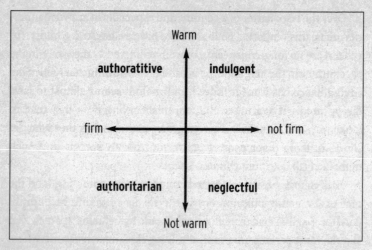

they're also firm, ensuring rules and routines to provide stability, security and safety – for instance, regular family meals, bedtime schedules and rituals, monitoring of TV viewing (and no television in the bedroom). The advice of every expert I spoke to while writing *Toxic Childhood* pointed towards an authoritative parenting approach. According to psychologists, a successful balance between warmth and firmness should produce 'self-regulating' children, well balanced, resilient, with plenty of initiative, optimism and genuine self-esteem. Such children are likely to do well at school, make (and keep) plenty of friends, and go on to lead happy, successful lives.

Parents who are firm with their children but lacking in warmth are labelled *authoritarian*. They tend to lay down the law, without listening to children's point of view or offering opportunities for discussion, choice or negotiation. Maybe they believe this law has been handed down to them from a higher authority; maybe they're replicating the parenting style they experienced themselves; or maybe they're just too unsure of themselves to brook any argument. Their regime means plenty of stability and security, but little consideration for the child's feelings or point of view. The outcome is generally a well-behaved, obedient child, but often with a poor self-image – and in a generally liberal society poor self-image can lead to problems (in terms of self-destructive or antisocial behaviour) once the child is out of the parents' immediate control.

On the other hand, parents with high warmth but low firmness rating are labelled indulgent: they're the ones who make a habit of loving 'not wisely but too well' – giving in to requests, letting children make more choices than is good for them, putting their offsprings' interests above other people's and automatically springing to their defence if they get into trouble. Some of these parents may be over-reacting to their own authoritarian upbringing; some may like the idea of being their children's 'friends' rather than parents; others may have let the child lead from the start – for instance, failing to establish family-friendly sleep schedules – then found themselves unable to recoup and establish parental control. The children of indulgent parents usually feel loved and are generally self-confident, but they often have problems conforming at school and getting along with other children or adults (as one teacher put it, 'Their sense of entitlement is breathtaking'). They may also go off the rails later – studies have found that as adolescents they're more likely to be involved in drug or alcohol abuse – or find it difficult to accept that the world doesn't owe them a living.

Evidence is also beginning to emerge that excessive indulgence accompanied by excessive praise can, in the case of certain children, stimulate 'narcissistic personality disorder' – a recent addition to journalists' psychobabble that I suspect we'll hear much more about in coming years.

The final parenting style – neither warm nor firm – is labelled neglectful, and involves giving one's children neither loving attention nor behavioural boundaries. It's sadly common among 'Mind the Gap' parents, who are often the result of a neglectful upbringing themselves and too preoccupied with the dramas of their own lives to expend much effort on their children. As Philip Larkin said, 'Man hands on misery to man. It deepens like a coastal shelf.' But it can also happen in more economically successful families when parents are simply too wrapped up in their work to spare the time for child-rearing. Children brought up in neglectful homes grow up with poor self-esteem and a far higher than average chance of behaviour problems – later leading to self-destructive and antisocial behaviour.

Most parents can probably recognise elements of their own parenting style in more than one category – these things are never clear cut. What's more, mothers and fathers sometimes have different styles and, unless they can find a happy medium, the resultant conflict is bad for their relationship as well as their children. But, whatever one's own shortcomings, it's obvious that authoritative parenting will lessen the effect of toxic childhood syndrome while the other styles will magnify it. So if we know the problem and we know the answer, why can't more parents move towards an authoritative style?

The case of the missing goal posts

Unfortunately, as pointed out in Chapter 3, to be authoritative you need to feel confident about what you're doing. In a world of tumultuous change, confidence is thin on the ground. The moral and social certainties that once produced the adult alliance have disintegrated, and there seems to be nothing to put in their place. If we think of society as acting like a parent to its citizens, the parenting style has moved – over the course of a couple of generations – from authoritarian to downright neglectful.

In the not very remote past, you couldn't move for rules for behaviour – many of them highly restrictive. Religious conventions, rigid class structures and long-established social norms all provided clear guidance for citizens, laying down the law in no uncertain terms. Not much more than half a century ago, for instance, English church-goers were still belting out the words:

'
     'The rich man in his castle,

     The poor man at his gate,

     God made them, high or lowly,

     And ordered their estate.'

There was certainly order, but – unless you were one of the lucky ones with a castle – it came at a cost.

Then suddenly the process of democratisation, which had been creeping slowly and steadily through Western civilisation for several centuries, shifted into electric speed. Within a couple of generations much of the old guidance was swept away. Respect for traditional authority figures declined, as the mystique on which they relied dissolved in the glare of the TV lights. Social attitudes relaxed and interactions became increasingly informal – even between people who'd always been considered of different status, such as boss and employee, teacher and pupil, or different generations. Religious traditions, deeply ingrained in the authoritarian culture of yesteryear, seemed increasingly irrelevant. Across much of the developed world, the old authoritarian social norms disappeared and no other value system – apart from a vague moral relativism – has emerged to replace them. For many people, self-realisation is now the only guiding star in a darkling sky.

Parenting styles have simply followed the same social and cultural trends. Parents know an authoritarian approach is 'old-fashioned', but without some sort of moral compass, they lack the confidence to be authoritative. So they're blown by the prevailing wind towards more indulgent behaviour. After all, in an egalitarian society, everyone has the same human rights as everyone else, so why shouldn't that apply to children too? If everyone's entitled to self-realisation, why should children be expected to defer to others just because of their age? Why should they give up their seat, hold their tongue, restrain their play so as not to offend some adult stranger?

In the case of 'warm' parents, this attitude blends neatly with their fear – born of Freudian psychology and nurtured by the advertising industry – that repressing children's natural inclinations will somehow damage their development. In the case of neglectful parents, it's a good excuse for letting children run wild. And the models of children's behaviour which parents see on TV shows and advertisements back up the impression that 'normal' children are sassy, quick-witted little characters who operate close to the edge of acceptable behaviour. These models are, of course, also available to children and – as we saw in Chapter 8 – there's considerable pressure from marketeers for children to exercise pester power and make a stand against figures of authority.

The late twentieth century also saw a great deal of talk about children's rights. The UN International Convention on the Rights of the Child, drafted in the late 1980s, ushered in even more uncertainty about how far children should be constrained by adults. The actual convention is sensible and fair, but it has spawned endless debates on what is or isn't acceptable behaviour, especially in terms of discipline. And then there's my personal pet theory about fathers being driven out of the discipline equation by the female 'tigress instinct' to defend her young against all comers.

In this contemporary social and ethical maelstrom, it's not surprising that many parents lack the moral confidence to be authoritative. But for the sake of their children's mental health and happiness, they have to find it from somewhere.

The pursuit of happiness

Most parents would say that, above all, they want their children to be happy. However, the World Database of Happiness, available on the web, shows that despite vast increases in wealth the people of the USA, Britain and Japan are no happier than they were fifty years ago. Our cultural quest for self-realisation – and the ability to pay through the nose for it – has not increased the sum of human happiness by one iota. And judging by the increases in mental health problems outlined at the beginning of this book, our children are actually getting unhappier. The influential British economist Richard Layard puts this down to a combination of consumerism and constant economic growth luring people in highly successful nations into over-competitiveness: 'Our fundamental problem today is a lack of common feeling between people – the notion that life is essentially a competitive struggle. With such a philosophy the losers become alienated and a threat to the rest of us, and even the winners can't relax in peace.'

Along with other political scientists, he argues that the success of a society depends just as much on its 'social capital' as on the monetary capital that drives economic growth. According to Harvard professor Robert Puttnam, social capital flows from 'the trust, reciprocity, information and cooperation associated with social networks', when people come together with a shared purpose. Social networks include religious congregations, political and pressure groups, sports or social clubs – anything from a bowling league to a book group. But as Westernised society stayed home nursing its 'affluenza', membership of such groups has declined considerably – society has splintered in the same way that family members are splintering into their own individual virtual worlds.

Being part of a social network – like being part of a successful family – involves time and commitment. But it's worth the effort. As Puttnam explains: 'People in relationships can reach goals that would have been far beyond the grasp of individuals in isolation' while at the same time enjoying 'the intrinsic satisfaction of association, of being part of a community'. There are other recorded advantages to this sort of social involvement – in a review of the research into what makes people happy, behavioural biologist Paul Martin found that 'connectedness' to a group was a critical ingredient of happiness. What's more, it makes you healthier – according to Puttnam's website, joining a group of some kind 'cuts in half your chances of dying next year'.

Perhaps the best way for parents to gain moral confidence in our changing world is to accept that self-realisation isn't just about making oneself (or one's offspring) happy but about working together with others for a common purpose. This isn't exactly a new idea – in fact it underpins every major religion and ethical system that's ever existed. But we don't have to sign up for church membership, political flag-waving or a moral crusade to take advantage of it. We just have to recognise that bringing up a child successfully involves collaborating with other people – and that to collaborate effectively, we must recognise that their happiness is as significant as our own.

Throughout this book there have been many detox recommendations that could lead to the creation of social networks – for instance, parents making contact with neighbours to provide eyes on the street (Chapter 2), or collaborating with childcare providers and schools to ensure children's success and well-being outside the home (Chapters 6 and 7). Many detox sections advise talking with other parents to establish general social norms (such as suitable bedtimes and attitudes to TV) and coming together to improve the local environment or stem the assault on children's minds by marketeers and other dark forces in the electronic village. All of these provide reasons for adults to work together for the common good – indeed, there can be no more important shared purpose than raising the next generation. Parents interested in detoxing childhood have strong motivation to re-establish the social capital that once underpinned the adult alliance.

Getting along in the real world

Unfortunately, as social change has made us preoccupied and suspicious, people have increasingly withdrawn from face-to-face contact within the community, and relied instead on virtual friendships online and watching other people's social lives on screen. But *Friends* in New York, *Neighbours* in Melbourne and helpful advisers all over cyberspace can never be as effective as real-life hands-on help with the day-to-day socialising of children. This requires real interaction within a real community. If we rely too heavily on virtual interactions and technological solutions, we jeopardise our children's chances of successfully growing into fully functioning human beings.

Perhaps, to refashion a splintered world, the present generation of parents needs help in greasing the wheels of everyday transactions with people outside their immediate circle. This skill – taken for granted in most communities in the past – isn't acquired through virtual relationships, where individuals assume complete control of their interactions with others (choosing the 'where', 'when' and 'how much' of all engagements, with the capacity to melt into cyberspace if anything goes wrong). Netiquette is different – and much easier – than getting along with real people in real time and space, especially if you don't know them very well. And especially now that our inter-national cultural revolution has swept away the hugely important social toolkit known as 'good manners'.

For many young people, manners are tarred with the same brush as deference and snobbery. But there's a huge difference between outdated rituals and sensible conventions for smoothing social contacts. The more each individual can put others at their ease, deal with misunderstandings and demonstrate respect through accepted conventions, the more easily the world turns on its axis. In this respect, good manners are simply part of the human survival kit. Fortunately, there's recently been a revival of interest in the subject – five books were published about manners in 2005 in the UK alone, including one by Lynne Truss, the woman who made apostrophes sexy.

Adopting a policy of mannerliness is the first step to creating social networks, and it's one that parents could easily take. By making an effort to be socially active, even on a very small scale, and ensuring that our exchanges are pleasant and respectful (even with people we don't really like the look of) we facilitate the growth of trust and reciprocity in the community. It may be difficult if others are surly in return but, on the other hand, it's immensely gratifying when they're responsive, and you feel that your politeness makes others around you polite too.

And, of course, the policy also works at home. Authoritative parenting has its origins in good manners, on the part of parents and children, to indicate respect and reciprocity between family members.

Social capital begins at home

Manners are habits of behaviour towards other people, and from their very earliest days on earth children can develop good habits or bad ones. In order to establish respectful behaviour parents have to accept responsibility, set up routines and rules for the family, and train infants to abide by them. This, of course, involves constantly demonstrating the same good manners yourself – children will copy what you do (and also what you say, so mind your language).

The firmness involved in establishing family rules should, of course, always be balanced by warmth. Children deserve warm praise for good behaviour and, if they question the rules, it behoves adults to listen and respond respectfully. Opportunities for children to make reasonable choices within agreed limits will also help the growth towards self-regulation. As children grow older and more able to think for themselves, the responsibility for defining appropriate behaviour is increasingly shared with them. The whole process of authoritative parenting involves mutual respect between parents and their offspring, based on mutual trust.

The family rules to be observed usually cover a number of areas:

- aspects of safety, health and hygiene
- social conventions such as table manners
- moral precepts (thou shalt take turns; thou shalt not hit thy sister, etc)

- simple practices to ease the running of the household, such as taking off muddy boots at the back door and closing doors to keep the heat in.

In a time of social upheaval and chaos, it may take a leap of faith to believe such rules can be agreed and kept by all. But if adults accept the responsibility for enforcing behavioural boundaries with reason and consistency (trying valiantly never to lose their temper), all the studies show that children soon learn to do-as-they-would-be-done-by and family life becomes much more enjoyable.

The extension of respectful behaviour to others outside the home shows children how the policy of doing-as-you-would-be-done-by reaches beyond the family circle, and makes sure they know how to behave respectfully to other adults. At the same time, parents and children begin to roll the snowball of trust and respect that builds communities.

In 2003, the Commission on Children at Risk, a panel of leading children's doctors, research scientists and youth-service professionals in the USA, recommended that the best way to address social concerns about children's deteriorating mental health was through 'authoritative communities'. By this they meant a culture of authoritativeness within all civic, educational, recreational, community service, business, cultural and religious groups that serve or include young people under the age of eighteen. Authoritative communities would be warm, nurturing, respectful to children's and teenagers' point of view, but would also set clear boundaries, encourage moral development and equal respect for all. If this could be brought about, I suspect we'd have achieved the ultimate detoxification of childhood.

Of course, it would help a lot if television – the window through which we now all see the world – could reflect the advantages of healthy social interaction, rather than concentrating so much attention on dysfunctional relationships and social breakdown. As the economist Richard Layard says, to create a society that values moral commitment to the welfare of others as well as ourselves, we have to 'change the relative prestige accorded to smart-arsed behaviour and that accorded to kindness'. Popular TV programmes – especially soap operas which are often watched by children – could help make that change.

Knowledge is power

While the simple ethical guiding star of do-as-you-would-be-done-by could do a lot to help parents feel more authoritative, there's another important route to confidence: knowledge. The more parents know about child development the better equipped they are to aim for a productive balance between warmth and firmness. But researching this book has taught me how little most adults know about children. As a teacher, working with them every day, one soon learns a few essential truths, otherwise one doesn't last long in a classroom. One important truth is that children – even very small children – are naturally manipulative. They have to be to ensure their survival – as the smallest and weakest of humans, they have to rely on psychology to make sure their needs are noticed. So they learn very early how to reward adults with smiles and punish them with screams, and as time goes on many become extremely adept at getting their own way.

Teachers learn about childish wiles through wide experience, but most parents' experience of children is limited. With the death of the extended family, contemporary adults' knowledge about child-rearing is often limited to vague memories of their own childhood, in a world vastly different from the world today, assisted perhaps by a few impressions from TV. As more families now stop at one child (meaning no points of comparison, and no need to share), parents are often at the mercy of their children – held to ransom by the power of love.

Parental love takes most people completely unawares. Take Julia Roberts' letter about her newborn twins, read out on *The Oprah Winfrey Show* at the beginning of 2005:

'The babies are amazing. The way they stare into your eyes, their exuberant smiles, how they begin each day all warm and sleepy, smelling of promise. I suppose I never realised it before – babies aren't really born of their parents, they're born of every kind word, loving gesture, hope and dream their parents ever had. Bliss.'

If you've gone through the experience of motherhood (or the more hands-on type of fatherhood), Ms Roberts's outpourings may bring a tear to your eye. If you haven't, it'll probably make you reach for the sick bag. The trouble is, there's a very fine line between the deep parental urge to care for a child and crippling sentimentality. If you land on the wrong side of it, even the youngest child – indeed, especially the youngest, with its charming gurgles and terrifying screams – could soon have you performing somersaults at its behest.

It seems only fair, therefore, to prepare parents for this experience. The media are already lending a hand with all those nanny programmes – but such TV crazes come and go, depending on the ratings. There are also some excellent books and courses available, such as the Australian Triple P: Positive Parenting Programme, which in a recent supervised trial was found to cut disruptive behaviour by half, while strengthening marriages and reducing parental stress.

Triple P uses new technology to great effect – videos, website links and so on. Indeed, as mentioned in Chapter 9, multimedia and the Internet show increasing potential to fill the gap in handing out knowledge left by the death of the extended family, village wise women and so on. But it's still up to parents to seek out support. If child-rearing is to take its rightful place at the centre of our culture, we need to ensure every parent knows the nuts and bolts of child development – and this probably means governments have to get involved. But here we run into the problem that's raised its head repeatedly throughout *Toxic Childhood* – how much should the state interfere in the way families function and children are brought up?

Can Nanny know best?

The question of state intervention into the way we rear our young always raises fierce opinions. There was, for instance, an extreme reaction in Germany in 2004 when a government minister, reporting that childhood obesity had reached near epidemic proportions, called for an initiative to change children's eating and exercise habits. Critics condemned her suggestion as 'reminiscent of regimented youth programmes under the Nazis and Communists' and a political opponent reflected that 'the whole thing raises an eery spectre, especially talk about mandatory PE and intimidating manufacturers into "doing the right thing"'. The following year, the British press had a field day when the government introduced its Childcare Bill, an innocuous framework for people looking after babies and toddlers outside the home, to regulate the hotchpotch of daycare provision that had sprung up around the country. One paper tried to start a panic about 'a national curriculum for babies' while another talked darkly about the child hatcheries of Aldous Huxley's *Brave New World*.

This particularly deep-rooted resistance to any sort of intervention in child-rearing seems to stem from a feeling that bringing up children is a 'natural' human process, not requiring guidance or regulation by the state. Yet one of the key factors behind toxic childhood syndrome is that profound social and cultural changes have cut parents off from the child-rearing lore that was once passed down through the female line. We no longer have any 'natural' access to knowledge about children and how they develop because we no longer live in extended families within tight communities, with grandmothers and other 'wise women' on hand to proffer help and advice. And unless we start acquiring this knowledge from somewhere else, the damage to children – especially in Mind the Gap families – seems likely to increase.

States around the world have often intervened to protect children's interests in the past. The banning of child labour and the introduction of compulsory schooling, two instances of the nanny state that are now normalised by custom, both arose in response to signficant social and cultural change, and were both at the time considered a gross infringement of parental rights. The state intervention I'm suggesting here is not government diktats or even advice on child-rearing. It's just that states should help pass on to *every* citizen the key messages learned from science about how children develop and what they need at different stages.

In the first instance, this could be done via the education system. At the moment, most countries provide sex education lessons, but nothing about the needs and nurture of the living products of sexual relationships – a strange and worrying omission. The best way to ensure a minimum baseline of knowledge for all adults would be to include the study of child development within the secondary school curriculum, when students are in their mid-teens. A short course on human development based on neuroscience and psychology could be both interesting and informative for teenagers, as well as arming them in advance for parenthood.

A second blast of information could be delivered through the health service as an integral part of antenatal and post-natal care – when prospective parents really have a reason to listen. And perhaps a third instalment could be provided through schools when parents enrol their children for full-time education. A short presentation at the antenatal clinic or school parents' meeting could convey the key facts about child development, using up-to-date technology to provide information as memorably as possible. Access to further detail and advice could then be available on demand via the web. As recommended elsewhere in this book, schools could also be valuable distributors of research-based advice for rearing healthy children – such as recommended bedtimes, information on healthy eating and guidance about electronic entertainment.

A recent cartoon in the *New Yorker* shows a pair of exhausted parents, surrounded by the products of global technology and telling their children, 'Your mother and I are feeling overwhelmed, so you'll have to bring yourselves up.' In the maelstrom of social change and moral disorientation, a few universally shared facts about children's developmental needs could help all parents feel less overwhelmed. And the reassurance that this shared information was based on up-to-date scientific knowledge should bolster their confidence to act authoritatively towards their children. At the very least, they might find it helpful to have the state's muscle behind them when explaining why early bedtime is important or a TV in the bedroom isn't a good idea.

At present, however, most governments dare not risk opening this particular can of worms. So the widespread ill-effects of contemporary culture on child development are not publicly debated, and there's no shared understanding in society about the difficulties of contemporary parenting. Parents continue to be overwhelmed, not only by tumultuous social and cultural change, but by the welter of information issuing from hundreds of different experts. And across the developed world children continue to grow up in an increasingly toxic environment.

*

Parenting is not just about looking inward, at the children in the centre of the family; it's about looking outward at the world where those children, and successive generations of children, will grow and live. Different cultures have always taken different attitudes to the moral and ethical education of their young, depending on religious, philosophical or political traditions. In terms of the relationship between individual and the state, the Japanese for instance have broadly recognised social conformity as the route to personal fulfilment, while the American dream is one of individual success eventually benefiting the whole of society. As the global village erodes tradition and brings us all closer together, the loss of cultural reference points adds to parental uncertainty. But whether you take the American view that 'it's the squeaky wheel that gets the grease' or, like the Japanese, believe that 'the nail that stands up must be hammered down', it's the balance of individual rights with social responsibilities that underpins life in a democratic society.

At present that balance is threatened by a terrible brew of market-driven self-indulgence, lack of moral direction and what sometimes seems like wilful misinterpretation of human rights legislation. And this confused state of mind is perpetuated by the media. As a frustrated headteacher wrote in *The Times Educational Supplement*, 'You can't watch daytime TV without being bombarded by commercials telling you that any accident you have should lead to compensation. Soap operas and magazines emphasise the rights of the individual to express themselves, be defiant, to shout as loudly as it takes to get their own way.'

Already many young people seem to be losing sight of the significance of social responsibility. Parents feel increasingly beset and isolated, and distrustful of those who once joined them in an adult alliance. Schoolteachers, neighbours and other members of the local community feel increasingly threatened by children's behaviour and parental distrust. Someone has to break this vicious cycle, and it probably has to be parents, since it's their children who have to live in the world we're creating today. As Julia Neuberger says in *The Moral State We're In*:

'Unless we rethink our social obligations and reassess the value of trust, we will become even more cynical, even more atomistic, ever more individualistic – and there really will be no such thing as society.'

DETOXING BEHAVIOUR

- Aim for an authoritative style in all dealings with your child. Try to be constantly aware of the need for *warmth* balanced by *firmness*.

- Parents' job is to give children what they need – this is not always the same as what they want. If your child wants something you know isn't good for him, it's your responsibility to stand firm.

- Authoritative parenting is much easier when all adults-in-charge agree (see 'Being an Adult-in-Charge: Some Things to Talk to a Partner About' page 164). If you can't agree, find ways to differ amicably – but keep a united front for the children.

- The younger the child, the more adults have to decide on the behaviour required and gently train the infant into that behaviour. The aim is to show children how to control their emotions so they can eventually become *self-regulating*. See for instance the advice on helping tiny babies become self-soothers (pages 85–87).

- The more you can ensure that the behaviour you want becomes ingrained as habit, the easier your child will find it to follow the rules – regularity, routine and consistency are critical, e.g., bedtime and ready-for-school routines, regular mealtimes and so on.

- Routine and regularity are also helpful to you. When particular aspects of the day-to-day grind are relegated to habit, you don't have to think about them. Then you can enjoy the chance to chat, think or perhaps listen to music as you get on with it.

- Decide with your partner on appropriate family rules and manners:

  - safety, health and hygiene rules
  - social conventions, such as table manners
  - moral rules to help children do-as-they-would-be-done-by
  - family rules to make everyone's life easier and more pleasant.

- Express rules positively as often as possible – what children should do, rather than what they shouldn't.

- Recognise that some of these rules (and the routines you embed them in) will change over time, as children get older, e.g., bedtimes. The older the child, the more important it is to involve him or her in discussions of family rules. Gradually, over the course of a child's first ten years, the aim is to move from parental regulation to self-regulation.
- Avoid falling into authoritarianism by remembering that children have to learn how to manage their *own* behaviour and emotions. The rules and routines parents establish are to help them towards this goal – they aren't holy writ. Don't let yourself get bogged down in petty issues of discipline.
- The language you use about behaviour should also be warm but firm:

  – praise good behaviour (don't take it for granted), but don't overdo the praise – if a child is praised to the skies for everything, it devalues real achievements
  – describe what your child has done that's made you pleased ('I love the way you're putting the bricks away!')
  – if your child behaves badly, explain what you don't like and why, but don't criticise more than is absolutely necessary (and never nag)
  – to elicit the behaviour you want, ask politely: if they don't respond, state firmly once more what you want the child to do – and expect it to happen.

- If your child states a point of view, listen respectfully and respond to it honestly. This shows you think the child competent and value his or her opinion. But it doesn't mean you have to agree – in the end, the responsibility for decisions rests with the parent.
- Be a good role model. Remember that your child will copy:
  – what you do and how you do it
  – what you say and how you say it.

RE-ESTABLISHING THE ADULT ALLIANCE

- Teach your child from the beginning to think about other people's feelings and needs, and to treat *everyone* with respect.
- Start when your child's a baby by acting in this way yourself. In public places (e.g., restaurants, church services, shops, museums, any sort of performance) try to position yourself where you can make a quick getaway if your child cries or misbehaves. Removing a distressed or disturbed infant means:

  – you don't disturb other members of the public
  – you can calm the child without risking the problem escalating.

- As well as trying to be considerate and trustworthy to others, it helps to assume that they'll reciprocate. While there are a few people around who can't be trusted, the vast majority are good-hearted. Start by hoping you can trust everyone, while keeping a wary eye open for any evidence to the contrary. Gradually teach your child to aim for the same balance.
- Explain that older people are less fit than younger ones, and age earns concessions (such as a seat on the bus or extra tolerance of irritating behaviour).
- This does not mean children should suffer behaviour that makes them uncomfortable or frightened – make sure they tell you about anything that worries them.
- Model respectful behaviour to other adults in the community yourself at all times. Don't be put off when other people don't keep up the same standards – someone has to start this ball rolling, and it's your child who should ultimately benefit from an increase in social capital.
- Make social contacts with other adults in your community, and – when an opportunity arises – talk about how important the adult alliance is. Listen to their opinions and concerns and try to draw them into re-establishing the alliance.
- If your child is disrespectful to an adult, apologise and show your

disappointment to your child. Explain later to your child what was wrong with the behaviour and why.

- Bear in mind that no child is perfect. Even a little angel may misbehave sometimes (I have seen delightful children lie through their teeth). If other people question your child's behaviour, listen respectfully to their point of view. Try to imagine how you'd feel if someone else's child had behaved in that way to you.

- If your child complains that an adult is behaving unpleasantly, talk it over and think about why they might be acting that way. (Once, when my daughter's teacher was being strangely snappy, we wondered if perhaps something was upsetting her outside school. My daughter decided to make her a 'My Favourite Teacher' card, and we were amazed at how much it cheered her up.)

- If all else fails, and an adult seems to have it in for your child, teach your child how to keep out of their way. And if that's impossible, help him or her learn the art of keeping a low profile to avoid incurring displeasure.

HOW TO DETOX A LITTLE MONSTER

- See 'detoxing behaviour' above. If your little monster's bad behaviour is deeply embedded, consult one of the books/websites on page 305. This short section cannot give more than a few starting points.
- Make sure you never inadvertently reward misbehaviour, e.g.:
  - by giving attention to a child who's misbehaving
  - by giving a treat to stop a child doing something
  - by laughing at bad behaviour.

All these will encourage the child to do it again.

- Choose your battles. You can't make a child perfect all at once. Decide which aspect of behaviour you're going to tackle first and ignore other aspects till you've made some headway with that. Then you'll have something positive to praise.
- With younger children, keep an eye out for behavioural flashpoints and distract your child before trouble starts, e.g.:

  - have a 'distraction bag', where you can stockpile interesting but safe items for ready access (see Chapter 8, 'How to Encourage Creative Play')
  - songs, games, rhymes, etc, make good distractions.

- With all ages, be prepared. The more you think through possibilities, the easier it is to deal with problems if they arise. If you know the sort of mischief your child's likely to get into, you can try to stop it happening, e.g.:

  - tell your child exactly what you want, discussing any difficulties he or she has with it
  - keep children occupied, e.g., with colouring books, songs and story tapes in the car
  - offer a reward for the behaviour you want (but only give it if you're satisfied)
  - use a system of incentives, e.g., a wall chart with stickers for good behaviour (but think this through carefully beforehand: if you start it, you have to stick with it, and reward systems can get very complicated)

– a simple reward system is the Marble Jar: put 20 marbles in a jar (well out of your little monster's reach) and take one away for every misdemeanour while adding one for every good deed. If by the end of a decreed period there are more than 20 marbles in the jar, convert them into a previously agreed reward.

- If possible, ignore silly, attention-seeking behaviour. The more fuss you make, the more likely your child is to repeat it.
- If you can't ignore it, nip it in the bud – don't let it escalate:

  – explain immediately and calmly what you don't like, what behaviour you want and what will happen if you don't get it – then expect your child to respond positively
  – don't get into an argument – wait for them to comply and if they don't, follow through calmly with the punishment.

- Don't ever let bad behaviour escalate to the point where you lose your temper, i.e., don't join in. Just look disappointed, act grown-up and continue to request the behaviour you're after. Don't give in and don't keep telling the child off. Just wait, if necessary restraining the child gently and guiding them into the behaviour you want. It can help to have a little mantra you recite to yourself on these occasions ('warm but firm, warm but firm' ...).
- Establish some sort of punishment for bad behaviour, e.g., time out on a naughty chair or docking pocket money, so you have something to use as a threat if your child misbehaves (plucking threats out of the blue is not a good idea because you can't always follow them through).
- The younger the child, the more immediate any punishment should be.
- If you threaten your child with anything, *always* follow through. If you don't, they'll just learn you didn't mean it.
- However, don't let yourself become focused on punishment. Find ways of being positive, such as praising good behaviour, and as soon as possible move into the general behavioural policies outlined in 'Detoxing behaviour'.
- There's much more specific advice in the books and websites listed throughout these detox pages.

Parent power: from authoritative parenting to authoritative communities

The suggestions throughout this book provide many vehicles for linking child-rearing to the re-establishment of social capital:

- Work with grandparents, extended family, neighbours and other parents to make communities safe for children.
- Collaborate with school and childcare agencies to look after *all* children's interests, not just your own.
- Develop social networks to help not only with raising your children, but also to establish a better work-life balance, find effective ways of policing the electronic village, and so on.
- Lobby for education about child development so the next generation don't have to try and find out about it haphazardly – a three-pronged approach would reach everyone:

  – a child development module in secondary citizenship classes
  – 'developmental needs 0–5' as part of ante- and post-natal care
  – child development meetings for parents when children start primary school.

It's only through families pooling their expertise and parents exercising their power as citizens that authoritative communities will come into existence.

Further reading

Tessa Livingstone, *Child of Our Time* (Bantam Press, 2005)

Norbert and Elinore Herschkowitz, *A Good Start in Life: Understanding Your Child's Brain and Behavior from Birth to Age 6* (University of Chicago Press, 2004)

Excellent self-help materials: Triple P: Positive Parenting Programme

Carol Markie-Dadds, Matthew Sanders, Karen Turner: *Every Parent's Self Help Workbook* and the Triple P Video: *Families: Every Parent's Survival Kit.* (Australia: Families International Publishing, 1999)

Useful websites

BBC parenting website: **www.bbc.co.uk/parenting**

Raising Kids: **www.raisingkids.com** (magazine format approach to child-rearing)

BBC/Open University child development and parenting: **www.open2net/childofourtime**

Mind the gap

I was walking down the road in a rundown English town behind two young mums. One had a babe-in-arms, the other was fielding a son of about two and a half. Suddenly this lad wanted to attract his mother's attention: 'Hey, bitch!' he cried, hitting her sharply on the arm. The two women laughed nervously. 'He gets it from his dad,' the mother explained to her friend.

The decline in standards of behaviour is all around us, but it's at its worst in areas of social deprivation. Mothers who have so little self-respect that they allow *anyone* to call them 'bitch' are unlikely to encourage self-regulation in their offspring, let alone a feeling of social obligation. Thus, general lack of respect is passed on through the generations, and antisocial behaviour swells in deprived areas, adding to the misery of poor families while generating even more bad behaviour.

Children growing up in such communities often have little option but to band together for protection. As a boy in Michigan told the child development expert James Garbarino, 'If I join a gang, I'm fifty per cent safe. If I don't join a gang, I'm nought per cent safe.' And in a morally relative society, once children are roaming in packs, there seems no way of putting a brake on their activities before gang behaviour spills over into law-breaking.

The English MP for Birkenhead, Frank Field, has described how the concerns of his constituents in rundown areas have changed over the twenty-odd years he's represented them. They used to bring queries about housing, jobs and benefits, but in the last ten years their main question has been, 'What can be done to stop our lives being made a misery by the unacceptable behaviour of some of our neighbours, or, more commonly, our neighbours' children?' After researching the subject for many years, he has concluded that draconian methods are necessary to stop the rot, including giving the police the power as surrogate parents to discipline out-of-control youths, and linking welfare payments to acceptable behaviour. I'm sure he's right: once social order has broken down to such an extent, top-down authoritarianism is probably the only way to patch it up.

But Field also believes that education in parenting and citizenship are essential if social cohesion is to be restored. That tackles the problem from the bottom up, hopefully ensuring that future generations of children will be reared to respect themselves and others. In the most advanced and advantaged civilisation in the history of the planet, we should all be ashamed when a two-year-old child has learned to call his mother 'bitch'.

CONCLUSION

DETOXING CHILDHOOD

It is the best of times, it is the worst of times. We live in an age of comfort, convenience and promise – a wonderful place for grown-up human beings to work and relax. But it's not always the best of all possible worlds for children. Deep in our hearts we all know it, but we're frightened to admit it. The world we've created is damaging our children's brains.

Neuroscientists can now describe what happens in the brains of children diagnosed with developmental disorders. They point to gluts or surfeits of particular chemicals, or to faulty neurological structures in particular areas, notably the prefrontal cortex. It's clear these symptoms can be inherited, or occur as the result of trauma before or during birth. But neuroscientists have also shown that the over-whelming majority of connections between neurons in the human brain, and the chemicals that enable those connections, are created during childhood, and are affected by children's experiences.

The eminent neuroscientist Susan Greenfield once wrote that there are as many neurons in a human brain as there are trees in the Amazonian rainforest, and as many connections between those neurons as there are leaves on those trees. To continue the analogy, the chemicals helping the neurons connect are like the sunshine, water, air and earth of the Amazonian forest.

With such a remarkable network of wiring and chemicals in our skulls, it's highly unlikely that a single environmental influence could cause much damage – just as in the vast tracts of the Amazon jungle, the occasional drought, heatwave or man with a chainsaw won't upset the complex ecology. But if a great many things go awry at once, if the build-up becomes so great it reaches tipping point, even an Amazonian rainforest can be endangered. I believe, along with a growing number of experts in the field, that the damaging factors in the daily life of many children in the developed world are perilously close to that tipping point.

I ❤ my attitude problem ... and my mum and dad ❤ me

Do you remember the child on the steps of the Uffizi? Ten years old at the most and the unhappiest of bunnies. How did she get like that? Perhaps she's spent ten years feeding on burgers, pizza and ice cream, washed down with sugary cola. Maybe she spends long hours in a virtual world of her own, absorbing the messages of the marketing men, playing computer games rather than real ones, staring at TV programmes rather than going out to play in the sunshine. Does she lie awake till the early hours, watching unsuitable TV and texting her chums? Has this sedentary, screen-based lifestyle led to problems at school in concentrating, controlling her temper or relating to other people? And are her parents bewildered that their beloved little girl seems so troubled, when they've provided her with every luxury money could buy?

Of course, her parents are products of contemporary culture too. It's no coincidence that toxic childhood syndrome seems worst in the four most economically successful nations on earth. The very characteristics that make those countries so rich – competitiveness, commitment to work, the capacity to embrace change – also create citizens ill-adapted to bring up children. So I imagine our little girl's parents have found raising a child a rather bewildering experience.

At school and work, they've been taught that it's good to work harder, aim higher, drive themselves to ever crazier deadlines. So they've probably taken the same approach to child-rearing, wanting their little princess to be the best, the first, the winner. I bet they enrolled her as early as possible in a day nursery that did 'proper work' and paid for lots of clubs and classes to ensure she was always one step ahead of the herd. Perhaps they pushed her to achieve at school, which (if toxic childhood has undermined her potential to learn) merely added to her angst. Out of school, they've certainly allowed her to grow up fast, letting her dress provocatively, like someone twice her age – although the ironic comment on her chest suggests that, actually, she still behaves like a very small child.

I also bet that, to keep their princess in consumer goods, both parents work long hours and bring projects home with them, ready to respond to emails and phone calls twenty-four hours a day. Parents who work so intensely often find it difficult to break away and slow down to the ancient, human rhythms of family life. What's more, their twenty-first-century minds are programmed to seek constant change and stimulation – not the same rites and rituals every day. So there's probably not been much stability and routine in their daughter's life, or the security of knowing what's coming next. Perhaps the most predictable elements of her day are the theme tunes of her favourite TV shows.

I shouldn't think mum and dad worry about how much TV she watches. As lifelong TV watchers themselves, they probably trust technology more than they trust the natural world, with its unpredictable weather, unknown physical hazards and people lurking with criminal intent. They feel safer knowing their daughter's tucked up with her telly and console games than outside interacting with all that threatening reality. It's never occurred to them that letting her wander alone in the electronic village now exposes her to far greater dangers than lurk in the average local park.

Above all, it's not difficult to imagine their parenting style – warm, but far from firm. When their little one was born they probably hadn't the foggiest idea what was involved in bringing up a child and thought that love would conquer all. She must have led them a merry dance from the beginning. Once the marketing men inveigled their way into her life, the poor parents didn't stand a chance – the need to supply more and more consumer goods ensured they were trapped for ever on their career paths, earning money to feed the monster their love had inadvertently created.

My heart goes out to those parents. Nobody told them about cultural side effects – nobody really knew. Indeed, having fallen into most of the same traps (albeit – thank God – in an earlier age, when the consequences weren't quite as dire), I have enormous sympathy for them both. They loved their princess not at all wisely, and far, far too well.

Tackling toxic childhood syndrome

We've seen that the following aspects of children's lives affect brain function and healthy emotional, social and cognitive growth. We've also seen that, in the lives of very many children, every one of them has undergone considerable changes in the last twenty to thirty years:

- the food children eat
- the amount of exercise, activity and unstructured play they engage in
- the amount of time spent outdoors, especially in natural surroundings
- the length and regularity of sleep
- the security and stability of lifestyle
- the potential for attachment in the first eighteen months
- the amount adults talk to them, and the way they talk
- the level of first-hand experiences they have throughout childhood
- the consistency of childcare arrangements
- the degree to which they're helped to be self-regulating
- the role models available to them
- the level of emotional security and stability throughout childhood
- the time available for social interactions within the family

- the ethos of the pre-school and schools they attend
- the confidence of parents in all aspects of child-rearing
- the 'adult alliance' of neighbourhood support.

These changes have resulted in the side effects of contemporary culture feeding toxic childhood syndrome. There are, however, many ways in which governments and other institutions can help to detox childhood. For instance, in various parts of the world, you'll find:

- healthy, compulsory school meals in pleasant surroundings
- banning of the sale of junk food in areas around schools
- initiatives to promote healthy eating, such as the Edible Schoolyard Project where children grow and prepare foods for school meals
- organised transport or 'walking buses' taking children to and from school
- child-friendly city planning, such as home zones and shared space, making safer streets for children to play outside
- movements for the greening of cities and creation of natural playgrounds
- well-funded child-centred pre-school provision for the under-sixes
- flexible, affordable, high-quality childcare, appropriate to various ages
- an exciting primary-school curriculum, with a balanced approach to literacy
- the banning of marketing to pre-teen children
- tight regulation of mobile phone ownership
- television programmes and websites to help parents
- successful, widely used parenting programs.

If every government adopted these policies for its future citizens, the sum of human happiness would be greatly increased. But while government action is important, parents are ultimately responsible for their children's well-being, as the detox sections at the end the preceding ten chapters make clear.

If you're a parent wondering where to start, don't panic – it's not a race. Neither do you have to be a perfect parent: just, in the words of psychologist Donald Winnicott, 'good enough'. Take a long look at your child's lifestyle, and talk with your partner, other family members and – if he or she's old enough – your child, to plan a strategy. Then remember the mantra 'Warm but firm, warm but firm', as you start putting it in place.

Once you get going, you'll probably find the detoxification process leads to some changes in your own life.

- You'll have to slow down, smell the roses and notice the real life going on around you.
- You'll have to spend time talking, doing, sharing, connecting with those close to you.
- To establish routines and habits for your child, you'll need to find ways of organising your life to give more time to home.
- This may mean re-examining your values and establishing what's really important to you and your family.
- With luck, you'll also become more involved with your real-life community – meeting other adults with interests that overlap with your own.

Interestingly, these are the same changes you'd pay a fortune to hear from a lifestyle guru, life coach or psychotherapist.

How detoxing childhood makes everyone happier

The beginning of the twenty-first century saw a glut of books about human happiness. They include lifestyle books, psychotherapy books, scientific tomes and, in 2005, Professor Richard Layard's *Happiness* – surely the most extraordinary (and readable) book on economics ever written. All of them tell us what science has shown: given a certain level of economic well-being, happiness in a social animal such as homo sapiens comes not from more money but from successful personal relationships with family and friends, and in the local community.

This finding is, of course, at odds with current economic theory, which stresses the importance of continued economic growth. To continue this growth, the market needs us to believe that the true route to happiness is through spending money. Hence the concerted drive of marketeers, aided by the miracles of technology, to divide and conquer. By splintering us off from our communities and our families, luring every man, woman and child into personalised virtual worlds where the advertisers can exploit their particular psychological vulnerabilities, the market creates the conditions in which to sell more stuff.

When you remove the TV from a child's bedroom and concentrate instead on real, human interaction, it's not only the first step in detoxing childhood, it's also the first step to becoming happier yourself. If you join with other parents to organise 'eyes on the street' or lobby for better child protection in the global village, you'll not only help the detoxification process for your children and others, you'll create the social capital communities need to thrive.

This doesn't mean turning our backs on the wonders of technology, sending Honey back into the kitchen, or failing to embrace exciting developments in the future. It doesn't mean stopping our children from enjoying TV, computer games or the excitement of the web. It simply means finding a balance between technological fixes and human needs – being warm but firm with ourselves about the extent to which we allow technology to determine our lifestyle. It also means addressing our work–life balance with the same warmth and firmness, and taking an authoritative hold on the way we choose to spend our time.

*

It seems to me that if we get the balance right for our children, we'll get it right for the whole electronic village. And if we start today, we might even be in time to save the world.

SURVEY OF PRIMARY TEACHERS

During 2004–5, I questioned 1,000 British primary-school teachers about how far they felt cultural factors were affecting children's learning. They came from schools all over the UK, both rural and urban and across the socio-economic range, but their opinions were remarkably homogenous.

The main question asked was:

'How much do you think each of the following factors affects the learning of the children you teach?'

The options were: 'Very much', 'Quite a lot', 'Not much' or 'Not at all'.

Very few answered 'Not at all' or 'Not much'. The graph below indicates the number of teachers who felt children's learning was significantly affected.

The list of factors was compiled in consultation with a group of teachers in 2003, in the very early stages of my research. As time went on, I wished I could add others (such as 'The effects of marketing') but for statistical reasons, I was stuck with the original categories. Nevertheless, over the year, it was instructive to receive constant reaffirmation of the impact of these cultural factors from people who spend their whole day interacting with real, live children. My thanks to all those teachers who filled in the form, especially those who provided a phone number so I could interview them further (and apologies to those I wasn't able to contact).

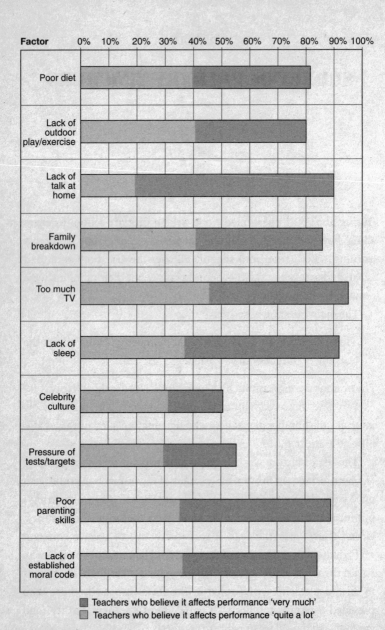

Teachers who believe it affects performance 'very much'
Teachers who believe it affects performance 'quite a lot'

NOTES AND REFERENCES

INTRODUCTION: TOXIC CHILDHOOD SYNDROME

What's happening to children?

- Mental health of young people: see Collishaw, Stephen, Maughan, Barbara, Goodman, Robert, Pickles, Andrew, 'Time Trends in Adolescent Mental Health', *Journal of Child Psychology and Psychiatry* No.8, pp.1350–63, November 2004; DeAngelis, Tori, 'Children's mental health problems seen as "epidemic"', *American Psychological Association: Monitor on Psychology*, Vol. 35, No. 11, December 2004. In August 2005, the UK Office for National Statistics reported that one in ten children in Great Britain aged 5–16 had a clinically recognisable mental disorder in 2004. Similar figures were reported at the same time in Germany: Rosenblatt, *Evidence-Based Mental Health*, 2005; 8: 28
- For general statistics on destructive teenage behaviour, see the World Health Organisation's ongoing study 'Young People's Health in Context': www.euro.who.int/eprise/main/who/informationsources/publications/catalogue/20040518_1. According to US government statistics for 2002, suicide is the third leading cause of death for young people (National Vital Statistics Reports, 2004) and the UK Office of National Statistics recorded one in fifty 11–15-year-olds trying to harm or kill themselves (*Children and Adolescents Who Try and Harm, Hurt or Kill Themselves*, 2001)
- Antisocial behaviour in Germany, for comment and review see 'Youth Violence on Rise in Germany' by Eric Geiger, Chronicle Foreign Service 17/3/01, reprinted in *Today* magazine of the International Child and Youth Care Network; for figures and carefully argued social solutions see 'Juvenile Delinquency – Facts, Problems and Challenges for Local Government' by Silke Pies and Christian Schrapper *Deutsche Zeitschrift für Kommunawissenschaft* Vol. 42 (2003) No. 1 on www.difu.de
- Elaine Lies, 'Japanese Girl, 11, cuts girl's throat', Reuters News, Tokyo, 3/6/04; 'Serious Crimes by Juveniles Under 14 on Rise' Kyodo News Service, Japan Economic Newswire 3/2/05

The 'special needs' explosion

- ADHD Wender, 2000
- ADHD statistics: American Academy of Pediatrics website, 2005 (www.aap.org)

cites between 4 per cent and 12 per cent of school-age children with ADHD
- Dyslexia: Snowling, 2000
- Dyslexia statistics: http://www.dyslexia-inst.org.uk/
- ASD: Frith, 1991
- ASD statistics: American Academy of Pediatrics website, 2005; UK autism figures: *Survey of the Mental Health of Children and Young People in Great Britain*, 2004 commissioned by the Department of Health and the Scottish Executive, carried out by the Office for National Statistics. These may be underestimates: at the International Meeting For Autism Research Conference in 2001, the noted autism epidemiologist Dr Eric Fombonne stated that the prevalence of autism is '68 per 10,000 or 1–147'.

Nature, nurture and behaviour

- Nature and nurture are vibrantly interactive: see for instance Rose, 2005, Greenfield, 2003
- Monkey research quoted in National Research Council, Institute of Medicine, *et al.*, 2000.

Learning to behave

- Experiment on deferred gratification: see Goleman, 1997, replicated by BBC *Child of Our Time* programmes, see Livingstone, 2005

A twenty-first-century report card

- The process of learning to read actually develops children's powers of thought and understanding – see Chapter 7, and Donaldson, 1978 and 1989
- Street-Porter, Janet, 'I've Changed My Mind Over Smacking', *Independent*, 4/11/04
- Increases in bullying are reported across the developed world, e.g., Ernest Gill 'Bullying Takes on Epidemic Proportions in German Schools' Deutsche Presse-Agentur, 7/7/05; Amelia Hill 'Children's Czar Warns of Huge Increase in Bullying' *Observer* 13/11/05
- Japanese literacy standards: 'Falling Academic Standards a Cause for Concern, Not Panic' Midori Matsuzawa, *The Yomiuri Shimbu* (Tokyo), 8/2/05

The blind men and the elephant

- Commentators have been complaining about reduced attention span ever since television became widespread in the 1950s, and over the last twenty years children's viewing has escalated wildly. e.g.,Winn, 2002
- The poem by John Godfrey Saxe, 'The Blind Man and the Elephant'

> It was six men of Indostan
> To learning much inclined,
> Who went to see the Elephant – (Though all of them were blind),
> That each by observation – Might satisfy his mind.
>
> The First approached the Elephant,
> And happening to fall
> Against his broad and sturdy side, – At once began to bawl:
> 'God bless me! but the Elephant – Is very like a wall!'
>
> The Second, feeling of the tusk,
> Cried, 'Ho! what have we here?

So very round and smooth and sharp? – To me 'tis mighty clear
This wonder of an Elephant – Is very like a spear!'

The Third approached the animal,
And happening to take
The squirming trunk within his hands, ffi Thus boldly up and spake:
'I see,' quoth he, 'the Elephant ffi Is very like a snake!'

The Fourth reached out an eager hand,
And felt about the knee.
'What most this wondrous beast is like ffi Is mighty plain,' quoth he;
''Tis clear enough the Elephant ffi Is very like a tree!'

The Fifth who chanced to touch the ear,
Said: 'E'en the blindest man
Can tell what this resembles most; ffi Deny the fact who can,
This marvel of an Elephant ffi Is very like a fan!'

The Sixth no sooner had begun
About the beast to grope,
Than, seizing on the swinging tail ffi That fell within his scope,
'I see,' quoth he, 'the Elephant ffi Is very like a rope!'

And so these men of Indostan
Disputed loud and long,
Each in his own opinion ffi Exceeding stiff and strong,
Though each was partly in the right ffi And all were in the wrong!

The past is another planet

- 'The past is a foreign country' L.P. Hartley, *The Go-Between* (Penguin, UK, 1953)
- Canadian media visionary Marshal McLuhan: see McLuhan and Fiore, 2001

Detoxing childhood

- Boseley, Sarah, 'Big Rise in Number of Children Given Mind-altering Drugs', *Guardian*, 18/11/04
- We could dole out drugs: Wong, I., Murray, M., et al., 'Increased Prescribing Trends of Paediatric Psychotropic Medications', *Archives of Disease in Childhood*, 89:1131–2, 2004
- Courtney Love quote, see Eberstadt, 2004

Mind the gap

- Decline of social mobility in UK: Buxton, J., Clarke, L., Grundy, E. and Marshall C.E., *The Long Shadow of Childhood: Associations Between Parental Social Class and Own Social Class, Educational Attainment and Timing of First Birth; Results From the ONS Longitudinal Study* (London School of Hygiene and Tropical Medicine 2005) quoted in News Release from UK Office of National Statistics, 29/10/05

CHAPTER ONE: FOOD FOR THOUGHT

- Dangers of unhealthy eating are widely reported, e.g. Olshansky, S., Passaro, D., et

al., 'A Potential Decline in Life Expectancy in the United States in the 21st Century'
New England Journal of Medicine, 253, 11, 17/3/05
- Quote about brain degeneration: report of plenary address by Anthony E. Kelly,
George Mason University, USA, to the OECD Brain Research and Learning Science
Symposium, Germany, 2003
- International food guidelines: Knight, Jonathan, 'Around the World in Three
Square Meals', *Nature*, 24/2/05; US 2005 food pyramid: www.mypyramid.gov
- US 2005 nutrition guidelines update: www.healthierus.gov/dietaryguidelines
- Quote about guidelines by Michael Jacobson, head of the Center for Science in the
Public Interest, a nutrition advocacy group in Washington DC, quoted in Butler,
Declan and Pearson, Helen, 'Flash in the Pan', *Nature*, 24/2/05

Junk-food junkies
- I'm indebted throughout this section to Dr Susan Jebb, Head of Nutrition and
Health Research at the Medical Research Council (HNR) Centre, Cambridge –
personal interview, 2004
- Sugar content of canned drinks: Warren S. Jafferian, Vice President, Worldwide
Education Market, Sodhexo USA – personal interview, 2004
- Addiction quote: Deanne Jade, psychologist and founder of the UK Centre for
Eating Disorders, reported by Rachel Newcombe, 'Is Junk Food Addictive?', *BUPA
Investigative News*, 19/7/03

Marketing messages
- Research on Coca-Cola's effect on the brain: Dr P. Read Montague of the Brown
Human Neuro-imaging Laboratory at Baylor College in Houston, Texas. Reported
in the *Independent*, 17/10/04
- Children and brands: from the Ofcom report: *Childhood Obesity – Food Advertising in
Context: Children's Food Choices, Parents' Understanding and Influence and the Role of Food
Promotions*, UK, July 2004
- Fruity snack advertising campaign: Felicity Lawrence, consumer affairs
correspondent, 'Revealed: How Food Firms Target Children', *Guardian*, 27/05/04. The
campaign was for Kellogg's Real Fruit Winders, a snack which is one-third sugar,
and Lawrence's article was based on the submission from an advertising agency to
the Institute of Practitioners of Advertising for an 'effectiveness award' in 2002

Trapped in the junk-food jungle
- Schools promoting unhealthy food: see National Union of Teachers guidelines
(http://www.teachers.org.uk/resources/pdf/EXPLOITATION05.pdf) or check out
a schools marketing site, inviting companies to 'target your market: put your
brands in their hands' (http://www.fim.uk.com/)
- For details of Jamie Oliver's magnificent campaign – www.feedmebetter.com
- Lack of parental control over diet: Ofcom report 2004 (see above)
- 'Not wisely but too well': *Othello*, Act 5, Scene 6

Sugar rush
- See also: 'Sugar Rush', Karen Schmidt in *New Scientist*, October 2002 and Ursell,
2005
- Review of studies about vitamin and mineral deficiencies: *Nutrition, Health and
Schoolchildren*, British Nutrition Foundation, 2003
- Bernard Gesch, Senior Research Scientist, Oxford Department of Physiology, in

Food on the Brain, Independent TV, UK, 29/4/05
- Study at University of Southern California: Jianghong Liu, Ph.D., Adrian Raine, D.Phil., Peter H. Venables, Ph.D., D.Sc., and Sarnoff A. Mednick, Ph.D., D.Med. 'Malnutrition at Age 3 Years and Externalizing Behaviour Problems at Ages 8, 11 and 16 Years', American Journal of Psychiatry 161:2005–13, November 2004

The additive cocktail
- See Ursell, 2005
- Review of 283 snack foods in Carrots or Chemistry: Snacking and Child Health, Lizzie Vann, 2004: see press release on www.babyorganix.co.uk/media/coc2.htm
- Dr Vyvyan Howard, toxico-pathologist, Liverpool University, quoted by Tim Utton, 'Children's Drinks Are a Chemical Cocktail', Daily Mail, 11/5/04
- Patrick Holford, nutritionist in Food on the Brain, Independent TV, UK, 29/4/05

Fats and fish oil
- I am indebted for information in this section (and general background information throughout this chapter) to Dr Alex Richardson, Senior Research Fellow, Mansfield College and the University Laboratory of Physiology, Oxford
- Japanese research into Omega 3 deficiency: Dr H. Okuyama and others Progressive Lipid Research, 1997 35(4): 409–57
- Among the contemporary illnesses that may be linked to an Omega 3/6 imbalance are inflammatory diseases (including heart disease, high blood pressure and strokes) and depression
- Fish oil supplement research study 2005 – Richardson, A.J., Montgomery, P., 'The Oxford-Durham Study: a Randomized Controlled Trial of Dietary Supplementation With Fatty Acids in Children With Developmental Co-ordination Disorder' Pediatrics 115 (5) 1360–6, 2005
- Professor Tom Sanders quoted by Robin McKie, Science Editor, 'Modern Diet Storing Up Mental Health "Time Bomb" Warns Experts', Observer, 27/6/04
- Felicity Lawrence, quoted by Glenda Cooper, 'What Your Kids Should Be Eating', The Sunday Times, 27/3/05
- Dr Alex Richardson trans-fats quote – further information on this and other nutrition research on the Food and Behaviour Research website: www.fabresearch.org
- Anne Kelley quote: reported by Rachel Newcombe, 'Is Junk Food Addictive?', BUPA Investigative News, 19/7/03

The decline of the family meal
- Sheila Pell's article: 'Family Dinner Minus Family', Washington Post, 11/1/05
- UK survey about family meals: Regional Eating and Drinking Habits, Mintel, 2001

Meals, manners and marijuana
- The table manners survey, by Brewsters Restaurant chain, quoted by Adam Powell, 'Pupils Get Lessons in How to Use Knife and Fork', Daily Mail, 7/4/05. He also provided following quote from a headteacher, which is typical of what teachers tell me everywhere I go in the UK (although, interestingly, less so in mainland Europe). 'There has been a trend in the last five years for children to come to school unable to hold a knife and fork or sit at the table properly because of the decline in family meals and the availability of convenience foods. I think you would find that the majority of family homes do not have a table any more, and the

only time the family is together is in the car. It's amazing how many children go
home in the evening just as their father is coming home and their mother is going
out to do an evening shift.'

- Quote from Dr Pat Spungin (www.raisingkids.com) in same article (also personal
interview, 2005)
- Decline of family meals in Japan: Yukio Hattori interviewed by Masami Ito, staff
writer, 'Food for thought', Japan Times, 2/11/05
- Solitary toddlers quote: Karen Pasquali Jones, editor of Mother and Baby, quoted by
Alexandra Frean, 'TV Meals Are "Eroding manners"', The Times, 31/3/04
- Social significance of family meals: Eisenberg, Marla E. et al., Correlations Between
Family Life and Psychological Well-Being Among Adolescents, Archives of Pediatrics and
Adolescent Medicine, Aug 2004, Vol. 158
- Survey of 20 years' worth of National Merit Scholars in the USA showing they all
ate family meals by the National Merit Scholarship Corporation, reported in 'The
Family That Eats Together ...' by Mimi Knight in Christian Parenting Today,
January/February 2002

Feeding a family

- The chopstickless tribe quote: Asako Aramaki in 'Pick Up Those Sticks: Chopstick
Use Seen as Sign of Healthy Diet', Trends in Japan, edited by Japan Echo Inc, 8/7/05:
http://web-japan.org/trends00/honbun/tj990708.html
- Long-established Italian feeding routine for babies – I was told about this by
several Italian mothers who swear by it, but couldn't find any official references –
I suspect it dates back to before the Second World War. However, thanks to the
miracle of the web, you can find it here, complete with suitable disclaimer:
http://www.epinions.com/content_4367097988
- Two-year-old fussiness: Cooke, L., Wardle, J., Gibson, E.L., 'Relationship
Between Parental Report of Food Neophobia and Everyday Food Consumption in
2–6-Year-Old Children', Appetite 41 (2003) 205–6 or Wardle, J., Cooke, L. et al.,
'Increasing Children's Acceptance of Vegetables; a Randomized Trial of Parent-
Led Exposure', Appetite Journal 40 (2003) 155–62
- What, when, where; how much and whether: Satter, 2000
- Susan Jebb quote – personal interview, 2004

Cutting back on snack attack

- Healthy snacks list: Better Health Channel, Victoria Australia,
www.betterhealth.vic.gov.au

CHAPTER TWO: OUT TO PLAY

- Stevenson, Robert Louis, Child's Garden of Verses, 'Good and Bad Children'

The fear of fear itself

- Research on effects of World Trade Center attack: see Restak, 2003
- Negative content of TV news: Szabo, Dr Attila, study by Nottingham Trent
University's School of Biomedical and Natural Sciences, UK, Press Release – 'TV
News Can Make Us Miserable', 22/3/05
- Quote about Beslan siege: Melanie McDonagh 'How close to home these terrified

children seemed', *Sunday Times*, 5/9/04
- Children's fears: see Cantor, 2001, Bourke, 2005
- Quote from Kansas professor: Eric M. Vernberg, 'Psychological Science and Terrorism: Making Psychological Issues Part of Our Planning and Technology', in http://merrill.ku.edu/publications/2002whitepaper/vernberg.html

Putting fear in its place
- Child safety kit: Laura Sessions Stepp, 'Teaching Timidity To Kids', *Washington Post*, 8/12/02
- Asthma boom research: see 'Factors associated with different hygiene practices in the homes of 15 month old infants' and 'Hygiene levels in a contemporary population cohort are associated with wheezing and atopic eczema in preschool infants', both by A. Sherriff, J. Golding and The Alspac Study Team in *Archives of Disease in Childhood*, 2002; 87; 26–9

How fear turns children into couch potatoes
- I am indebted for much of the information in this section to Dr Amanda Kirby, Director of the Dyscovery Centre for Learning Difficulties, Cardiff, UK – personal interview, 2004
- Quote from Dr Christine Mcintyre, from a presentation at the Early Years Education Conference, Harrogate, 23/9/05: see also Macintyre and McVitty, 2004
- Sunshine avoidance: for information about vitamin D see Gillie, 2004 and www.healthresearchforum.org.uk
- Overweight two-year-olds: Reilly, J.J., Methven, E., McDowell, Z.C., Hacking, B., Alexander, D., Stewart, L., Kelnar, C.J.H., 'Health Consequences of Obesity', *Lancet*, January 2003

Getting children off the couch
- Info re deaths from accidents: Brown, Hester, Living Streets, 'School Run Mums Have Some Thinking to Do', *Independent*, 10/12/04
- Dr Amanda Kirkby – personal interview, 2004

PE, playtime and paranoia
- Japanese children's physical fitness: Ihara, Atsushi, 'Japan Perspective; Kids, Society Becoming Weak', *Daily Yomiuri*, 9/8/02
- Swiss children's fitness: Hershkowitz, 2002
- Decline of raijo taiso: Alice Gordenker, 'Better Off Sleeping Than Working Out', *Japan Times*, 16/8/02

The decline of the free-range child
- I'm indebted for many of the ideas in this and the following two sections to Tim Gill, Director of Rethinking Childhood – personal interview, 2004
- Research on children's loss of freedom: Simon Crompton quoting Professor Colin Pooley, Lancaster University UK, 'Look Out, No Kids About', *The Times*, 14/8/04
- Real and virtual risk assessment: Corinne Usher, clinical psychiatrist, quoted in *The Times*, 14/8/04, as above

Places to play, people to play with
- Loss of outdoor play space: Tim Gill, farewell lecture: *Bred into Captivity?* Children's Play Council, 20/9/04 – www.ncb.org.uk/cpc/cpcgilllecture.pdf

- Boring playgrounds: *Urban Myths About Children's Playgrounds*, Report of the Child Accident Prevention Trust, 31/8/05

Re-establishing children's right to roam
- Issy Coles-Hamilton, UK Children's Play Council, *Best Magazine*, May 2003
- The term 'eyes on the street' was coined by Mary Eberstadt: Eberstadt, 2004

Safer streets
- Ben Hamilton-Baillie, urban designer, address to Royal Society of Arts, Bristol, and personal interview, 2005
- Home zones – see www.homezonenews.org.uk
- Yellow school buses: successful pilot schemes in Wrexham and Hebden Bridge by the Sutton Trust were reported in 'It's Time for the Yellow Solution' by Hilary Wilce, *Independent* 16/6/05
- Walking buses in Japan: see Ashby, 1994. British example: http://www.worcestershire.gov.uk/home/large_text/cs-sus-transport-ooschool-plan-walking_buses
- *The Child in the City*, Degen-Zimmermann, D., Hollenweger, J., *et al.*, Zwei welten: Zwischenbericht zum Projekt 'Das Kind in der Stadt'. Zurich, Marie-Meierhofer-Institut fur das Kind (1992)

Happy play in grassy places
- Effects of greenery on ADHD: Taylor, A.F., Kuo, F.E. and Sullivan, W.C., *Go Out and Play: Nature Adds Up for ADD Kids*, University of Illinois, 2001
- Japanese *sanson ryugaku*: Alice Gordenker, 'City Kids Bring Diversity to Countryside Schools', *Japan Times*, 19/8/04
- Japanese tendency to tidy nature: Kerr, 2001
- Research on Japanese children and nature by Professor Tetsuro Saito of the Kawamura Gakuen Women's University, reported in the Sankei Shimbun 28/11/04 – in *Nature? What's That?* www.accj.journal (February 2005)
- The Canadian Evergreen movement: www.evergreen.ca
- Parks in Freiburg: Tim Gill – 'In need of an unlevel playing field', *Guardian*, 3/8/05
- Scottish playground – the Balmaha Playscape in Loch Lomond and Trossachs National Park: see Melville, 2005
- *Learning Through Landscapes*: www.ltl.org.uk
- Playwork – for information on playwork and playworkers, I'm indebted to Sue Palmer, Head of School of Film, Television and the Performing Arts, Leeds Met University – personal interview, 2005

CHAPTER 3: TIME FOR BED

- General background on sleep – Martin, 2003
- US National Commission on Sleep Disorders Research, *Wake Up America: a National Sleep Alert* (Washington DC, Dept of Health and Human Services – 1993)

Tired families
- Recommended sleeping hours and 2004 sleep poll: the US National Sleep Foundation – www.sleepfoundation.org

A good night's sleep

- For advice on this and the next two sections, I'm indebted to sleep researcher Dr Jan Born, Director of Neuroendocrinology at Luebeck University, Germany – personal interview, 2005

Learn while you sleep?

- The National Sleep Foundation (see above) points out that 'children who get enough sleep are more likely to function better and are less prone to behavioural problems and moodiness'. Many studies back this up, e.g., Fallone, G., Acebo, C., Seifer, R. and Carskadon, M.A., 'How Well Do Children Comply With Imposed Sleep Schedules at Home?', *Sleep Medicine Review*, 25, 739–45, USA, 2002
- Dr Gillian Nixon in Talk About Sleep, 2003 www.talkaboutsleep.com
- For a comprehensive summary of recent sleep research, see Martin, 2003
- Sleep provides opportunity for brain to reorganise and prune: Terry Sejnowski, Director of Computational Neurobiology Laboratory, Salk Institute, USA, quoted in *Time Magazine*, 2005

Why it's important to 'sleep on it'

- REM sleep and learning: Maquet, P., Laureys, S., *et al.*, 'Experience-dependent changes in cerebral activation during human REM sleep', *Nature Neuroscience* pp.831–6, August 2000
- Slow-wave sleep and learning: Huber, R., Ghilardi, M., *et al.*, 'Local Sleep and Learning', *Nature*, Vol. 430, 1/7/04
- Born, J., Gais, S., 'Low Acetylcholine During Slow-Wave Sleep is Critical for Declarative Memory Consolidation', PNAS Vol. 101 No. 7 2140–4, February 2004
- Born's creative thinking experiment: personal interview, 2005

Hush, little baby ... stopping sleep problems before they begin

- My overview of recommendations was taken from the American Academy of Pediatrics, the National Sleep Foundation and, in the UK, Livingstone, 2005
- Tessa Livingstone quote: Livingstone, 2005

The babies who haven't read the book

- One of the most popular books of recent years is *The Contented Little Baby Book* (Ford, 1999) – parents of babies who respond well to its strict sleep regime seem to love it; those whose babies respond badly tend to hate it.
- 'Fussy' babies: see Shimada, M. and Takahashi, K., 'Emerging and Entraining Patterns of the Sleep-Wake Rhythm in Preterm and Term Infants' in *Brain Development* 21, 1999 and National Research Council Institute of Medicine, 2000
- For more information on ways of soothing children, see Woodhouse, 2003
- If you've tried all the recommended techniques, and your child still has problems going to sleep and/or staying asleep beyond the age of nine months, check with a doctor or paediatrician, and perhaps ask for referral to one of the new 'sleep clinics' springing up all over the developed world

Time for a nap

- Why naps are important: Weissbluth, 2003
- TV and naps: Winn, 2002

Sleepy schoolchildren

- Research on children's lack of sleep: Silentnight Beds poll, reported in the

Guardian, 1/5/03; Chervin, R.D., Archbold, K.H., Dillon, J.E. *et al.*, 'Inattention, Hyperactivity and Symptoms of Sleep-Disordered Breathing', *Pediatrics*, 2002;109:449–56; Yoshimatsu, Shingo and Hayashi, Mitsu, 'Bedtime and Lifestyle in Primary School Children', *Sleep and Biological Rhythms*, Vol. 2, Issue 2, p.153, June 2004

- Brillat-Savarin, Jean-Anthelme, *The Physiology of Taste*, France, 1825
- Caffeine counter at www.sleepfoundation.org
- Among studies linking sleep with obesity: Horvath, T.L., Xiao-Bing, G., 'Imput Organization and Plasticity of Hypocretin Neurons, Possible Clues to Obesity's Association With Insomnia', *Cell Metabolism*, Vol. 1, Issue 4, pp.279–86, April 2005

Snoring and other worries

- Snoring research: Gozal, David *et al.*, 'Sleep Disordered Breathing and School Performance in Children', *Pediatrics* Vol. 102, No. 3 pp.616–20, September 1998; Chervin, R.D., Archbold, K.H., Dillon, J.E. *et al.*, 'Inattention, Hyperactivity and Symptoms of Sleep-Disordered Breathing', *Pediatrics*, 2002;109:449–56; see also Weissbluth, 2004
- Quote about tonsillectomy by Professor Jim Horne of Nottingham University: 'In the US experts have found that 20 per cent of children with mild to moderate forms of ADHD seem to have a disturbance of their sleep due to chronic colds, enlarged tonsils and breathing problems. The implication is that these sleep disturbances are the cause of mild to moderate ADHD behaviour but parents should make sure their children are not experiencing a sleep disorder before checking for ADHD. Sometimes, just removing a child's tonsils, for example, can solve the problem' in Niki Chesworth's 'How Lack of Sleep Can Turn Little Angels into Nightmares' in *Sunday Express*, 4/8/04

A regular bedtime

- Changes in children's behaviour due to sleep improvements: Dahl, R.E., Pelham, W.E., Wierson, M., 'The Role of Sleep Disturbances in ADD Symptoms' *Journal of Pediatric Psychology*, 16, 1991 and Gozal, Dr David, *et al.*, 'Sleep and Neurobehavioural Characteristics of 5 to 7-Year-Old Children With Parentally Reported Symptoms of ADHD', *Pediatrics* Vol. 111, No. 3, March 2003

The monsters in the bedroom

- TV and sleep problems: Owens, J., Maxim, R., McGuinn, M., *et al.*, 'Television Viewing Habits and Sleep Disturbance in School Children', *Pediatrics* Vol. 104, No. 3 September 1999; The Brown University Child and Adolescent Behaviour Letter, January 2000
- Figures for TVs in bedrooms: under-fours – US Kaiser Family Foundation survey 2003; over-fives – ChildWise Monitor Trends Report 2005, www.childwise.co.uk/trends.htm
- Resetting circadian rhythms: John Herman, Associate Professor of Psychiatry, in press release from the University of Texas Southwestern Medical Center, Dallas, USA, 30/9/02
- Effects of TV lights: Salti, R. and Galluzzi, G. *et al.*, 'Nocturnal Melatonin Patterns in Children', *Journal of Clinical Endocrinology and Metabolism*, Vol. 85, No. 6, 2137–44, University of Florence, Italy, 2000
- Long-term sleep problems: Johnson, J.G. *et al.*, 'Association Between Television

Viewing and Sleep Problems During Adolescence and Early Adulthood', *Archives of Pediatrics and Adolescent Medicine* 2004, 158, 562–8

- Mobile phones disturbing sleep: Van den Bulck, Jan, Senior Lecturer in Psychology, Catholic University of Leuven, Belgium, Letter to the *Journal of Sleep Research*, 2003:12:263
- Figures on mobile phone ownership: Campbell, Denis, 'Mobiles, Mp3s, DVDs: Raising a Generation of Techno-kids', *Observer*, UK, 13/02/05 – www.childwise.co.uk
- Franklin, Benjamin, *Poor Richard's Almanack for the Year 1735*

CHAPTER 4: IT'S GOOD TO TALK

- Communication by thumb. In Japan texters are known as 'the thumb tribe' ('*oyaj ubi zoku*') – this used to refer to people who spent their time playing a card game. Now it means those who prefer texting to speaking face to face

Language, literacy and learning
- For information on the British National Literacy Strategy, see www.standards.dfes.gov.uk/literacy
- American teachers' concerns: Healy, 1990
- German research: Herschkowitz, 2004
- Japanese teachers' concerns: '80 per cent of teachers say language skills declining', *Daily Yomiuri*, 8/8/02 quotation from Hidefumi Arimoto, Senior Researcher for National Institute For Educational Policy Research

Here's looking at you, kid
- 'The Dance of Communication': Dr Colwyn Trevarthan, personal interview, 2005
- The Epidemic: Shaw, 2003
- Early parent–child communication has been the subject of much interest in recent years, e.g. Gopnik *et al.*, 1999, Bloom, 2004
- For more on the significance of infant 'mind-reading' see Bloom, 2004; but also important is the extent to which mothers read their children's minds – see E. Meins, C. Fernyhough, R. Wainwright, D. Clark-Carter, M.D. Gupta, E. Fradley, and M. Tuckey. 'Pathways to Understanding Mind: Construct Validity and Predictive Validity of Maternal Mind-Mindedness' in *Child Development*, Vol. 74, Issue 4, 2003. This is an *interactive* process

The cradle of thought
- *The Cradle of Thought*, Hobson, 2002, and personal interview, 2005
- The second 'insight' gained in the triangle of interrelatedness is known as 'theory of mind' and is very popular at present among psychologists and philosophers, e.g., see Bloom, 2004
- The importance of children's symbolic play was clarified by the Russian psychologist Lev Vygotsky. He believed it was humans' ability to use symbols that set us apart – symbols are 'mental tools' which help us extend our control over our mental world in the same way that physical tools such as hammers and levers help us extend our control over the physical world. See also the article 'Lev Vygotsky' by Galina Dolya and Sue Palmer, on my website: www.suepalmer.co.uk (first

published in *The Times Educational Supplement*, July 2004)
- Most early years practitioners recognise symbolic play as critical to children's cognitive development, e.g., Bergen, Doris, 'The Role of Pretend Play in Children's Cognitive Development', *Early Childhood Research and Practice*, Vol. 4 No. 1, Spring 2002
- 'A growing body of neuroscientific research suggesting Hobson is right' – this case is powerfully argued in Gerhardt, 2004. See also the work of Dr Bruce Perry and others at the Baylor College of Medicine in Houston, Texas (www.childtrauma.org)

How contemporary culture disrupts the dance
- The descriptions of parents failing to communicate with children are anecdotal evidence, gathered from health visitors, speech and language therapists, and nursery practitioners on home visits – the same story is told all over the UK
- The Talk To Your Baby website (www.talktoyourbaby.org) is run by the National Literacy Trust. Information on pushchair design was provided by TTYB director Liz Attenborough at a steering group meeting, summer 2004

Tuning in or turning off
- Noise affecting children's school achievement, e.g., Hygge, S., Evans, G.W., and Bullinger, M., 'The Munich airport noise study – effects of chronic aircraft noise on children's cognition and health' *7th International Congress on Noise as a Public Health Problem*, Sydney, Australia, 268–74, November 1998
- TV noise affecting children's reading at six: research reported in review by the Kaiser Foundation: *Zero to Six: Electronic Media in the Lives of Infants, Toddlers and Preschoolers*, 28/10/03, see www.kff.org
- Sally Ward's research – personal interview, written up in several articles, e.g., 'Time for Teletubbies?', *Independent*, 30/10/1997. See also Ward, 2000
- Survey of headteachers about children's deteriorating speech and listening by National Literacy Trust, UK 2003; survey of nursery staff by I CAN (speech and language charity), UK, 2005: both referenced in 'Why the Au Pair May Be Damaging Children's Speech' by Julie Henry, *Sunday Telegraph*, 20/11/05
- Steady beat research – see Kuhlman, K. and Schweinhart, L.J. *Basic Timing and Child Development* (High/Scope Educational Research Foundation, Ypsilanti, Michigan, USA, 2000) and Palmer and Bayley, 2004
- Songs and rhymes on the web, e.g., http://www.nurseryrhymes4u.com/; http://www.bbc.co.uk/cbeebies/
- The recent craze for babysigning is another way of promoting parent–child interaction and communication, see www.babysign.com and www.babysigning.co.uk
- American Academy of Pediatrics recommendations on TV – *Television and the Family* – http://www.aap.org/family/tv1.htm

The language instinct
- The title of this section was taken from Steven Pinker's 1995 book, which summarises the Chomskian arguments, but doesn't acknowledge the importance of exposure to a particular language in order to internalise it – see Tomasello, 2003, Palmer and Bayley, 2004
- Early language development – Herschkowitz, 2004; Law, 2004; Woolfson, 2002

The power of words

- Dr Pat Spungin, social psychologist and founder of *Raising Kids*: personal interview, 2005
- UK study recommending 'sustained shared thinking': Siraj-Blatchford, I., Sylva, K., Muttock, S., Gilden, R., Bell, D., *'Researching Effective Pedagogy in the Early Years'*, Institute of Education, University of London, Department for Educational Studies/University of Oxford, UK, updated November 2004
- Quote from Iram Siraj Batchford – personal interview, 2004
- *How to Talk So Kids Will Listen, and Listen So Kids Will Talk*, Faber and Mazlish, 2001

How technology can dumb our children down

- Vincent's story told by Professor Jean Aitchison, Professor of Language and Communication, Oxford – personal interview, 2005
- Review of research into effects of TV and video – Close, Dr R., on behalf of the National Literacy Trust, 'Television and Language Development in the Early Years', March 2004

Stories and screens

- There have been many studies showing that reading to children helps them in school, e.g., 'The Importance of Parental Involvement in their Children's Literacy Practices', National Literacy Trust, 2004. In a recent book (Levitt, *et al.*, 2005) the authors argued that the practice is unhelpful – they didn't, however, give any good arguments or evidence to this effect, so I think they were just trying to be clever. For further arguments as to why reading is helpful, see Palmer and Bayley, 2004 and Bayley and Broadbent, 2005
- The lovely quote from RLS is in *Essays of Travel*, ii

The joy of txt

- Queen Victoria's letters – display at Buckingham Palace, World Writer's Day, 2003
- Steven Pinker's quote about the telegram and definition of TweenSpeak – Lindstrom, 2004
- The intuitive nature of computer literacy – see Johnson, 2005

Mind the gap

- Hart and Risley, 1995

CHAPTER 5: WE ARE FAMILY

Revolution, relationships and roles

- 2004 evaluation of the family: Williams, 2004

The mommy wars

- The expression 'mommy wars' has been used in the press since at least the mid-nineties to describe contemporary women's dilemma
- Women's 'resigned understanding' of working conditions: Report on British Social Attitudes, *Horizons* magazine, UK National Statistics Office, March 2005
- 'Women, Work and Marriage': Brinig, Margaret F. and Allen, Douglas W., *These Boots Are Made For Walking: Why Wives File For Divorce*, American Law and Economics Review, 2000

- *I Don't Know How She Does It*, Pearson, 2002
- 'After the age of forty, a third of women are infertile', Lord Robert Winston, British fertility expert, interviewed in the *London Evening Standard*, 9/8/05
- www.womendoingitall.com
- 'Pink medicine' babies, mothers who 'do it all' but have very little: see Heyman, 2000.

The mother of all dilemmas
- Madonna quote: *I'm Going to Tell You a Secret*, Channel 4 TV, 1/12/05

What are fathers for?
- Ruth Hill quoting Laurie Taylor, sociologist, and Jack O'Sullivan, Director of Fathers Direct in 'How New Man Turned into a Distant, Confused New Dad', *Observer*, 20/6/04
- Marion Salzman quote: Salzman, 2005
- Fathers' relationship with children: see Motherhood Project, 2001 and Livingstone, 2005
- Fathers' influence on child development: see Lamb, 2004

Old and new dads
- Young, Toby, 'Baby sling? All that says is 'eunuch on board' . . .', referring to 'Dad' magazine, *Night and Day*, 3/10/04
- Stepford Husbands survey: Future Laboratory, a consumer forecasting consultancy, interviewed 2,500, 20 to 45-year-olds in urban areas on behalf of www.match.com (a dating agency), 14/2/05

How technology comes between parents and children
- 'Attention deficit is the "paradigmatic disorder of our times"', Rekstak, 2004; see also Honoré, Orion Books, 2004
- *The Time Bind* reference: Hochschild, 1997
- The problems of Japanese salarymen: 'Family Support Policies in Japan' by Pat Boling www.yale.edu/leitner/pdf/Boling.doc
- Review of work–life balance research: Pocock, Prof. Barbara, Adelaide University, Australia, 'Can't buy me love?' *The Australia Institute*, February 2004

Happily ever after...?
- Gary Becker quote from *A Treatise on the Family*, Harvard University Press, 1981
- Marriage now merely 'an arrangement' – Wilson, James Q., 'The Decline of Marriage', *San Diego Union-Tribune*, 17/2/02
- 'Women Prefer Bricks to Rings', www.BBC.co.uk, 11/8/03
- Divorce rates: (http://www.divorcereform.org/rates.html, www.contemporaryfamilies.org)
- Ono, Hiroshi, economist, 'Divorce in Japan: Why it Happens, Why it Doesn't', *EIJS Working Paper Series* 201, The European Institute of Japanese Studies, 2004
- John Baker quote, personal interview, 2005

Breaking up is hard to do
- Emotional repercussions of divorce: Brown, Alex; Young, Ellie and Allen, Melissa, 'The Effects of Divorce on Children', *NASP Communique*, Vol. 32, 3, November 2003
- Is divorce becoming less traumatic for children?: Neale, Bren and Flowerdew, Jennifer, *Parent Problems: Looking Back at Our Parents Divorce: No.2* (Young Voice), 22/9/04

- Charlotte's quote: Dodd, Celia and Guest, Katy, 'How to Survive Divorce Without Damaging Our Children', *Independent on Sunday*, 10/10/04
- Long-term results of divorce: Sun, Y., 'Family Environment and Adolescents' Well-being Before and After Parents Marital Disruption: a Longitudinal Analysis', *Journal of Marriage and Family*, 63, 697–713, 2001

Minimising the trauma

- Talking to teddy quote: Professors Douglas, Butler, Murch and Fincham, family law specialists, Cardiff and Keele Universities, UK, *Family Law Journal*, May 2001
- Dr James Kraut quote in 'Children Centered Divorce': www.divorcesource.com/FL/ARTICLES/kraut1.html

Children in the centre

- For advice on this and the following section I am indebted to family experts Pat Spungin and Jill Curtis, personal interviews, 2005
- Information on Anna Wahlgren's work: Cecilia Weiler, personal interview, 2005

Forging a family

- I found the expression 'economy-friendly families' in the chapter by Richard Reeves in Diamond, *et al.*, 2004
- 'What makes a normal family' quote – see Hart and Risley, 1995
- The Archbishop of Canterbury, Speech at Queen Mary, University of London, UK, press release from Lambeth Palace Press Office, 11/4/05, www.Archbishopofcanterbury.org

Mind the gap

- One-parent families and poverty – Department for Works and Pensions survey, 2003 quoted in Diamond, *et al.*, 2004
- Births to single mothers: Barrett H.: *UK Family Trends, 1994–2004: Executive Summary*, National Family and Parenting Institute, 2004
- Problems of lone mothers in juggling work and childcare: see Heyman, 2000
- David T. Lykken, Dept of Psychology, University of Minnesota, in 'Parental Licensure', *American Psychologist*, November 2001
- Leon Feinstein research: 'Not Just the Early Years – the Need for Developmental Perspective for Equality of Opportunity' in *New Economy* 10:4, Dec. 2003
- Quote about state intervention from a recent Fabian Society pamphlet: Diamond, *et al.*, 2004.

CHAPTER 6: WHO'S LOOKING AFTER THE CHILDREN?

- Background information on international approaches to childcare: Childcare in a Changing World conference, Netherlands, 2004 and Organisation for Economic Cooperation and Development research project *Babies and Bosses* – www.oecd.org
- Neuroscientific research: the most comprehensive survey to date was commissioned by the US government in the late 1990s and published in 2000: *From Neurons to Neighbourhoods*, see National Research Council, Institute of Medicine, 2000. For a clear summary of key issues in brain development for parents, see Herschkowitz and Herschkowitz, 2002

For love or money ...

- *Babies and Bosses – Reconciling Work and Family Life* (OECD Publishing), Vol. 1: Australia, Denmark, The Netherlands, 12/11/02; Vol. 2: Austria, Ireland and Japan, 13/11/03; Vol. 3: New Zealand, Portugal, Switzerland, 5/11/04; Vol. 4: Canada, Finland, Sweden and the United Kingdom, 27/5/05
- Renate Schmidt, German Family Minister quoted by Kristine Ziwica in 'Germany Struggles to Close Daycare Gap', *Deutsche Welle*, 21/7/04
- 'Invisible curriculum of childcare' quote: Todd and Risley, 1995
- 'Cabbage patch' quote: Shirley Burgraff quoted in Reeves, R., 'Economy Friendly Families' – Diamond, *et al.*, 2004

Childcare on the cheap

- Falling birth rates: Lutz, W., Scherbor, S., Sanderson, W. 'The End of World Population Growth', *Nature*, 412 (2001)
- German low birth rate reference: Emma Pearse, 'Germany in Angst Over Low Birthrate', *Women's eNews* 11/4/05 http://www.womensenews.org/article.cfm/dyn/aid/2253
- Foreign Press Centre Japan Brief 10/6/05: *Concern Deepens over Continuing Slide of Birth Rate in Japan, No Stop in Sight*, www.fpcj.jp/e/

The hot housing rat race

- For background on early learning and brain development, see Nutbrown, 1999, Pinker, 2003. Also, with particular reference to hot-housing, Blakemore, Dr Sarah-Jayne, 'Life Before Three: Play or Hot-housing?' *RSA Journal*, February 2005
- Steve Petersen quote: see Bruer, 1999
- Canadian research into pushy mothers: Joussemet, M., Koestner, R., Lekes, N., Landry, R., 'A Longitudinal Study of the Relationship of Maternal Autonomy Support to Children's Adjustment and Achievement in School', *Journal of Personality*, Vol. 73, Issue 5, pp.1215–36, Oct. 2005
- Recent UK summary quote: Blakemore and Frith, 2005

Home sweet home

- Bowlby attachment quote: cited in Park, 2002
- For details on childcare options see national websites, e.g., in UK the Daycare Trust www.daycaretrust.org.uk; National Network for Childcare www.nncc.org; Child Care Link www.childcarelink.gov.uk
- Grandmothers acting as carers: research by Mintel *Women's Changing Lifestyles*, 30/11/05 suggested that as many as one in three grandmothers take on childcare duties
- Family members looking after children: research from both UK and USA suggests informal arrangements are generally less successful than formal ones: Gregg. P., Washbrook, L., 'Working Mums: What Impact on Children's Early Years Development?' *University of Bristol, CMPO Market and Public Organisation*, Issue 9, August 2003 and Bernal, R. (North Western University), Keane, M.P. (Yale) 'Maternal Time, Child Care and Cognitive Development: the Case of Single Mothers' preliminary version 22/8/05 on www.niu.edu. However, both research projects were concerned with children's progress in schoolwork: as a spokeswoman for the charity Working Families pointed out in the UK magazine *Children Now* (31/8/05 – 6/9/05), 'What isn't measured in the research is the

emotional health of the child.' Children cared for in happy secure surrounding, should be able to catch up later at school, and in this respect the anecdotal evidence I gathered about grandparents caring for children was generally pretty favourable.

- Summary of research on favourable effects of pre-school education from three: Goodman, Alissa and Sianesi, Barbara, *Early Education and Children's Outcomes: How Long Does the Impact Last?* Institute for Fiscal Studies, July 2005

Birth to three: the great daycare controversy

- 1997 report on effects of childcare on attachment: Belsky, Professor Jay, *et al.*, NICHD Study of Early Child Care Research Network 'The Effects of Infant Child Care on Infant–Mother Attachment Security', *Child Development*, 68, 1997; see also Belsky, Professor Jay, 'Developmental Risks (still) Associated With Early Child Care', *Journal of Child Psychology and Psychiatry*, 2001
- 2004 report: Professor Ted Melhuish quoted in 'The Effective Provision of Pre-School Education (EPPE) Project: Final Report', Institute of Education, University of London, November 2004
- 2005 Families, Children and Childcare survey quotes from 'Official: Babies Do Best With Mother' by Yvonne Roberts in the *Observer* 2/10/05. For further information on this survey see www.familieschildrenchildcare.org
- Biting in day nurseries: Eberstadt, 2005
- Penelope Leach quoted in 'Fear on Nursery Care Forces Rethink' by Madeleine Bunting, *Guardian*, 8/7/04
- Effects of attachment on brain development: Gerhardt, 2004
- Belsky quote: in 'The Debate Over Childcare Isn't Over Yet' by Beth Azar in *Monitor on Psychology*, Vol. 31, 3, April 2000, magazine of the American Psychology Association, www.apa.org

Three to six: the quest for quality pre-school provision

- The Belgian head teacher is right that it's the Anglo-Saxons. The Welsh have just amended their curriculum for the under-sevens to a more European model, the Northern Irish have also changed their approach to early years education, and there are indications of change in several Scottish education authorities. However, in the USA a previously child-centred approach to kindergarten teaching has become increasingly formalised
- International comparisons of achievement: PIRLS 2001 International Report: IEA's Study of Reading Literacy Achievement in Primary Schools, Mullis, I.V.S., Martin, M.O., Gonzalez, E.J., and Kennedy, A.M. (2003), Chestnut Hill, MA: Boston College
- Sylva, Kathy, Melhuish, Edward, *et al.*, 'The Effective Provision of Pre-School Education (EPPE) Project: Final Report', Institute of Education, University of London, November 2004
- Children from 'later start' countries overtaking others: see 'Completing the Foundation for Lifelong Learning: An OECD Survey of Upper Secondary Schools', OECD Publishing/Studienverlag Ges m.b.H, Centre for Educational Research and Innovation, 10/2/04
- Comparison of behaviour in Scandinavia and UK: *The Education of Six Year Olds in England, Denmark and Finland* Ofsted, UK, 22/7/03

- No benefit in extending pre-school hours: Sylva, Kathy, Melhuish, Edward, Sammons, Pam, *et al.*, 'The Effective Provision of Pre-School Education (EPPE) project: Findings from the Pre-School Period', Institute of Education, University of London, March 2003

Six to eleven: home from home?
- I'm indebted to Sue Palmer, Head of School of Film, Television and the Performing Arts, Leeds Met University, for many of the ideas in this section – personal interview, 2005
- Dr Christopher Arnold, Senior Educational Psychologist at Sandwell Metropolitan Borough Council, addressing the Division of Educational and Child Psychology Annual Conference, Bournemouth UK, 5/1/06
- American research quote from Nilda Cosco and Robin Moore *Playing in Place: Why the Physical Environment is Important in Playwork*, 14th Play Education Annual Play and Human Development Meeting: *Theoretical Playwork*: Ely, Cambridgeshire, UK. January 26–7, 1999 on www.naturalearning.org

Money can't buy me love
- Carl Honoré quote: Honoré, 2004

Mind the gap
- Savings made by early years help: see Diamond, *et al.*, 2004
- Quote re Headstart: Levitt and Dubner, 2005
- Study on long-term effects of too formal an early start: Schweinhart, L.J. and Weikart, D.P., 'Lasting Differences: The High/Scope Preschool Curriculum Comparison Study Through Age 23', *Monographs of the High/Scope Educational Research Foundation*, Ypsilanti, MI: High/Scope Press, 1997

CHAPTER 7: THE BEST DAYS OF THEIR LIVES

- Lyrical neuroscientists: Gopik *et al.*, 1999

Shades of the prison house
- Wordsworth quote: Intimations of Immortality from Recollections of Early Childhood, 1803–06
- Boys more likely to be affected than girls: there's gathering evidence (e.g., Baron-Cohen, 2004, Biddulph, 1998, Sax, 2005) that girls and boys have different strengths. Boys take longer to develop phonological discrimination, language development and fine motor control, which means slower progress in literacy skills often causing problems in the primary years
- William Crane quote in Alliance for Childhood, 2004

Why reading is important in a multimedia age
- Reading's effect on the brain: Blakemore and Frith, 2005; see also Donaldson, 1990
- Neil Postman quotes: Postman, 1994
- J.K. Rowling's *Harry Potter* books have inspired millions of children to read

Why Johnny still can't read ... and how he might
- Phonological basis of reading problems: Snowling, 2000
- Resumé of current state of research into reading problems: TV programme *The*

Dyslexia Myth produced by David Mills, Channel 4, 8/9/05; professional conference: The Death of Dyslexia, London 21/10/05

The educational rat race

* Amplification as opposed to acceleration: I'm indebted for ideas in this section to Galina Dolya, researcher at the Russian Academy of Education and co-author (with Professor Nickolai Veraksa) of the *Key to Learning: Developmental Cognitive Curriculum for Early Years* – personal interviews 2004–5
* Reports of aggression in early primary years: USA 'School Violence Hits Lower Grades', Greg Toppo *USA Today*, 13/1/03; UK *Child Education*, September 2005
* Marion Dowling quote from keynote speech to Early Years Conference, Harrogate UK, 24/9/2005
* Japanese politician quote: Nariaki Nakayama, minister of education, culture, sports and science and technology, in 'Academic Abilities Decline' Foreign Press Centre/Japan, 13/12/03
* Dropout rate for five-year-olds: there are no statistics for this, but at present 15 per cent of children in England fail to reach the expected minimum reading level at seven: experience has shown that very few are retrieved

Winners and losers

* Professor Joe Frost, 'Bridging the Gaps: Children in a Changing Society', University of Texas, 2003
* Thomas Jefferson quote – quoted from a letter to J. Bannister, Paris, 15 Oct. 1785, contained in *Memoirs, Correspondence, and Private Papers of Thomas Jefferson*, Vol. 1, Thomas Jefferson Randolph, ed., 1829, pp. 345–7
* Homer Simpson quote from *I Love Lisa*

Thinking in blinkers

* In 2005, all the teaching unions in England joined together to condemn the effects of high-stakes testing: *Key Stage 2 Assessment: a Joint Union Statement*, A joint statement by ATL, NAHT, NASUWT, NUT, PAT and SHA, 12/9/05
* Mullis, I.V.S., Martin, M.O., Gonzalez, E.J., and Kennedy, A.M., PIRLS, 2001 International Report: IEA's Study of Reading Literacy Achievement in Primary Schools, Chestnut Hill, MA: Boston College, 2003
* Policy Speech by Prime Minister Ryutaro Hashimoto to the 142nd Session of the Japanese National Diet, 16/2/98
* New Japanese curriculum: Michael Fitzpatrick 'Dawn of a New Creativity' in *The Times Educational Supplement*, 18/6/99 see also *Japan: Context and principles of education* on http://www.inca.org.uk/2162.html (updated 9/6/05)

The great e-learning revolution

* For more about Seymour Papert's work: http://www.papert.org/ and http://www.mamamedia.com
* Info on US technology spending etc, see Alliance for Childhood, 2004
* Munich Research: Fuchs, T., Woessmann, L., 'Computers and Student Learning: Bivariate and Multivariate Evidence on the Availability and Use of Computers at Home and at School', October 2004, presented at the Royal Economic Society's 2005 Annual Conference at the University of Nottingham, 23/3/05
* The great calculator scandal: see Ben Preston, 'Inquiry into Pupils' Use of Calculators', *The Times*, 23/5/95

- Greg Pearson quote in Alliance for Childhood, 2004

Parents and teachers

- I am indebted for ideas about this section to Hilary Wilce, author of *Help Your Child Succeed at School*, personal interview, 2005

Bullying tactics

- Bullying definition – www.direct.gov.org.uk

Dealing with discipline

- Nurture groups: see Bennathan and Boxall, 2002, Boxall, 2002
- United Nations Convention on the Rights of the Child, 1989 – see www.unicef.org/crc

Mind the gap

- Private schools in UK: see Patrick O'Flynn, 'Blair Admits State Scandal; Clamour to Be at Private Schools', *Daily Express*, 8/7/04 and Matthew Taylor, 'Fall in Private Pupils as Fees Rise', *Guardian*, 10/5/05 (The fall turns out to be related to falling birth rate.) There has also been an increase in parents removing children from school and teaching them at home: see http://www.home-education.org.uk/ and http://www.nheri.org/
- UK education secretary quote: Ruth Kelly in a speech to an IPPR seminar see 'Education Reforms Aid the Better Off' by Richard Garner, *Independent*, 27/7/05

CHAPTER 8: THE WORD ON THE STREET

- Hillary Clinton, *It Takes a Village* (Touchstone, 1996)
- Influence of wider community, Pinker, 2003

From creative play to 'toy consumption'

- Real play – 'The Increasing Role of Electronic Toys in the Lives of Infants and Toddlers – Should We Be Concerned?' Diane E. Levin and Barbara Rosenquest in *Contemporary Issues in Early Childhood*, Vol. 2, No. 2, 2001
- Marketing references: Lindstrom, 2003

Strangers on screen

- Background on marketing to children: see Schor, 2004, Linn, 2005
- Research on children's understanding of advertisements summarised in *Childhood Obesity – Food Advertising in Context: Children's Food Choices, Parents' Understanding and Influence and the Role of Food Promotions*, UK, July 2004
- James McNeal quote, see McNeal, 1992

Children as customers

- For further information on guilt money, pester power and 'winning for brands', see Schor, 2004
- Children's influence on car choice: research by ad agency Millward Brown, cited on Brandchild website: www.dualbook.com
- 100 per cent children affecting food purchases: Griffin Bacal ad agency survey cited in 'Preschoolers: an Emerging Consumer Set', *Kidscreen: Reaching Children Through Entertainment*, 1999 – www.kidscreen.com

- Sales decline by a third if children don't ask: Idell, C, 'The Nag Factor', Western Media Initiative, 1998
- Brand awareness at different ages: Lindstrom, 2003
- Nancy Shalek quote cited in 'Why They Whine: How Corporations Prey on Our Children' in *Mothering*, November–December 1999

Sugar and spice ...

- Background on gender differences: see Baron-Cohen, 2003, Sax, 2005
- Barbie website: www.everythinggirl.com
- Little Kitty website: www.hellokitty.com
- 'I love brands' quote: Lindstrom, 2003

... and all things nice

- Further background on KAGOY: Lindstrom, 2003, Schor, 2004
- Dissatisfaction with body image: Kate Fox, 'Mirror, Mirror: a Summary of Research Findings on Body Image', Social Issues Research Centre, Oxford, UK, 1997
- Survey of seven-year-olds: Dohnt, H., Tiggemann, M., 'Peer Influences on Body Dissatisfaction and Dieting Awareness in Young Girls' British Journal of Developmental Psychology, Vol. 23, No. 1, March 2005
- *'Sometimes I don't feel comfortable about my body and the spa helps me'* – Taylor Hawkins aged ten reported by Amelia Hill, 'Why Beauty Spas Thank Heaven for Little Girls', *Observer*, 1/5/05
- Canada – BBC News 'Eating Disorders Rife in Girls', 4/9/01

Slugs and snails ...

- Background on dominion and computer games: see Linn, 2005

... and puppy dogs tails

- Boys who want to wear popular labels: see Mayo, 2005
- Background on Nickelodeon, see www.nick.com
- The Nickelodeon 'empowerment' agenda is explained in Kevin Sandler's 'A Kid's Gotta Do what a Kid's Gotta Do' in *Nickelodeon Nation*, reviewed in *Academia*, February 2005 (www.ybp.com/acad/reviews)
- Mark Crispin Miller quote from *The Merchants of Cool* broadcast on PBS 27/2/01 (full transcript on www.pbs.org/wgbh/pages/frontline/shows/cool/etc/script.html)
- *The Economics of Acting White*, David Austen Smith and Roland G. Fryer Jr., National Bureau of Economic Research working paper, USA 2003 quoted in Levitt and Dubner, 2005

Heroes and villains

- Fictional character survey by Tomy Toys, reported on CBBC News 24/4/03
- Bart Simpson quote: www.thesimpsonsquotes.com
- Children and irony: see *Humor: its Origins and Development*, Paul E. McGhee (W.H. Freeman, 1979)
- Britney Spears story: see Linn, 2005
- Research from Australia in 2003 – Street, H., Durkin, K. *et al.*, *Childhood Conceptions of Happiness and Vulnerability to Depression*, presented at the British Psychological Society's annual conference, Bournemouth, UK, March 2003
- Ed Mayo quote from 'The Onslaught' by Jonathan Freedland, *Guardian Unlimited* special report, 25/10/05

Mind the gap
- Camilla Batmanghelidjh quote in Mayo, 2005

CHAPTER 9: THE ELECTRONIC VILLAGE

The electronic babysitter
- Tots' TV in Japan – 1986 survey by S.I. Kodaira, 'Television's Role in Early Childhood Education in Japan', Tokyo Broadcasting Culture Research Institute, 1987
- Smart rats research: Dr Marian Cleeves Diamond, professor of neuroanatomy at the University of California, addressing the Department for Health and Human Services Conference, 'Television and the Preparation of the Mind for Learning', 1992. Quoted in Winn, 2000
- Plonking in front of telly quote: Rosemary Duff, research director ChildWise in Anil Dawar, 'One in Four Under Eights Has a Mobile', *Daily Mail*, 15/2/05
- Good educational TV can stimulate children to copy the activities: e.g., Huston, A.C., Wright, J.C. *et al.*, 'Development of TV Viewing Patterns in Early Childhood: A Longitudinal Investigation' in *Developmental Psychology*, 26, 1990; *Watching Children Watch Television and the Creation of Blues Clues*, Daniel R. Andersen in Hendershot, 2004; *Deferred Imitation From Television During Infancy*. Rachel Barr, Georgetown Early Learning Project, Georgetown University, 28/10/05
- CBeebies information: Clare Elstow, Director of Pre-School, BBC – personal interview, 2005
- Attention deficit from early TV watching: Research by Dimitri Christakis Associate Professor of Pediatrics at University of Washington and Children's Hospital in Seattle, published in Christakis, D.A., Zimmerman, F.J., DiGuiseppe, D.L., McCarty, C.A., 'Early television exposure and subsequent attentional problems in children', *Pediatrics*, 113: 708–13, April 2004
- Default activity quote: Dr David Walsh, President of the National Institute on Media and the Family, 2002, www.MediaFamily.org

The splintering family
- The first children's channel Nickelodeon began in 1979, and was available initially to only 600,000 subscribers in Columbus Ohio. It now reaches almost 3 million households worldwide. www.nick.com: 'everything nick – history'
- Rideout, V., Vandewater, E., Wartella, E., 'Zero to Six: Electronic Media in the Lives of Infants, Toddlers and Preschoolers, *The Kaiser Family Foundation / Children's Digital Media Centers*, Pub. no. 3378, 28/10/03
- Figure of 80 per cent of 5 to 16-year-olds having TVs in bedroom is from ChildWise Market Research Group, UK, 2005
- Survey of 1,200 children's virtual worlds – statistics from *Observer*, 13/2/05
- Denis Campbell, 'Mobiles, DVDs and MP3s Send Under Eights to Techno Heaven', *Observer*, 13/2/05
- MyRoom, see Leo Lewis 'Thinking Inside the Box: How to Deal With Noisy Husbands', *The Times*, 27/5/05
- Hikikomori – term coined by Tamaki Saito, author of *Shakaiteki Hikikomori* (Hikikomori as a Social Phenomenon), *Hikikomori Bunkaron* (The culture of

Hikikomori) and other works – estimates sufferers of condition number 1.2 million

- David McNeill, 'Japan's Lethal Teenage Angst: the Social Outsiders Who Hide Indoors', *Independent*, 6/12/04
- Quote from Ryu Murokami, novelist and film director in 'Japan's Lost Generation: In a World Filled With Virtual Reality, the Country's Youth Can't Deal With the Real Thing', *TIMEasia*, 1/5/00
- Satoru Saito, psychiatrist, Tokyo 2002 – quoted by Michael Zielenziger, Knight Ridder News Service – same article is in several American newspapers under a different title e.g., 'Stagnant Japanese are Becoming a Lonely Crowd', *Miami Herald*, 22/12/02
- Social isolation is an international problem. The following quote is from a British market researcher: 'Many of today's children do seem to be experiencing greater isolation from family life ... Sadly, it does seem that in many cases modern technology has replaced the family unit, so that everyone does what they want, when they want, even if it means doing it on their own'. Jenny Catlin, press release 'Modern Technology Replaces Traditional Family Values', 25/8/04, regarding the report 'Marketing to Children Aged 11–14', MINTEL, July 2004, UK

The dark side of the village

- 2005 survey of children's viewing *Remote, no control* by Matt Born, *Daily Mail*, 25/7/05
- Quote from press release 'Modern Technology Replaces Traditional Family Values', 25/8/04, (see above)
- Parents unsure about Internet filtering software: Livingstone, S., Bober, M., *UK Children Go Online: Final Report*, London School of Economics, 2005 http://www.children-go-online.net/
- Violence/sexual references/bad language in music and music videos – there is as yet no concrete evidence that children are damaged by these, but there's also no doubt that the content is becoming more explicit – see Roberts, D.F., Christenson, P.G. and Gentile, D.A.: 'The effects of violent music on children and adolescents' in *Media Violence and Children* ed. Gentile, D.A. (Praeger, 2003). Parents and others are particularly worried by the content of rap music – see Eberstadt, 2004 in USA; Giles Hattersley: '*!@**! Where did that come from?' *The Sunday Times*, 31/7/05 in UK; Ruth Elkins: 'Rap Music and the Far Right; Germany Goes Gangsta; a New Wave of Rap Music is Sweeping Germany: sexist, violent, often', *Independent*, 17/8/05 and 'Youth and Violent Music,' Issue Brief Series (2000). Studio City, CA: Mediascope Press + others in 'Children and Media'
- Psychologists believe ... emotionally destabilising: see Joanne Cantor, *The Psychological Effects of Media Violence on Children and Adolescents*, presented at the Colloquium on Television and Violence in Society, Montreal, 19/4/02

A question of rights

- Parents calls for restrictions – see Linn, 2005
- 2000 institutions calling for restriction on violence: American Academy of Pediatrics, *Joint Statement on the Impact of Entertainment Violence on Children*, presented at the Congressional Public Health Summit, Washington DC, 26/7/00 (http://www.aap.org/advocacy/releases/jstmtevc.htm). For further details on

desensitisation research, see *Effects of televised violence on aggression* in *The handbook of children and media* eds Dorothy G. Singer and Jerome L. Singer (Thousand Oaks, CA: Sage, 2001)

- The three effects of screen violence are listed in the AAP *et al.* statement above
- Arguments against screen violence/aggression link: see 'Playing With Fire?' Tony Reichardt, *Nature*, Vol. 424, 24/7/03
- British researcher's comment: Professor Kevin Browne (forensic and family psychology unit) and Catherine Hamilton-Giachritsis, Birmingham University: 'The Influence of Violent Media on Children and Adolescents – a Public Health Approach' *Lancet*, Vol. 365, Issue 9460, 702–10, 19/2/05
- Ed Richards quote: Westminster Media Forum, Ofcom Annual Lecture 20/7/05 – Trends in Television, Radio, and Telecoms http://www.ofcom.org.uk/media/speeches/2005/07/nr_20050720

Electronic friends ... and enemies

- Mobile Phone Ownership: Childwise Monitor Survey 2004/2005 – www.childwise.co.uk
- Health risks of mobiles: Sir William Stewart (Chairman), *Mobile Phones and Health: A Report By the Board of* NRPB, Vol. 15, No.5, Chilton, 2004
- www.bbc.co.uk/cbbc – CBBC
- www.playstation.co.uk – PlayStation

Village politics

- BBC booklet: *Chatguide: a Guide for Parents on How to Keep Children Safe Online and on Mobiles*, BBC, 2004 available on www.bbc.co.uk
- 'Tina Bell' paedophile research and article: Richard Barry, 'Chatroom Danger: Opinion – When Online Chats Leads to the Crying Rooms', *ZDNet UK*, 15/3/01
- Information on Internet blocking devices, see www.getnetwise.org
- John Giacobbi of Web Sheriff's suggestions for Internet policing: 'How We CAN clean up the Internet', *Mail on Sunday*, 11/9/05
- www.virtualglobaltaskforce.com
- Lars Kongshem, 'Filters or Free Speech?' *Electronic School*, March 1998
- Livingstone, S., Bober, M., 'UK Children Go Online: Final Report', 28/4/05

And now the good news ...

- I am indebted to Dr Jackie Marsh, Sheffield University, for her help in reviewing the overall positive effects of technology on children's development – personal interview, 2005
- American psychologist Paul Bloom, see Bloom, 2004
- Liz Cleaver quote, from speech to BBC Seminar *Can Entertainment Educate?*, London, 30/9/05

Village wisdom

- Family help websites: these are referenced throughout *Toxic Childhood*
- *Les maternelles*: see www.lesmaternelles.com
- BBC *Child of Our Time* www.bbc.co.uk/childofourtime and for academic support www.open2.net/childofourtime See also, Livingstone, 2003
- www.supernanny.net
- Jill Curtis quote: personal email

CHAPTER 10: MANNERS MAKETH MAN

The parental balancing act

- Authoritative parenting – for summary of research see Martin, 2005. Although most researchers use the term 'authoritative', other terminology varies from study to study. I've chosen what seemed to me the simplest, clearest vocabulary for the concepts involved. The claims that an authoritative parenting is most successful applies to child-rearing in Westernised democratic societies – in different cultural circumstances other styles may be more appropriate.
- 'Man hands on misery to man' Philip Larkin from 'This Be the Verse' in *High Windows*, 1974
- 'The rich man in his castle' is a verse from the hymn 'All Things Bright and Beautiful' by Cecil Alexander's *Hymns for Little Children*, 1848
- The Freudian theory that frustration of childhood desires leads to neurosis has been hotly contested by many psychotherapists, including his daughter Anna. In lectures at Harvard Anna Freud claimed her father actually said that 'the incapability to overcome frustration can lead to neurosis', i.e., that children need to learn the self-regulatory skills that allow them to deal with frustrated wishes – thanks to Professor Norbert Herschkowitz for this reference
- United Nations Convention on the Rights of the Child, 1989 – see www.unicef.org/crc

The pursuit of happiness

- Veenhoven, R., *World Database of Happiness, Distributional Findings in Nations*, Erasmus University Rotterdam. Available at: www.worlddatabaseofhappiness.eur.nl (2005)
- Richard Layard quote from Layard, 2005
- Robert Puttnam and social capital, see Puttnam, 2000, quote from Puttnam and Feldstein, 2003 see also www.bowlingalone.com and www.bettertogether.org
- Happiness quote, in Martin, 2005
- The five books on manners published in UK in 2005 were:
- *Talk to the Hand: the Utter Bloody Rudeness of Everyday Life*, Lynn Truss (Profile Books)
- *Blaikie's Guide to Modern Manners*, Thomas Blaikie (Fourth Estate)
- *Manners From Heaven: the Easy Way to Better Behaviour for all the Family*, Sean Davoren and Sue Carr
- *The Done Thing: Negotiating the Minefield of Modern Manners*, Simon Fanshawe (Random House)
- *Mind Your Manners: A Guide to Good Behaviour*, Robert O'Byrne (Prion)

Social capital begins at home

- Authoritative communities: *Hardwired to Connect: The New Scientific Case for Authoritative Communities* (YMCA of the USA, Dartmouth Medical School, Institute for American Values, 2003), Researchers' PowerPoint presentation available on www.americanvalues.org
- Richard Layard quote – personal interview, 2005

Knowledge is power

- Julia Roberts quote: *Oprah Winfrey Show*, USA, 10/02/05
- Triple P Parenting Programme – details on p.305

- Triple P study: Felicia A. Huppert, 'A Population Approach to Positive Psychology: the Potential for Population Interviews to Promote Well-being and Prevent Disorder' in *Positive Psychology in Practice* eds P.A. Linley and Stephen Joseph, 2003 (NJ John Wiley and Sons Inc)

Can Nanny know best?
- German dismay at suggestions of Minister Renate Kunäst – *Deutsche Welle*, 17/6/04 www.smh.com.au
- Headteacher quote from Geoff Barton, Suffolk, UK, in *The Times Educational Supplement*, March 2005
- Julia Neuberger quote: Neuberger, 2005

Mind the gap
- Michigan quote: Garbarino, 1995
- Frank Field quote and recommendations: Field, 2003

CONCLUSION: DETOXING CHILDHOOD

- Neuroscience and developmental disorders: see Snowling, 2000, Wender, 2000, Blakemore and Frith, 2005
- Rainforest analogy: see Greenfield, 1997

Tackling toxic childhood syndrome
- International detox measures demonstrating what is possible may be found in many countries, including:
    – Excellent school meals – Finland, Spain, France
    – Banning of junk food near schools – Germany
    – 'Edible Schoolyard Project' – California, USA
    – Walking buses – Japan
    – Child-friendly city planning – Netherlands, Germany
    – City-greening – Canada
    – Natural playgrounds – UK
    – Excellent pre-school provision – Scandinavia
    – Banning of marketing to under-twelves – Sweden
    – Tight regulation of mobile phone ownership – France
    – Successful, widely used parenting programme – Australia
- A good enough parent – see Bettelheim, 1995

How detoxing childhood makes everyone happier
- *Happiness* – Layard, 2005

BIBLIOGRAPHY

Abbott, John and Ryan, Terry, *The Unfinished Revolution: Learning, Human Behaviour, Community and Political Paradox* (Network Educational Press, 2000)

Adams, Sian and Moyles, Janet, *Images of Violence – Responding to Children's Representations of the Violence They See* (Featherstone Education Ltd, 2005)

Aitchison, Jean, *The Seeds of Speech – Language Origin and Evolution* (Cambridge University Press, 2000)

Alderson, Priscilla and Goodey, Christopher, *Enabling Education: Experiences in Special and Ordinary Schools* (The Tufnell Press, 1998)

Alliance for Childhood, *Tech Tonic* (Alliance for Childhood, 2004)

Ashby, Gwynneth, *School Under a Volcano* (Longman Group, 1994)

Athey, Chris, *Extending Thought in Young Children – A Parent–Teacher Partnership* (Paul Chapman Publishing Ltd, 1990)

Baron-Cohen, Simon, *The Essential Difference: Men, Women and the Extreme Male Brain* (Allen Lane, 2003)

Bayley, Ros and Broadbent, Lynn, *Flying Start With Literacy* (Network Educational Press, 2005)

Bennathan, Marion and Boxall, Marjorie, *Effective Intervention in Primary Schools: Nurture Groups*, second edition (David Fulton Publishers, 2002)

Bettelheim, Bruno, *A Good Enough Parent: Guide to Raising Your Child* (Thames and Hudson, 1995)

Biddulph, Steve, *Raising Boys: Why Boys are Different, and How to Help Them Become Happy and Well-balanced Men* (HarperCollins, 1998)

Blakemore, Sarah-Jane and Frith, Uta, *The Learning Brain – Lessons for Education* (Blackwell Publishing, 2005)

Bloom, Paul, *Descartes' Baby: How Child Development Explains What Makes Us Human* (William Heinemann, 2004)

Bloom, Paul, *How Children Learn the Meanings of Words* (A Bradford Book, The MIT Press, 2000)

Blythe, Sally Goddard, *The Well Balanced Child* (Hawthorn Press, 2004)

Borkowski, J., Ramey, S., Bristol-Power, M. (eds), *Parenting in the Child's World: Influences on Academic, Intellectual and Socio-economic Achievement* (Lawrence Erlbaum Associates, 2002)

Bourke, Joanna, *Fear: A Cultural History* (Virago Press, 2005)

Boxall, Marjorie, *Nurture Groups in Schools: Principles and Practice* (Paul Chapman, 2002)

Bradley, Alan and Beveridge, Jody, *How to Help the Children Survive the Divorce* (Foulsham, 2004)

Bruer, John, *The Myth of the First Three Years* (Free Press, 1999)

Burrell, Andrew and Riley, Jeni, *Promoting Children's Well-Being in the Primary Years* (Netword Educational Press/Right from the Start, 2005)

Byron, Dr Tanya and Baveystock, Sacha *Little Angels: The Essential Guide to Transforming Your Family Life and Having More Fun With Your Children* (BBC Books, 2003)

Cantor, Joanne, *Mommy, I'm Scared: How TV and Movies Frighten Children and What We Can Do to Protect Them* (Harvest Books, 2001)

Collins, Andrew, *Where Did it All Go Right? Growing Up Normal in the 70s* (Ebury Press, 2003)

Cragg, Arnold, Dickens, Sarah, Taylor, Cheryl, Henricson, Clem, Keep, Gill, *Researching Parents: Producing and Delivering Parent Information Resources – A Qualitative Research Study and Practice Guide* (National Family and Parenting Institute, 2002)

Curtis, Jill, *Find Your Way Through Divorce* (Hodder & Stoughton, 2001)

Dalrymple, Theodore, *Life at the Bottom: the World View That Makes the Underclass* (Ivan R. Dee, 2003)

Diamond, P., Katwala, S., Munn, M., *Family Fortunes: the New Politics of Childhood* (Fabian Society, 2004)

Damasio, Antonio, *Looking for Spinoza – Joy, Sorrow and the Feeling Brain* (Vintage, 2004)

Donaldson, Margaret, *Children's Minds* (Fontana Press, 1978)

Donaldson, Margaret, *Human Minds: an Exploration* (Allen Lane, 1992)

Donaldson, Margaret, *Sense and Sensibility: Some Thoughts on the Teaching of Literacy* (Reading and Language Information Centre, 1989)

Eberstadt, Mary, *Home Alone America: the hidden toll of daycare, Behavioural Drugs and Other Parent Substitutes* (Sentinel, 2004)

Editors of Scientific American, *The Scientific American Book of the Brain (Introduction by Antonio R. Damasio)* (The Lyons Press, 1999)

Elkind, PhD, David, *The Hurried Child: Growing Up Too Fast Too Soon* (Da Capo Press, 2001)

Erikson, Martha Farrell and Aird, Enola G., *The Motherhood Study: Fresh Insights on Mother's Attitudes and Concerns* (Institute for American Values, 2005)

Faber, Adele and Mazlish, Elaine, *How to Talk So Kids Will Listen and Listen So Kids Will Talk* (Piccadilly Press, 2001)

Faber, Adele and Mazlish, Elaine, *How to Talk So Kids Will Learn at Home and in School* (Scribner, 1995)

Field, Frank, *Neighbours From Hell: the Politics of Behaviour* (Politico's Publishing, 2003)

Ford, Gina, *The Contented Little Baby Book* (Vermilion, 2002)

Frith, Uta, *Autism and Asperger Syndrome* (Cambridge University Press, 1991)

Frost, Jo, *Supernanny* (Hodder & Stoughton, 2005)

Garbarino, James, *Raising Children in a Socially Toxic Environment* (Jossey-Bass, 1995)

Gavin, Mary L., Dowshen, Steven A., Izenberg, Neil, *Fit Kids: a Practical Guide to Raising Healthy and Active Children – From Birth to Teens* (Dorling Kindersley, 2004)

Gerhardt, Sue, *Why Love Matters: How Affection Shapes a Baby's Brain* (Brunner-Routledge, 2004)

Gillie, O., *Sunlight Robbery* (Health Research Council, 2004)

Goleman, Daniel, *Emotional Intelligence* (Bantam Books, 1997)

Gopnik, Alison, Meltzoff, Andrew N., Kuhl, Patricia K., *The Scientist in the Crib: What Early Learning Tells Us About the Mind* (HarperCollins, 1999)

Greenfield, Susan, *The Human Brain: a Guided Tour* (Phoenix, 1997)

Greenfield, Susan, *Tomorrow's People: How 21st Century Technology is Changing the Way We Think and Feel* (Allen Lane, 2003)

Hart, Betty and Risley, Todd R., *Meaningful Differences in the Everyday Experience of Young American Children* (Baltimore, 1995)

Hartley-Brewer, Elizabeth, *Raising Confident Boys: 100 Tips for Parents and Teachers* (Da Capo Press, 2001)

Healy, Jane M., *Endangered Minds – Why Children Don't Think – and What We Can Do About It* (Simon & Schuster, 1990)

Herschkowitz MD, Norbert and Chapman Herschkowitz, Elinore, *A Good Start in Life: Understanding Your Child's Brain and Behaviour From Birth to Age 6* (Dana Press, 2002)

Heymann, Jody, *The Widening Gap: Why America's Working Families are in Jeopardy – and What Can Be Done About it* (Basic Books, 2000)

Hobson, Peter, *The Cradle of Thought: Exploring the Origins of Thinking* (Macmillan, 2002)

Holford, Patrick, *Patrick Holford's New Optimum Nutrition Bible* (Piatkus Books Ltd, 2004)

Holloway, Susan D., *Contested Childhood: Diversity and Change in Japanese Preschools* (Routledge, 2000)

Holmes, Jeremy, *John Bowlby and Attachment Theory* (Brunner-Routledge, 1993)

Honoré, Carl, *In Praise of Slow: How a Worldwide Movement is Challenging the Cult of Speed* (Orion Books, 2004)

Johnson, Steven, *Everything Bad is Good for You* (Allen Lane, 2005)

Kerr, Alex, *Dogs and Demons: The Fall of Modern Japan* (Penguin Books, 2001)

Kirby, Jill, *Choosing to Be Different: Women, Work and the Family* (Centre for Policy Studies, 2003)

Lamb, Michael (ed), *The Role of the Father in Child Development*, fourth edition (John Wiley and Sons, 2004)

Law, Professor James, *Johnson's Learning to Talk: A Practical Guide for Parents* (Dorling Kindersley, 2004)

Layard, Richard, *Happiness: Lessons From a New Science* (Allen Lane, 2005)

Levitt, Steven D. and Dubner, Stephen J., *Freakonomics: a Rogue Economist Explores the Hidden Side of Everything* (Allen Lane, 2005)

Lindstrom, Martin, (with Seybold, Patricia B.), *BRANDchild* (Revised Edition) (Kogan Page Limited, 2003)

Linn, Susan, *Consuming Kids: the Hostile Takeover of Childhood* (New Press, 2005)

Livingstone, Tessa, *Child of Our Time: How to Achieve the Best for Your Child from Conception to 5 Years* (Bantam Press, 2005)

Louv, Richard, *Last Child in the Woods: Saving our Kids From Nature-Deficit Disorder* (Algonquin Books, 2005)

Lucas, Bill and Smith, Alastair, *Help Your Child to Succeed: the Essential Guide for Parents* (Network Educational Press, 2002)

Macintyre, Christine and McVitty, Kim, *Movement and Learning in the Early Years – Supporting Dyspraxia (DCD) and Other Difficulties* (Paul Chapman, 2004)

Martin, Paul, *Counting Sheep – the Science and Pleasures of Sleep and Dreams* (Flamingo, 2003)

Martin, Paul, *Making Happy People: the Nature of Happiness and its Origins in Childhood* (Fourth Estate, 2005)

Matsumoto, David, *The New Japan: Debunking Seven Cultural Stereotypes* (Intercultural Press, 2002)

Mayo, Ed, *Shopping Generation* (National Consumer Council, 2005)

McEvedy, Flora, *The Step-Parents' Parachute: the Four cornerstones to Good Step-parenting* (Time Warner, 2005)

McLuhan, Marshal and Fiore, Quentin, *The Medium is the Massage* (Gingko Press, 2001)

McNeal, James U., *Kids as Customers: a Handbook of Marketing to Children* (Lexington Books, 1992)

Medhus MD, Elisa, *Hearing is Believing: How Words Can Make or Break Our Kids* (New World Library, California)

Melville, Sandra, *Places for Play* (Playlink, 2005)

Motherhood Project, The, *Watch Out for Children: A Mothers' Statement to Advertisers* (Institute for American Values, 2001)

National Association of Elementary School Principals, *Standards for What Principals Should Know and Be Able to Do* (National Association of Elementary School Principals, 2004)

National Research Council, Institute of Medicine, *From Neurons to Neighborhoods: The Science of Early Childhood Development* (National Academy Press, 2000)

Neuberger, Julia, *the Moral State We're In: a Manifesto for a 21st-century Society* (HarperCollins, 2005)

Noel, Brook, *Back to Basics: 101 Ideas for Strengthening our Children and our Families* (Champion Press Ltd, 1999)

Nutbrown, Cathy, *Threads of Thinking: Young Children Learning and the Role of Early Education*, second edition (Paul Chapman Publishing Ltd, 1999)

Orrey, Jeanette, *The Dinner Lady: Change the Way Your Children Eat, for Life* (Bantam Press, 2005)

Orange, Teresa and O'Flynn, Louise, *The Media Diet for Kids* (Hay House, 2005)

Paley, Vivian Gussin, *The Kindness of Children* (Harvard University Press, 2000)

Parentline Plus, *Being a Parent* (Hawthorn Press, 1999)

Pearson Alison, *I Don't Know How She Does It*, (Chatto & Windus, 2002)

Phillips, Melanie, *All Must Have Prizes* (Time Warner Paperback, 1998)

Pinker, Steven, *The Language Instinct* (Penguin Books, 1995)

Pinker, Steven, *The Blank State* (Penguin Books, 2003)

Pipher PhD, Mary, *The Shelter of Each Other – Rebuilding Our Families* (Ballantine Books, 1997)

Postman, Neil, *Amusing Ourselves to Death* (Random House, 1985)

Postman, Neil, *The Disappearance of Childhood* (Vintage, 1994)

Putnam, Robert D., *Bowling Alone: the Collapse and Revival of American Community* (Simon & Schuster, 2000)

Putnam, R.P. and Feldstein, L., *Better Together* (Simon & Schuster, 2003)

Ramachandran, Vilayanur, *The Emerging Mind* (Profile Books, 2003)

Restak, Dr Richard, *The New Brain: How the Modern Age is Rewiring Your Mind* (Rodale Ltd, 2004)

Rich, Diane, Myer, Cathy, Durrant, Andrea, Drummond, Mary Jane, Dixon, Annabelle, Casanova, Denise, *First Hand Experience – What Matters to Children* (Rich Learning

Opportunities, 2005)

Richardson, Alex, *They Are What You Feed Them* (HarperCollins, 2006)

Rose, Steven, *The Making of Memory – From Molecules to Mind* (Vintage, 2003)

Rose, Steven, *The 21st Century Brain: Explaining, Mending and Manipulating the Mind* (Jonathan Cape, 2005)

Salzman, Marian, *The Future of Men* (Palgrave MacMillan, 2005)

Satter, Ellyn, *Child of Mine: Feeding With Love and Good Sense* (Bull Publishing Company, 2000)

Satter, Ellyn, *How to Get Your Kid to Eat ... But Not Too Much* (Bull Publishing, 1987)

Sax, Leonard, *Why Gender Matter:– What Parents and Teachers Need to Know About the Emerging Science of Sex Differences* (Doubleday, 2005)

Schor, Juliet B., *Born to Buy* (Scribner, 2004)

Shaw MD, Robert, *The Epidemic: the Rot of American Culture, Absentee and Permissive Parenting, and the Resultant Plague of Joyless, Selfish Children* (Regan Books, 2003)

Sheppard, Philip, *Music Makes Your Child Smarter: How Music Helps Every Child's Development* (Artemis Editions, 2005)

Sigman, Aric, *Remotely Controlled: How Television is Damaging our Lives and What We Can Do About it* (Vermilion, 2005)

Snowling, Margaret J., *Dyslexia*, second edition (Blackwell, 2000)

Stevens M.S., Laura J., *12 Effective Ways to Help Your ADD/ADHD Child: Drug Free Alternatives for Attention-Deficit Disorders – A Guide to Controlling Attention and Hyperactivity Using Nutrition and Other Safe, Natural Methods* (Avery, 2000)

Storr, Anthony, *Music and the Mind* (HarperCollins, 1992)

Tomasello, Michael, *Constructing a Language: a Usage Based Theory of Language Acquisition* (Harvard University Press, 2003)

Ursell, Amanda, *What Are You Really Eating?: How to Become Label Savvy* (Hay House, 2005)

Ward, Dr Sally, *Babytalk* (Century, 2000)

Weissbluth MD, Marc, *Healthy Sleep Habits, Happy Child* (Random House, 1998)

Wender MD, Paul H., *ADHD Attention-Deficit Hyperactivity Disorder in Children, Adolescents and Adults* (Oxford University Press, 2000)

Whalley, Margy and the Pen Green Centre Team, *Involving Parents in Their Children's Learning* (Paul Chapman Publishing Ltd, 2001)

Whittingstall, Jane, *The Good Granny Guide* (Short Books, 2005)

Wilce, Hilary, *Help Your Child Succeed at School* (Piatkus, 2004)

Williams, Fiona, *Rethinking Families* (Calouste Gulbenkian Foundation, 2004)

Winn, Marie, *The Plug-in Drug: Television, Computer, and Family Life* (Penguin Books, 2002)

Woodhouse, Sarah, *Sound Sleep: Calming and Helping Your Baby or Child to Sleep* (Hawthorn Press, 2003)

Woolfson, Dr Richard C., *Small Talk: From First Gestures to Simple Sentences* (Hamlyn, 2002)

INDEX